Short Essays

MODELS FOR COMPOSITION

Short Essays

MODELS FOR COMPOSITION

GERALD LEVIN

The University of Akron

HARCOURT BRACE JOVANOVICH, INC.

New York   Chicago   San Francisco   Atlanta

ISBN: 0-15-580912-1

Library of Congress Catalog Card Number: 76-29166

Printed in the United States of America

preface

Almost all these 57 short essays appear here for the first time in a freshman reader. Almost all are only three or four pages long—about the length usually assigned in composition courses. For this reason they are especially appropriate in classes where a detailed discussion of the essay is a necessary preliminary to writing an essay. Students of all abilities perhaps find it easiest to study the organization and development of ideas by reading short essays, but instructors who want longer examples will find several in this book, including those by Dwayne Walls, Elaine Kendall, Phyllis McGinley, Lewis Yablonsky, Rust Hills, and Truman E. Moore.

The essays are concrete, contemporary, and pertinent to the world and experience of freshmen. A variety of interests are represented, such as urban and rural living, sports, work, changing values in American life, and growing up. The essays are presented complete, with only two exceptions—Jim Brown's "Growing Up on Long Island" and Leo Rosten's "Shlemiel," which have been slightly cut. A number of them are self-contained sections from chapters of books—Angelou, Kendall, Walls, Pettit, Brainerd, Deford, the section from *The Foxfire Book,* Updike, Trillin, Tyrrell, Mannes, Clarke, and Toffler. Several are complete chapters—Craig, Dillard, Hobbs. Many of the essays connect in theme, so that certain subjects recur from fresh points of view. I have suggested these connections in the thematic table of contents and in many of the Suggestions for Writing, which invite the students to compare their own ideas and points of view with those of the other essayists. The Instructor's Manual offers still other suggestions for comparison.

The Questions generally begin with the content and rhetoric of each essay and conclude with the students' responses to its ideas and experiences. The Vocabulary Study is designed to supplement these questions, to teach the uses of a dictionary in reading and composition, and to demonstrate that what a word means very often depends on the context in which it appears.

Each essay illustrates rhetoric topics other than the one under which I have included it, and instructors may want to switch essay and topic to fit the needs of their classes. The Instructor's Manual suggests many such alternative combinations. In the text I have kept discussion of these topics as simple as possible, omitting such complex considerations as classification as a refinement of division and the forms of deductive reasoning. The essays present an intellectual challenge to students of all writing abilities, without presenting the complex reading problems that prevent many essays from being useful models for composition.

I wish to thank Andrea A. Lunsford (Ohio State University) and Ann Raimes (Hunter College of the City University of New York) for their careful criticism of the original manuscript and their many useful suggestions for revision. I owe thanks to my colleagues at the University of Akron, with whom I have discussed freshman composition over many years. I also owe a very special debt to five superior teachers who have long shared with me their experiences and ideas: William A. Francis, Bruce Holland, Alice J. MacDonald, Sally K. Slocum, and Arlene A. Toth, all of the University of Akron. My wife, Lillian Levin, assisted me in preparing the manuscript for publication. Eben W. Ludlow and Natalie Bowen, both of Harcourt Brace Jovanovich, encouraged this project from its inception to its completion, and I am grateful to them for their help.

GERALD LEVIN

contents

SENTENCE VARIETY 255

PARALLELISM 269

CONCRETENESS 276

FIGURATIVE LANGUAGE 290

USAGE 301

THEMATIC
TABLE OF CONTENTS

AMERICAN LIFE

SPORTS

PEOPLE

NATURE

LANGUAGE

VALUES

ISSUES AND CONTROVERSIES

Short Essays

MODELS FOR COMPOSITION

thesis

The main idea of an essay organizes the many subordinate ideas and details. In argument, this main idea is called the *thesis,* and this word is also used for the main idea of the expository essay, the kind of essay that explains and illustrates ideas. Essays of personal experience and other types are also organized through a controlling idea or impression.

Occasionally the thesis of an essay appears in the first sentence, particularly if the essay is a newspaper or magazine article:

> Parents want two opposite things at once: they want their children to excel, and they want their children to be docile. But the two don't go together and never have.—Sydney J. Harris, *Parents Must Make Up Their Minds*

But it is more usual to build to the thesis statement at the end of the first paragraph or the beginning of the second, or later in the essay. Introductory comments and details prepare the reader for the idea. Here is an opening paragraph that builds to the thesis statement:

> Males and females do not receive equal educations under our present coeducational system. Their educations reflect the roles that society intends them ultimately to occupy. In our society the male, rather than the female, is taught to achieve, to advance, to create. *This deference to the male is particularly evident in the textbooks used by children in primary grades.*—Marjorie B. U'Ren, *The Image of Women in Textbooks* (thesis italicized)

Sometimes the thesis appears toward the end of the essay. One reason for this delay is that the idea will not be clear without considerable explanation and examples. Another reason is that the idea gains special emphasis when it is placed toward the end of the essay. The more controversial the thesis, the later in the essay it may appear, for the writer may wish to make the reader receptive to it before actually stating it. Finally, the writer may not state the thesis but will let details suggest it. In this kind of essay, the thesis is said to be *implied.*

GOING MY WAY

Martin L. Krovetz

Martin Krovetz was born in 1945. He grew up in Rochester, New York, and finished high school in Miami Beach, Florida. He is assistant principal of Carmel High School in Carmel, California. His essay supplies other biographical details.

[1] We live in an age of change and mobility. The person who has had the same job for twenty years and has lived in the same house for that time may have trouble understanding my thoughts expressed here.

[2] Until I was 15 years old I lived in Rochester, N.Y. During that time I attended three elementary schools, one junior high school and one high school. My last two years of high school were in Miami Beach. I then attended a large state university for four years to earn my B.A., followed by four more years at a second large university where I earned my Ph.D. I spent no more than four years at any one of these eight schools. I am employed in my third major job. I left the other two voluntarily after three years each and went on to something new. Now after two years in my present position I'm actively considering what should come next.

[3] Everything has come in two-, three- or four-year cycles. No roots here, no roots there. Upward mobility is the theme. What's next, what's right to get there, thinking more of the future than the present . . .

[4] I was an excellent student in school. My Phi Beta Kappa key reminds me that I played by most of the rules. I realize now, as

many people do, that most of the book learning has slipped my mind, but the messages given by the teachers all those years still ring loud and strong. Elementary school prepares you for junior high school. Junior high school prepares you for high school. High school prepares you for college. College prepares you for graduate school. Graduate school prepares you for a job. (There are a lot of Ph.D.'s unemployed these days, I hear.) If you work hard enough at the first job, the second job will offer more prestige, power and pay. If you work hard at the second job . . . The endless cycle of a prosperous and *worthwhile* life. What better example of Marshall McLuhan's "the medium is the message."

⁵Somewhere a part of me has been lost. There have been many whos at each stop, but it gets harder and harder to give of myself to others when I know that the relationship will be shortlived, based on the life-style I have chosen for myself to date. I tell myself that the next stop may not be lasting, but it will be longer. The next stop is where the roots will grow and flourish. I sound too much like the aspiring law student who plans to play by all the rules until he is president of the General Motors Corp. and will then change the world.

⁶Every year, I try to get back to Florida to visit with my father, sister, grandparents, nieces and nephew, aunts and uncles and two people who have been my closest friends since the first days of college. Two weeks out of 52 my extended family is a reality. A couple of times a year I correspond with friends from graduate school. We are spread all over North America now, but over the last four years I have seen several of them once or twice during someone's vacation.

⁷At the same time, if I'm not moving, someone else probably is. As an educator, I have become close friends with many of my past students. Their lives too are spent in two-, three- and four-year cycles. They too are now spread all over North America.

⁸Needless to say, I'm not sure that I want to change my lifestyle. I have an advantage that reportedly a majority of Americans do not have: I like my work. Each change of jobs has been stimulating and has caused me to grow as a person. I am away from my extended family, but I spend a lot of time with my nuclear family and find my relationship with my wife and three children to be very rewarding. I have made friends all along the way. I have hated to leave any of them, but I have enjoyed watching us change and grow

with each move and with each new group of friends. Life is a learning process and by living in a number of places in the United States I have come to recognize and appreciate the pluralism within this country. Also, intellectually at least, I allow myself to think that I am somewhat of a free thinker, a person who will take risks and state his views even if it happens to endanger his job security; I pride myself on this, in fact.

[9]The dilemma facing me is at least somewhat clear. Do I choose the professional and personal satisfaction that I perceive comes from a life-style characterized by mobility, or do I choose the shelter and satisfaction that come from choosing a more stable life-style and then try to find ways to achieve the other satisfactions? I notice as I write this that the ingrained biases are evident to me; I cringed slightly as I wrote the word "shelter." Protection and shelter have negative connotations for me; strength, power and fame are positive. I am not at all sure that these ideas are mutually exclusive; I know that the valences are questionable, but I will need to reevaluate my value system in order to be able to make a valid judgment.

[10]I suppose that I see the world as made up of "them guys" who choose to not take chances, to work 40 hours a week at a boring job, drink lots of beer and watch "Let's Make a Deal" on television; and "us guys" who are willing to take chances, speak up, move, drink wine, eat cheese and read lots of newsmagazines. Along the way a number of "them guys" have been my friends, and they have admitted that they are jealous of the way I choose to approach life. I now wonder if I'm a little jealous of some of what they have as well.

[11]I suspect that I will allow this dilemma to be waged inside me for a few more years and perhaps through several more moves. At some point, however, I shall choose to at least try to look at my new house and new community as *home*. In the long run I still might choose to remain there for only three or four years; but once at least I should allow myself to think that the soil is rich and permit my roots to grow.

COMMENT

Krovetz begins with an observation about American life: "We live in an age of change and mobility." He then develops it through his personal experience. For him, as for other Americans, life is experienced in "two-, three- or four-year cycles," the result being the loss of "shelter" and stability. Krovetz says at the beginning of paragraph 5 that "Somewhere a part of me has been lost." This statement is his controlling idea or thesis: the opening four paragraphs build to it. The remainder of the essay develops this idea through his experiences and his thoughts about their advantages and disadvantages. The final sentence of the essay restates it, adding a partial solution to the problem. Krovetz reminds the reader of his controlling idea in his references to his visits home, to his new jobs, and to the "several more moves" he probably will make. At no point does he stray to an unrelated topic. In general, the first part of the essay states a problem; the second part explores a solution.

QUESTIONS FOR STUDY AND DISCUSSION

1. Why is the solution suggested at the end only partial? Is Krovetz saying he *will* grow roots?

2. What personal qualities does Krovetz stress in explaining his way of living? How do these qualities show the ways in which he is different from "them guys"?

3. Does Krovetz suggest that the disadvantages of his life-style outweigh the advantages—or the reverse? Or does he consider the advantages and disadvantages equal?

4. Do you agree with Krovetz's assessment of American values, given your experiences? Was "upward mobility" the theme of your education, or were you taught other values? Were you taught the same values at home and at school?

5. Do you agree that the world is made up of "them guys" and "us guys," or do you see another way of distinguishing attitudes toward work and personal relationships?

VOCABULARY STUDY

1. Krovetz states that the words *protection* and *shelter* have "negative connotations" for him, that is, unpleasant associations. What other words in the essay probably have negative connotations for him too? Notice his statement that *strength, power,* and *fame* have positive connotations for him. Think of three or four other words that probably also would seem positive to him.

2. Rewrite paragraph 9 in your words. In particular find substitute words and phrases for *dilemma, mobility, ingrained, biases, valences, re-evaluate,* and *valid.*

SUGGESTIONS FOR WRITING

1. Write your own essay on the topic "Going My Way." Introduce your thesis or controlling idea in your opening paragraph and keep it before your reader in the whole essay.

2. Compare two of your friends through their attitudes toward change and mobility. You might wish to compare them to Krovetz or discuss whether they are "them" or "us" guys. Use your comparison to make a point, and underline this controlling idea.

3. Discuss what experiences you want now in a job, or will want later. You might discuss the influence of your friends on your attitude toward work. Build the discussion to a statement of your controlling idea in your final paragraph. In your opening paragraph you may wish to introduce yourself and the topic of the essay.

RAZE LOW THE ROOF BEAM, CARPENTERS

Caskie Stinnett

Caskie Stinnett was born in Remington, Virginia, in 1911. He graduated from the College of William and Mary in 1932, worked as a reporter for a Virginia newspaper, and was an information specialist for the United States government from 1936 to 1945. He worked from 1945 to 1962 for the Curtis Publishing Company, and wrote humor and satire for numerous periodicals including *The Saturday Evening Post, Atlantic Monthly,* and *Holiday.* He also edited several magazines including *Holiday* and *Travel and Leisure.* Much of his writing is about New York City.

[1] A handsome brownstone house is being razed across the street from us, thrusting us into a conflict between two seemingly irreconcilable groups: the progress-at-any-price group, who seem determined to turn New York into a city of glass, and the stodgy holdouts, who feel that the nontransparent brownstone offered comfort, livability, and the charm of a gracious and bygone period. The cornice of a magnificent bay has just tumbled to the ground in a cloud of mortar-dust, as we write this, and the workman is gazing over the edge, as though shocked at his own vandalism. Our position is with the holdouts; we harbor a dread that the whole activity is tragically misdirected. Rachel Carson showed us how, aiming at a weevil, we exterminated the eagle; aiming to save man from malaria, we have probably given him cancer. Now, seeking to create the all-efficient, sterile, living-factory of the planners, we have probably eliminated the home.

[2] There is some peculiar private quality to wallpaper, and one recoils slightly at the sight of it exposed on a partly demolished wall. Across the way, on what is left of a third-floor bedroom, a yellow wallpaper flecked with a small design is revealed amid the debris. It is like a lady whose slip is showing. Was it a pleasant bedroom, we wondered, and did that design, slight as it was, irritate the occupant when he was sick abed, and spent the day staring at the walls and ceiling? With no trouble at all, we can trace out to this day the design in the wallpaper of the room where, as a child, we sweated out a case of scarlet fever.

[3] This particular brownstone was sturdily built, and we can't help exulting in the stubborn way that it resists the wreckers. A few months ago it took three workmen, straining at their wrecking bars, to pry off the top of a window sill. A pigeon came in suddenly, without tower clearance, and was refused permission to land. After coasting over the wreckage, with eye cocked first right and then left, it glided on uptown. Everybody is fascinated by destruction.

[4] The man in the next office, to whom we have just called, estimates the brownstone was built around 1875. (He also said, "Isn't it a shame?" which places him, too, on the side of the holdouts—as the losing group is known.) The mechanics of the home have undergone many changes since the house was built. An electric refrigerator, for example, was brought in ("It makes its own ice,

From *Back to Abnormal* by Caskie Stinnett, © 1963 by Caskie Stinnett, with the permission of Bernard Geis Associates, Inc.

right there in the kitchen") and in our mind's eye we can see the excitement that caused: those first few days when it was turned up too high with the result that the milk and eggs froze, and the owner threatened to have it removed. With a brownstone like this, the owner was certain to have been a sort of Father Day figure. By the time the oil burner replaced the coal furnace, with the coal bunkers converted into laundromats, the house was accustomed to change, and most of the hight had gone out of it. But a house like this had pride, and knew that glass was a material for windows and not for walls.

[5] An endless train of trucks is moving down Fifty-third Street now to cart away the rubble, and in a couple of days the premises will be level and ready for the new temple of crystal. We are sure it will be glistening, and soundproof, and sterile, and free of soot in the air and dust underfoot. And also, alas, free of memories, warmth, and the cry of a human infant in a nursery whose wall is covered in yellow wallpaper flecked with a small design.

COMMENT

Stinnett presents his thesis at the end of the first paragraph: "Now, seeking to create the all-efficient, sterile, living-factory of the planners, we have probably eliminated the home." He might have started the essay with this sentence, but that would have been an abrupt beginning—and a formal one, unsuited to the informal discussion that follows. Stinnett introduces the reader to his world—through the building being razed and his thoughts on the cost of modern improvements. He focuses on the cost in the remainder of the essay. As he describes the demolition of the building, he imagines the changes that took place in it and its differences from the building that will replace it. These considerations are related to his theme—the gradual disappearance of the home, in face of technological progress.

QUESTIONS FOR STUDY AND DISCUSSION

1. Having described the final stages of the demolition, how does Stinnett remind the reader of his thesis?

2. Throughout the essay Stinnett contrasts age and disorder with order and efficiency. What details develop this contrast? How does this contrast support the thesis?

3. What other subordinate ideas are introduced to show that progress is sometimes harmful to people?

4. Does Stinnett state or imply a solution to the situation he describes? Can you recommend a solution?

5. Do you believe Stinnett would agree with Krovetz's assessment of American values?

VOCABULARY STUDY

Write sentences of your own using the following words. Let the content of the sentence clarify the meaning of the words, as in the following:
The *razed* building lay in heaps of stone and wood.

> *stodgy*   *exterminated*   *flecked*
> *vandalism*   *recoils*

SUGGESTIONS FOR WRITING

1. Develop a thesis relating to the changes that appliances have made in your life, in particular in your personal habits. Underline each full or partial statement of your thesis.

2. Describe how a house, an apartment, or a room—a kitchen or living room—influences or determines how you live your life, for example, how you eat, or listen to music, or watch television, or read, or in general live with members of your family. Build the discussion to a thesis, and be careful to connect your comments and details to it.

ON THE A TRAIN

Maeve Brennan

Since 1953 the short-story writer and essayist Maeve Brennan has written in the guise of "The Long-Winded Lady" for *The New Yorker*. Her sketches and commentaries on New York City life appear in "The Talk of the Town," a collection of unsigned editorials, commentaries, personal essays, and sketches at thè beginning of the magazine. "The long-winded lady" reports her experiences and observations in a rambling but engaging style, which conveys a special point of view and humor.

There were no seats to be had on the A train last night, but I had a good grip on the pole at the end of one of the seats and I was reading the beauty column of the *Journal-American,* which the man next to me was holding up in front of him. All of a sudden I felt a tap on my arm, and I looked down and there was a man beginning to stand up from the seat where he was sitting. "Would you like to sit down?" he said. Well, I said the first thing that came into my head, I was so surprised and pleased to be offered a seat in the subway. "Oh, thank you very much," I said, "but I am getting out at the next station." He sat back and that was that, but I felt all set up and I thought what a nice man he must be and I wondered what his wife was like and I thought how lucky she was to have such a polite husband, and then all of a sudden I realized that I wasn't getting out at the next station at all but the one after that, and I felt perfectly terrible. I decided to get out at the next station anyway, but then I thought, If I get out at the next station and wait around for the next train I'll miss my bus and they only go every hour and that will be silly. So I decided to brazen it out as best I could, and when the train was slowing up at the next station I stared at the man until I caught his eye and then I said, "I just remembered this isn't my station after all." Then I thought he would think I was asking him to stand up and give me his seat, so I said, "But I still don't want to sit down, because I'm getting off at the next station." I showed him by my expression that I thought it was all rather funny, and he smiled, more or less, and nodded, and lifted his hat and put it back on his head again and looked away. He was one of those small, rather glum or sad men who always look off into the distance after they have finished what they are saying, when they speak. I felt quite proud of my strong-mindedness at not getting off the train and missing my bus simply because of the fear of a little embarrassment, but just as the train was shutting its doors I peered out and there it was 168th Street. "Oh dear!" I said. "That was my station and now I have missed the bus!" I was fit to be tied, and I had spoken quite loudly, and I felt extremely foolish, and I looked down, and the man who had offered me his seat was partly looking at me, and I said, "Now, isn't that silly? That was my station. A Hundred and Sixty-eighth Street is where I'm supposed to get off." I couldn't help laughing, it was all so awful, and he looked away, and the train fidgeted along to the next station, and I got off as quickly as I possibly could and tore over to the downtown platform and got a local to 168th, but of course I had missed my bus by a minute, or maybe two minutes. I felt very much at a loose end wandering around 168th Street, and I finally went into a rudely appointed but friendly bar and had a Martini, warm but very soothing, which only cost me fifty cents. While I was sipping it, trying to make it last to exactly the moment that would get me a good place in the bus queue without having to stand too long in the cold, I wondered what I should have done about that man in the subway. After all, if I had taken his seat I probably would have got out at 168th Street, which would have meant that I would hardly have been sitting down before I would have been getting up again, and that would have seemed odd. And rather grasping of me. And he wouldn't have got his seat back, because some other grasping person would have slipped into it ahead of him when I got up. He seemed a retiring sort of man, not pushy at all. I hesitate to think of how he must have regretted offering me his seat. Sometimes it is very hard to know the right thing to do.

COMMENT

Brennan saves her thesis for the final sentence of the essay: "Sometimes it is very hard to know the right thing to do." Brennan's thesis is really an afterthought—a momentary reflection on her amusing experience aboard the A train. She might have opened the essay with this thought—or omitted it. If she had omitted it, the reader would still understand the point of her narrative, for each detail is selected to illustrate it. Even the description of the man who offered her his seat contributes to our understanding.

QUESTIONS FOR STUDY AND DISCUSSION

1. If the man who gave up his seat had not seemed shy, how would her response to the situation have been different?

2. What personal qualities does Brennan reveal to us in her telling of the episode, and how do these contribute to our understanding of her concluding statement? What do her long rambling sentences show?

3. Where in the essay might a new paragraph begin? What is gained by developing the episode in a single paragraph?

4. How does the author anticipate her final sentence in earlier statements? Would the essay be just as effective if she had opened with her final statement?

5. Brennan has developed her idea humorously. What experiences of city life could be used to develop the idea seriously? Could you draw upon your experiences at home or at school in the same way?

VOCABULARY STUDY

1. Identify words in the essay that have negative connotations and be ready to discuss how they reveal the feelings of the author.

2. How do the details of the essay explain the italicized words in this sentence?

   He seemed a *retiring* sort of man, not *pushy* at all.

SUGGESTIONS FOR WRITING

1. Develop in a single, well-developed paragraph the final sentence of Brennan's essay. Use a similar experience of your own, and be careful to select only those details that clearly illustrate it.

2. Use another experience to illustrate an idea of your own. But this time omit any statement of it, so that your point or thesis is implied. Remember that you will succeed in communicating the thesis to your reader only if your details directly illustrate it.

PICKING COTTON

Maya Angelou

Maya Angelou was born in St. Louis in 1928, and grew up in Stamps, Arkansas, where she was raised by her grandmother, who operated the only black general store in town. In 1940 she moved to San Francisco to live with her mother. She later studied dancing and taught it in Italy and Israel, after performing professionally. Angelou has served as an official of the Southern

Christian Leadership Conference, and she has traveled and lived in Africa, teaching school and writing for newspapers in Egypt and Ghana. Returning to the United States, she worked in the theater and taught writing. Her description of cotton pickers in Stamps is a complete section of an early chapter of her autobiography, *I Know Why the Caged Bird Sings* ((1969).

[1]Each year I watched the field across from the Store turn caterpillar green, then gradually frosty white. I knew exactly how long it would be before the big wagons would pull into the front yard and load on the cotton pickers at daybreak to carry them to the remains of slavery's plantations.

[2]During the picking season my grandmother would get out of bed at four o'clock (she never used an alarm clock) and creak down to her knees and chant in a sleep-filled voice, "Our Father, thank you for letting me see this New Day. Thank you that you didn't allow the bed I lay on last night to be my cooling board, nor my blanket my winding sheet. Guide my feet this day along the straight and narrow, and help me to put a bridle on my tongue. Bless this house, and everybody in it. Thank you, in the name of your Son, Jesus Christ, Amen."

[3]Before she had quite arisen, she called our names and issued orders, and pushed her large feet into homemade slippers and across the bare lye-washed wooden floor to light the coal-oil lamp.

[4]The lamplight in the Store gave a soft make-believe feeling to our world which made me want to whisper and walk about on tiptoe. The odors of onions and oranges and kerosene had been mixing all night and wouldn't be disturbed until the wooded slat was removed from the door and the early morning air forced its way in with the bodies of people who had walked miles to reach the pickup place.

[5]"Sister, I'll have two cans of sardines."

[6]"I'm gonna work so fast today I'm gonna make you look like you standing still."

[7]"Lemme have a hunk uh cheese and some sody crackers."

[8]"Just gimme a coupla them fat peanut paddies." That would be from a picker who was taking his lunch. The greasy brown paper

sack was stuck behind the bib of his overalls. He'd use the candy as a snack before the noon sun called the workers to rest.

[9]In those tender mornings the Store was full of laughing, joking, boasting and bragging. One man was going to pick two hundred pounds of cotton, and another three hundred. Even the children were promising to bring home fo' bits and six bits.

[10]The champion picker of the day before was the hero of the dawn. If he prophesied that the cotton in today's field was going to be sparse and stick to the bolls like glue, every listener would grunt a hearty agreement.

[11]The sound of the empty cotton sacks dragging over the floor and the murmurs of waking people were sliced by the cash register as we rang up the five-cent sales.

[12]If the morning sounds and smells were touched with the supernatural, the late afternoon had all the features of the normal Arkansas life. In the dying sunlight the people dragged, rather than their empty cotton sacks.

[13]Brought back to the Store, the pickers would step out of the backs of trucks and fold down, dirt-disappointed, to the ground. No matter how much they had picked, it wasn't enough. Their wages wouldn't even get them out of debt to my grandmother, not to mention the staggering bill that waited on them at the white commissary downtown.

[14]The sounds of the new morning had been replaced with grumbles about cheating houses, weighted scales, snakes, skimpy cotton and dusty rows. In later years I was to confront the stereotyped picture of gay song-singing cotton pickers with such inordinate rage that I was told even by fellow Blacks that my paranoia was embarrassing. But I had seen the fingers cut by the mean little cotton bolls, and I had witnessed the backs and shoulders and arms and legs resisting any further demands.

[15]Some of the workers would leave their sacks at the Store to be picked up the following morning, but a few had to take them home for repairs. I winced to picture them sewing the coarse material under a coal-oil lamp with fingers stiffening from the day's work. In too few hours they would have to walk back to Sister Henderson's Store, get vittles and load, again, onto the trucks. Then they would face another day of trying to earn enough for the whole year with the heavy knowledge that they were going to end the season as they started it. Without the money or credit necessary to sustain a family

for three months. In cotton-picking time the late afternoons revealed the harshness of Black Southern life, which in the early morning had been softened by nature's blessing of grogginess, forgetfulness and the soft lamplight.

COMMENT

Angelou's description begins with her grandmother's rising at four o'clock in the morning; it ends with a picture of workers mending their sacks under coal-oil lamps at night. The details at the beginning suggest a softness of life: "The odors of onions and oranges and kerosene had been mixing all night and wouldn't be disturbed until the wooded slat was removed from the door"; the sounds and smells of morning "were touched with the supernatural," she tells us in a later passage. In contrast to the morning, the late afternoon is harsh and ordinary, and she gives details of that world in the remaining paragraphs. The concluding sentence of the essay combines these impressions and states the thesis of the essay. Angelou is writing for an audience that perhaps holds a stereotype of the Southern black; that audience must be immersed in the sounds and feelings of the real Southern black world if it is to lose that stereotype. Angelou saves her thesis for the end of the essay as a way of involving the reader in the real world, intellectually and emotionally.

QUESTIONS FOR STUDY AND DISCUSSION

1. What details in the essay suggest "nature's blessing of grogginess, forgetfulness and the soft lamplight"? What details suggest "the features of the normal Arkansas life"?

2. The author is recalling an incident of her childhood. How does she suggest the child's view of the world?

3. How does she state or imply the influence of this experience on her feelings about her race?

4. How do the details contradict the stereotype of the Southern black? What other stereotypes is she possibly criticizing?

5. What experiences would you describe in order to attack a familiar stereotype?

6. What different pictures do morning and evening experiences of your own suggest? Do they also suggest a thesis?

VOCABULARY STUDY

1. Some of the words in the essay are colloquial (words used conversationally and informally) and some are dialect (words restricted to a particular part of the country). You may have to look them up in a dictionary of American English or slang if your college dictionary does not define them. Look up the following words to find out how widely they are used: *six bits, vittles.*

2. Look up *paranoia.* Is Angelou using the word in its technical or general sense in paragraph 14?

SUGGESTIONS FOR WRITING

1. Describe an experience of your childhood that reveals something important about your world or upbringing. Build your details to a statement of your controlling idea. Remember that you are seeking details that reveal the typical quality of life in that world.

2. Describe an experience of your childhood from two points of view— that of the child and that of the young adult remembering the experience. Then comment on the differences between what the child experiences and what the adult remembers. Use these differences to arrive at a thesis.

topic sentence

The *topic sentence* of a paragraph is what its name suggests—the statement of the subject or topic of the paragraph, sometimes in the form of a phrase or brief transitional sentence at the beginning:

> Christmas time! That man must be a misanthrope indeed, in whose breast something like a jovial feeling is not roused—in whose mind some pleasant associations are not awakened—by the recurrence of Christmas.—Charles Dickens, *Sketches by Boz*

> Now comes the moral of the story—for it has a moral after all. —Dickens, *Sketches by Boz*

More commonly, the topic sentence is the central or controlling idea of the paragraph, which the various details and ideas of the paragraph develop:

> In our time it is broadly true that political writing is bad writing.

> In our time, political speech and writing are largely the defense of the indefensible.

> But if thought corrupts language, language can also corrupt thought.

These topic sentences open paragraphs of George Orwell's essay "Politics and the English Language." Placed at the beginning of the paragraph, the topic sentence gains prominence, and guides the attention of the reader. The topic sentence, however, may appear anywhere in the paragraph—at the beginning, the middle, or the end—and on occasion it may be divided between two sentences:

> As I have tried to show, modern writing at its worst does not consist in picking out words for the sake of their meaning and inventing images in order to make the meaning clearer. It consists in gumming together long strips of words which have already been set in order by someone else, and making the results presentable by sheer humbug.

In the paragraph that these sentences introduce, Orwell illustrates his topic idea through a long series of examples.

In many paragraphs a series of details builds to the topic sentence:

> At his press conference Smith could not answer questions about unemployment and pollution problems in his district. He admitted that he had not visited the district or talked to people living there since his election to the State Senate. An investigation last year confirmed that he had accepted bribes during his tenure as road commissioner. *These are reasons enough not to vote for Smith again.*

If the details are revealing enough to make the point by themselves, the topic idea may not be directly stated; it is then said to be *implied.*

It is useful to think of the topic sentence as a miniature thesis, to which all ideas and details of the paragraph connect, and which in turn develop the thesis of the whole essay.

THE GOLDEN TOKEN

Dwayne E. Walls

Dwayne E. Walls was born in 1932, and raised in Southern Appalachia. He joined the Air Force in 1951, where he gained newspaper experience, and later studied at Lenoir-Rhyne College and the University of North Carolina. Since 1956 Walls has worked as a journalist, and has received numerous awards for his reporting; he was nominated three times for the Pulitzer

Prize in journalism. His book *The Chickenbone Special* (1971) is mainly about rural black people in North Carolina.

[1] It is still winter when the planting cycle begins for the tobacco farmer. It is cold and wet and dreary, not the way New York is cold in winter and not the way Florida is wet in summer. It is clammy wet, muddy wet, the way it is when the land and the air are filled with dampness and the skies will neither heat nor freeze the dampness and be done with it.

[2] The dampness clings to the land and everything on the land. In cities like Durham and Richmond and Winston-Salem, it weaves itself into the rich aroma of processed tobacco rising from the cigarette factories. The invisible shroud thus formed drops over the cities, testing the olfactory sense of the natives and reassuring their sense of economic security. In the fields the dampness engulfs the machinery and fertilizes the germ of rust. It bathes and swells the doors of the barns and the privies and the little tenant houses so that the doors will not shut tight, allowing the dampness into the houses. It creeps in on the wind, through the cracks in the doors and windows and walls. It rises on air currents through the floor. It seeps in with the rain that spatters onto the tin roof and trickles into the nail holes and seam cracks, permeating the tenant houses; and then it attacks the tenants.

[3] Along the highways, men who can afford winter vacations begin noticing the strange-looking barns somewhere north of Rocky Mount, where the Interstate ends and U.S. 301 becomes, for a while, the main route for the Florida tourist trade. The barns stand high, as barns are supposed to stand. But they are not big the way barns are supposed to be, because they are not built to hold feed and livestock and equipment, and most of the year they stand empty. Except at harvesttime, when the tobacco must be hung inside them to roast under three or four days of intensive heat, the curing barns stand like tar-paper obelisks, commemorating nothing at all but hard labor.

[4] The tourist sees the barns and then he sees the houses, and he shakes his head and asks of his wife: Which is the barn and which is the house, for Christ's sake? Oh, yeah. That's the house. See the car

From "The Golden Token" in *The Chickenbone Special,* copyright © 1970, 1971, by Dwayne E. Walls. Reprinted by permission of Harcourt Brace Jovanovich, Inc.

out front? See the stove and refrigerator and wringer washing machine on the front porch? See the TV antenna?

[5]Now his wife shakes her head and asks of her husband: What kind of people would live in a place like that? Why don't they fix the place up a little? You'd think the least they could do is paint it. Paint doesn't cost that much, for heaven's sake.

[6]Lazy people. Shiftless people. Black people, the husband says. And then he puts them out of his mind. It is more pleasant to think of Florida and the sun, and that great little bar on Collins Avenue.

[7]Inside the farmhouses in the mean winter months, life is a torpid wake for what was and what will be again when spring comes. If he is resourceful and lucky, the farmer can get occasional work and come home to the smell of meat frying on the kitchen stove. He will lie down on a pallet or on the bare floor behind the kitchen stove and let the healing warmth penetrate his arthritic joints, and for a while he can put out of his mind everything else in his world except the heat, the smell and the sound of grease crackling in the pan above him, and the beauty of his wife's hips as she moves about the kitchen. In another room, his children will huddle close to a space heater, staring at a television set turned up deafeningly loud because one of his children is partially deaf from too many colds that turned into too many untreated ear infections. The family will eat and sleep around the stoves. The pallet in the kitchen will become the bed for one of the middle boys. The parents and the babies will sleep in the two beds in the front room. The remaining one or two rooms are not heated, and the older children will sleep there, sometimes three or four to a bed.

[8]The farmer's wife cannot do much laundering in the winter months because the laundry cannot be washed and dried in one day, and then someone must sleep without bedding, and someone will be left without socks or shirt or trousers because there is not enough clothing and bedding to restock the wet laundry. Sometimes the wash will not dry in a week, and the house has about it all winter the smell of urine-soaked bedding and sweat-soaked clothing. The passing tourist does not know that the car and the front-porch appliances are impotent symbols of possession. They do not work except in the sense that each is a refrigerator of sorts in winter and a storage closet in summer. Washing, even personal hygiene, is accomplished by carrying water in from the back-yard well, pouring

it into pots on the stove and then pouring it again into wash pans or buckets. The television set does work. But if the family is receiving welfare, they must be careful of the television set. Families who own fifteen-dollar used sets are not considered impoverished enough to draw welfare.

[9]And what of the man who is not resourceful, not lucky? Society, of course, looks after him. He can buy food stamps if he can borrow the money, or he can pick up free surplus commodities once a month if he can find some way to haul them home from the county seat. There is a chance that he can draw welfare. More than likely, he will end up mortgaging himself into bondage for another year by turning to the landlord or the country merchant who carries him or furnishes him if the farmer's landlord approves the credit. For a price only fifteen or twenty per cent higher than it would be if he had cash—plus ten-per-cent interest at settling-up time next fall, of course—the farmer can feed and clothe his family through another winter. The farmer considers his family and his chance of ever bettering his lot. He agrees to plant another crop and takes a bag of groceries home to his wife. The cycle begins again.

[10]The work starts in January with the preparation of the plant bed. The millions of tiny seeds must be planted safe from the wind and in the warmth of the sun, and so the farmer favors a clearing in the woods or a piece of new ground on the southern edge of the woods. He looks for a gentle slope that will allow good drainage, and scratches out a rectangle in the skin of the black earth—long and narrow and typically equal to about twenty yards of narrow rural highway. He doses the wound liberally with chemicals to kill the weeds and fungus and covers the whole thing carefully with a clear plastic bandage; then he leaves, hoping that he has selected a good spot, that the chemicals will do their work, and that the elements will cooperate with him or, at the very least, do him no harm. He is in debt again now. But this year, maybe this year, he will get good plants, make a good crop, and maybe there will be something left over at settling-up time. There is an old joke in tobacco country in which the smiling landlord announces to his tenant, "Well, Sam. We came out even again. You don't owe me a thing."

[11]In late winter, when the chemicals and the sun's rays have had six weeks or so to cleanse and enrich the soil in the plant bed, the farmer returns to plow the soil again—to feed it, to water it, to

spread the seed and change the plastic bandage for one of cheese-cloth. Later, when the seeds have taken hold and the little plants have begun to shoot up, he will return to the bed once more to remove the cover altogether.

[12] The time of transplanting begins in Florida in March and moves north with the sun, so that the Georgia-Florida crop has already started ripening when the ancient ritual of transplanting begins in North Carolina and Virginia.

[13] From transplant to harvest is the best time for the tobacco farmer. It is good even though that is when the work is most demanding, when the fields become blistering hot. It is good because there is work to be done, because the farmer has survived another winter to rejoice in the sunlight. It is a time when family and neighbor work together, sharing labor and meager equipment. While the men ready the fields to receive the plants, the women and children remove the young shoots from the plant bed and prepare them for transplanting.

[14] Alternately squatting among the plants and bending in that peculiar stoop that black mothers of the fields pass on to generations of daughters—feet planted wide, knees almost straight, body bent in a right angle at the hip, back horizontal to the ground—the women work rhythmically through the beds. The tender plants must be pulled gently from the soil and examined for maturity and health. The damaged plants must be discarded, along with those whose oversize leaves will block the sun's rays from the plant stem.

[15] The good plants are shaken lightly to remove the old soil and carefully stacked for the planters.

[16] The youngsters work more slowly than the women, partly because of inexperience and partly because of romance. Even in good plant beds the tobacco shoots sometimes are born with a tiny vine clinging to them. These infected shoots also must be discarded, and the search for them is a diligent one. For every youngster in tobacco country knows the little parasite as a "love vine" said to possess magical powers over matters of the heart.

[17] If you find a love vine, it is said, then you must lay it on a bush and leave it there overnight. If the vine is still alive the next morning, you know that your sweetheart loves you. It is a hardy vine that will survive on almost any living plant. Even the old women look for the love vines, and the discovery of one may bring a secret smile under a broad straw hat, or sometimes a burst of

raucous laughter. It is a good time to talk with friends about church, scattered families and old loves.

[18]When the plants are ready for setting into the fields, the farmer rigs his tractor with a water barrel and hitches a two-seat mechanical planter onto the rear. With his children or his neighbors feeding the plants into the planting wheel, he moves slowly down the rows. Carefully, symmetrically—forty-two inches between rows, twenty-two inches between plants—a plow on the planter cuts a furrow into the dark, sandy loam, drops a plant and a spurt of water into the cut, and then squeezes the soil up against the plant to keep it upright. The tractor moves slowly, and most small farmers can cover only one row at a time—one going and one coming and every fifth row left vacant for the sled at harvesttime.

[19]Some of the plants will not live, and the farmer must set new plants to replace them. If there is a good rain soon after the transplanting is completed, the ministers in the little Negro churches will offer a special thanksgiving, and the collection plates will be heavier with silver.

[20]The crop will grow for two months, and for the entire growing season it has to be treated with fungicide and insecticide, and chemicals to control the growth of suckers—damaging shoots that grow from the junction of the leaf stem and the stalk. As the tobacco matures, the blossoms that sprout at the top of the plant must be broken on every stalk so that they will not produce seed and retard the growth of the leaf.

[21]And then, one hot summer day, the farmer looks across his field and sees that the leaves at the bottom of the man-high stalk have faded from green to ripe yellow and it is time for the first priming. Each leaf must be picked at just the right stage of maturity, beginning at the bottom of the stalk and working toward the top. Thus, each field must be primed, or harvested, five, six, even seven times. Each harvest must be strung on sticks and hung in the barn for about three or four days of curing by artificial heat produced by oil or gas burners.

[22] The small, boxlike barns are not so much barns as kilns. The summer temperature in the upper rafters is already intense as the tobacco sticks are passed upward to small boys standing precariously on cross poles. Soon after the barn is packed to the bottom and the door bolted with a wooden peg, the heat inside becomes humanly unbearable. The leaves must be drained of every bit of moisture,

leaving them almost crisp enough to crumble between the fingers. The curing process is completed, the farmer's work is almost done, when the dried leaves are stacked and allowed to regain their moisture naturally. But the farmer cannot celebrate his harvest until his crop is auctioned on the warehouse floor.

COMMENT

Walls begins his essay by showing the reader the black tobacco-farming world as strangers see it—the winter travelers on their way to Florida— and as the farmers see it themselves. In this way he stresses what is unusual about that world. He also wants to show that the process of growing and harvesting tobacco is a human as well as a natural one—the natural process the more important one, because it reveals qualities of the human world. The topic sentences clarify the stages of the natural process and also those human qualities of the farmer's life. Most of the topic sentences state the central idea of the paragraph fully. One of them is mainly transitional: "And what of the man who is not resourceful, not lucky?"

QUESTIONS FOR STUDY AND DISCUSSION

1. What are the physical experiences—the smells, the feeling of the air and the earth—peculiar to tobacco farming? How does the author help the reader experience these sensations?

2. How do these physical experiences shape the life of the tobacco farmer?

3. What is gained by introducing the attitude of the travelers toward the barns and houses, in addition to showing what is unusual about these buildings? Is the author attacking a stereotype, as Maya Angelou does, or is he merely pointing up a contrast?

4. In how many ways does the author reveal his attitude toward the tobacco farmer and his world?

5. How do the topic sentences connect the paragraphs, in addition to stating the subject of the paragraph and perhaps the full idea?

6. What details help the reader visualize the process of growing tobacco? Why is that visualization necessary, given the purpose of the essay?

7. How similar is Walls to Angelou in purpose and ways of achieving it? Does he make the same assumptions about his audience?

VOCABULARY STUDY

1. Use the following words in sentences of your own. Let the content of the sentence clarify the meaning of the word: *seeps, permeating* (paragraph 2); *torpid* (paragraph 7); *hygiene* (paragraph 8); *commodities* (paragraph 9); *loam* (paragraph 18); *retard* (paragraph 20); *primed* (paragraph 21); *precariously* (paragraph 22).

2. Rewrite the third paragraph, supplying equivalent words and phrases for the following: *clings, weaves, shroud, engulfs, fertilizes, bathes, swells, creeps in, attacks.*

SUGGESTIONS FOR WRITING

1. Describe a kind of work—tending a gas pump, operating a service truck, cooking short orders—through the physical experiences associated with it.

2. Show how the conditions and environment of a kind of work shapes the lives of the workers and perhaps their families.

3. Compare the attitude of Walls toward the black tobacco farmer with that of Maya Angelou toward the black cotton pickers. Comment on the ways they reveal these attitudes.

FAST FOOD

Elaine Kendall

Elaine Kendall was born in 1929 in New York City, and lives now with her husband and two children in Princeton, New Jersey. She has written extensively about American life for *Vogue, Mademoiselle, Horizon, Harper's Magazine, Saturday Review,* and other periodicals. The essay printed here is part of a chapter from her book *The Happy Mediocrity* (1971).

¹ The recent boom in the food franchising business amounts to a rare and almost perfect example of American historical inevitability at work. The public companies that have been formed during the past ten years to purvey hamburger, fried chicken, and hot dogs to America have been the glamor stocks of the 1960's, and their track records make old champions like AT&T, General Motors, and electronics look lame by comparison. In a single year some of the food franchisers have shown price increases so huge as to be incredible—McDonald's up 346 percent from 1967 to 1968; Kentucky Fried Chicken up 700 percent; Lum's, essentially a frankfurter operation, up 1,280 percent. Nineteen seventy was a letdown. Lum's earnings rose only 165 percent, Kentucky Fried a mere 26 percent; McDonald's was up 30 percent. Everyone got hurt in 1970, but the investor who was up to his elbows in fast food seems to have escaped with relatively slight first-degree burns. In each case the triteness of the food contrasts sharply with the novelty of the stock quotations. Nothing much is new except the figures. The successful franchisers all work on the same fundamental principle, which is to sell their formulas, their names, and generous helpings of psychological support to individual entrepreneurs across the country. To emphasize their slight difference from their antecedents in the catering business, the franchisers like to refer to themselves as "systems," a word that hints at a new direction in American gastronomy. As the market reports prove, these "systems" are still all go. Every one of these companies is built on certain basic American attitudes toward food, attitudes that have been plain enough all along, but have suddenly become considerably plainer and almost certainly irreversible. The wonder is only that it took so long to happen.

² As befits a prototype, the McDonald's Hamburger Empire illustrates these attitudes beautifully. Although Ray Kroc, the president of McDonald's, doesn't attribute his success to anything as vague or chancy as historical inevitability, he certainly hasn't sold more than five billion hamburgers without a profound understanding of his market and the forces that shaped it.

³ Fifty seconds is regarded as the optimum length of time to prepare a McDonald's meal, which typically consists of a hamburger, a milk shake, and an order of french fries. McDonald's stores

have an eerily exaggerated resemblance to seventeenth-century New England dining rooms. Most contain no chairs, though a few experimental units with seating have been tested. "Things change," says Mr. Kroc, "and so do we." When and if America ever becomes a nation of two- or three-minute epicures, Mr. Kroc will be ready, but for the time being, the Puritan code is strictly enforced. Adults as well as children stand to feed, and there's no lolling around a McDonald's. "We never allow a jukebox, a cigarette machine, a vending device, a pinball game, or a telephone in a McDonald's restaurant," says Mr. Kroc. The lack of these amenities is intended to discourage teen-agers, a group that McDonald's can easily do without. The company even prefers not to hire waitresses, thereby reducing the temptation still further. When Mr. Kroc looks for a site, he counts "church steeples, signs of substantial family neighborhoods." This policy was widely publicized toward the end of 1968, just as Mr. Kroc was embarking on his second thousand set of stands.

[4]The ideal location for a McDonald's is the "above-average residential area." "We want young families," say the McDonald's scouts, and unlike the older highway drive-ins, which relied heavily on a snack trade, McDonald's attracts and gets a family dinner business. If they don't choose to lean against the bare walls inside for the time it takes to swallow the food, Mom, Dad, Sis, and Junior can sit in their car, depreciating their own upholstery, running their own heater, and listening to the radio. For 19 cents they get the hamburger, but customers are encouraged to supply their own shelter and ambience. McDonald's, however, serves an important side dish of security with each order. Every burger is guaranteed to be just like every other. The possibility of variation has been finally routed, thereby averting invidious comparisons with burgers past, as well as eliminating squabbling among the children for the biggest, the rarest, or the best. A McDonald's burger puts a moratorium on that kind of table (or back-seat) talk forever. The last one and the one before that, all the way back to 1955, were identical in every respect. The roast beef sandwich has been discontinued completely. It had an unfortunate tendency to deviate from a single standard.

[5]Each stand must be managed by a certified graduate of McDonald's "Hamburger University" where the curriculum consists of courses in Q.S.C.—Quality, Service, and Cleanliness. "We at McDonald's," says Mr. Kroc, "believe in these fundamentals and

really live by them." Although Hamburger University has a limited catalogue, it maintains an active research and development program. For instance, by the end of 1970, the company had adopted a scoop that delivers the same number of french-fried potato pieces every time, regardless of who is running the machine or where. The company laboratories, of course, have long since arrived at the perfect meat-fat ratio, the perfect size (3½ inches by ³⁄₁₆ inch B.C.— Before Cooking), and the perfect roll measurement (3¾ inches), thus assuring a bun surround of no less than ¼ inch. The university seems to have a strong science and math department.

⁶There is still another, subtler factor that contributes to the success of these plans. Franchise shops are not dependent on that rare and mercurial personage, the chef. The chef's place in this country has always been awkward and ambiguous—a man doing woman's work, a kind of super-servant who has to be treated like an artist or, at least, a craftsman. Few people have ever been attracted to so dubious a profession, but lots of Americans are available and willing to press buttons and work levers. There is nothing effeminate about that. Franchised food is manufactured, rather than "cooked" in any true sense. Its components are delivered to the shop already blended, assembled and portioned. The store only heats it. The methods have been scientifically developed, and the serving is done according to the assembly-line principles that we approve. The new food is simply bought and consumed, out of stock. The identical recipe serves everyone.

⁷The bespoke meal, like the bespoke suit or shoe, seems destined to become a special privilege for the quirky few. The trend is clearly away from the custom restaurant, and although a few such places may linger in the cities for some time to come, it is doubtful whether Americans will put up with so costly, so complex, and so essentially undemocratic an institution much longer. The franchisers have something far more appropriate to offer, something that Alexis de Tocqueville hinted at when he said that "the majority possesses a power which is physical and moral at the same time; it acts upon the will as well as upon the actions of men, and it represses not only all contests, but all controversy. . . ." In 1835, of course, the only kind of despotism De Tocqueville really feared was political.

⁸The food that Americans eat at home has been thoroughly branded, standardized, and nationalized for more than fifty years,

and it should have been obvious that the public would welcome—
would eventually *demand*—the same sort of reassurance and the
same monotony in the food they consumed elsewhere. The chain
restaurants like Howard Johnson's recognized the mood long ago,
but a chain is only as strong as its weakest link. Howard Johnson's
was a great plan, but it stopped short of the ideal.Twenty-eight
flavors of ice cream are twenty-six flavors too many, when 90
percent of the people are content with chocolate or vanilla. Howard
Johnsons are cluttered with tables, chairs, rest rooms, telephones,
and banks of vending machines. They employ waitresses, a proved
and expendable hazard. While the newer outlets along the turnpikes are considerably more functional, they are apparently not as
austere as America would like. Some HoJos even serve whiskey, a
practice known to encourage talking and lingering over meals,
slowing down turnover, and contributing to wear and tear on the
premises. For Howard Johnson it's almost too late to change, and it
seems destined to become the sybarite's chain. The germ of franchising was there from the start, but it was not fully exploited. Howard
Johnson's had a distinctive quasi-Colonial architectural style; it had
the limited menu, the moderate price, and a central commissary to
assure the public that variation in the appearance and quality of
HoJo food would be held to a minimum. All the choicest locations
were theirs, and by the end of the 1950's when most of the turnpikes
were complete, there was hardly anywhere else to eat without
taking a long and time-wasting detour. HoJo grew and thrived, but
not as dramatically as the franchising companies have done. The
reason is simple and economically sound. Howard Johnson's continued to spend company money every time a new store opened. The
franchisers do not. The required capital is put up by the franchisee,
a refinement which allows corporations like McDonald's, Lum's, and
the various chicken systems to proliferate at a far more rapid rate
than any old-fashioned chain could hope to do. The franchisers are
thus in a position to crowd everyone else right off the map.
McDonald's, for example, receives an infusion of $97,000 every time
a new outlet opens. By September 30, 1970, there were 1,481 of
them, and the home office has a perpetual waiting list of 100 people
with funds in hand, marking time until there is an available seat in
Hamburger University. There are no scholarships in HU. Every
student not only pays his own way, but actually *endows* the
institution.

[9]Ninety-seven thousand dollars is double or even triple the amount of capital the other franchisers require, but the McDonald's franchisee, like the Harvard freshman, is a very special person. He is, according to corporate records, between thirty-five and fifty years old with a solid business background. (Failures do not accumulate or borrow ninety-seven grand very readily.) He has, in many cases, tried the Organization Life and rejected it. Unlike the product he merchandizes, the McDonald's man tends to be a strong individualist. He's not afraid of hard work. The stands are open all day seven days a week until late in the evening. A McDonald's franchisee, in fact, seems to represent something close to the early American business tradition. Each candidate is assured that he can count on an annual revenue of $300,000—approximately five times the average for drive-in restaurants and considerably more than can be realized by investing $97,000 somewhere else. Once the shop is under way, 10 percent of this gross goes right back to the parent company for "counseling services," local and national advertising, and rental of the premises. These appropriations are rigidly fixed. The initial investment buys the sign, the university course, the recipe, and the right to the magic name. After that, the acceptee is on his own, though troubleshooters from Papa Kroc's regional offices are readily available for advice and support. The lease is for twenty years, and it represents a thoroughgoing commitment to cheap hamburgers, as well as a promise to the American public that this is no mere fad. There's every assurance that McDonald's will be with us in 1990. So far there are no officially acknowledged instances of a McDonald's stand having failed, though there are undoubtedly some that have changed hands or even reverted to the parent company. McDonald's maintains a few hundred house shops so that radical innovations like chairs, apple pie, and larger hamburgers may be tried at no risk to the private investor. The triple-decker Mighty Mac was launched this way and is now considered a major factor in McDonald's stability during otherwise lean 1970.

[10]Most of the other franchisers use the McDonald's system as a paradigm, though often on a more limited scale. Even if the investment is only half what McDonald's requires, however, there is bound to be "education," advice, and continuing control. McDonald's may get particularly solvent types—"former dentists, retired Navy officers, and even a man who was once former assistant Secretary of Labor," but such impressive credentials are not required for a

Lum's, a Chicken Delight, a Colonel Sanders', a Burger Chef, Minnie Pearl's, a Denny's, a Nathan's Famous, a Big Boy, a Dairy Tastee, King, Queen, or Freeze, or the pizza establishments. (There are, after all, not enough ex-dentists, naval officers, or Labor Department assistants in the country to buy into all these places.) In general, the franchisee is a man who would like to be on his own but still needs the special props: the moral support and business assistance that the franchising companies can provide. He has usually accumulated $30,000 to $50,000 and wants an assurance that he's not jeopardizing it. He is looking for a tested, accepted, certified, sure thing, and the franchisers seem to have it.

[11]These success stories thoroughly disprove the notion that the American people dine out in order to have something that they can't get at home. The franchisers sell only those items that can be prepared quickly and easily by anyone. The food is comparatively cheap, but you can still have a bigger, juicier hamburger for your 19 cents if you divide a pound of ground meat into quarters. The burger systems get *ten* to a pound, a ratio rarely approached by even the most grudging housewife. What the franchisers seem to be selling is the antithesis of warmth, charm, atmosphere, social life—or even nourishment. They are actually anti-restaurants, judged by any of the usual definitions.

[12]If these places existed only to cater to people caught on the road at mealtime, they'd be readily explainable, but that's not the case. The fact that they often serve that purpose is really quite incidental to the whole idea. They are on the road because America is mostly road, but as Mr. Kroc says, and the others agree, residential and business neighborhoods make the most desirable locations. The idea is for someone in the office to bring back a bag of hamburgers for the steno pool or for Dad to pick up dinner while the family waits in the car or in front of the TV. That sort of trade accounts for two-thirds of the total volume. Between-meal business is just lagniappe.

[13]The fried chicken franchisers of which there are now dozens, rely almost entirely upon a regular mealtime trade. A bucket of fried chicken is hardly anyone's idea of a mid-morning, after school, or bedtime snack, and it's not something that an officeworker can keep on the desk while getting through the paper work. The chicken shops go far beyond the hamburger and shake concept, which, despite its newer refinements (or lack of refinements), can still be an

impulse purchase. The 19-cent hamburger is small enough not to spoil the appetite, and despite the hoopla about secret recipes and carefully guarded formulas, there's not much you can do with 1.6 ounces of anything. Fried chicken is different. It constitutes a genuine meal, both in price and in substance. Morever, chicken does take some time to prepare, and the differences between methods of frying chicken can be noticeable. The chicken systems are not as dependent on the car as the hamburger empires. Chicken Delight will even deliver a bucketful to your very door in less time than it takes to warm up the oven. Chicken Delight is actually selling a total freedom package—from the hot stove, the freezer, the supermarket, the automobile, and the decision. This variation of the idea is essentially foreign in origin, though that fact is not stressed in any publicity. Nevertheless, in India and many other "emerging" countries of the Orient, peddlers push barrows down the poorer streets selling hot meals to those who have no cooking or food storage facilities. The notion that such a technique would work in America, where kitchen equipment is the grandest and most elaborate in the world, is delightfully provocative. We may be working not only toward the antirestaurant, but toward the antikitchen as well.

[14]The capital of the takeout chicken business is Nashville, Tennessee, the home of Kentucky Colonel Sanders, Eddy Arnold's Tennessee Fried, and the recently formed Mahalia Jackson System, aimed at what is euphemistically known as the "ethnic" market. Minnie Pearl's is in Nashville too, but that one has not got very far out. To get ahead in chicken franchising, it apparently helps to be able to carry a tune. (Ballplayers have not proved to be as handy in the kitchen.) Both Eddy Arnold and Minnie Pearl are *Grand Ole Opry* stars, and Mahalia Jackson can belt out a song better than either of them. Kentucky Colonel Sanders, however, is an important exception. He seems to have created his coast-to-coast $35,000,000 business entirely on the strength of his snow-white mustache, his secret blend of herbs and spices, and his two-step cooking process, which involves tenderizing the chicken under pressure before frying it. Singing may help, but it isn't the *sine qua non*. Neither, apparently, is chicken itself. The Kentucky Colonel sells everything to its franchisees *except* the chicken. The parent company supplies all the real essentials—the special cooking equipment, the signs, the napkins, the paper pails with the colonel's instantly recognizable likeness, and the precious blend of seasonings. The franchisee must find

the chickens wherever he can. Under the circumstances, the accessories become crucial to the entire operation, because chicken has a disconcerting tendency to vary in taste and quality. Some are bound to be better or worse than others. The illusion of sameness therefore rests heavily on the paper goods and the equipment. People do not buy just "chicken"—they buy Colonel Sanders' chicken, and it has to be dependable every time, spring, fall, summer, and winter. These accessories do for all those different chickens what the McDonald's laboratory technicians do for the hamburger—make it all look, smell, and taste the same. How wonderful for an American riding around Cuernavaca to come upon Colonel Sanders' pink and white face on the sign and know that while he may be getting a Mexican chicken, it will be a naturalized Kentucky Fried Mexican chicken, wrapped in a virtual affidavit proving that it's not some unknown, foreign *pollo*. The future of the franchising business, in the day of the 747 jets, really bends the mind. The franchisers are enlarging their Hamburger Universities and Fried Chicken Colleges, their Pizza Institutes and their Frankfurter Prep Schools, and accepting exchange students from all over the world. Colonel Sanders, always a leader, has recently entered into an agreement with Mitsubishi to establish Japanese Kentucky Chicken outlets.

[15]Wall Street has many experts on this newest of the wonder businesses, and while these sages agree that "quality issues of franchising stock are no longer on the bargain counter," they are still considered reasonably sound long-term investments, less speculative than a lot of more venerable industries. Donald Trott, of Jas. H. Oliphant and Company, says, with some restraint, that "the franchise stocks should eventually prove highly rewarding, as earnings continue to build up at about twenty to fifty percent annually." Of course, Mr. Trott suggests some caution. Scores of undercapitalized fly-by-night imitations have arrived on the scene, and they have presented a serious threat to the concept. A franchiser needs time to set up his university and find a qualified faculty. He must have good locations, and he must avoid obvious mistakes like offering too broad a menu. Certain food items are inherently unsuitable for franchising. It is important to settle on something that is totally accepted by the entire American population, and the quality must be either controllable, as in the case of hot dogs or hamburger, or disguisable, as with fried chicken. Corned beef, for instance, would be a very poor risk because it varies tremendously from one cut to

another. Nathan's Famous, however, is experimenting with it on a small scale. Tacos and enchiladas go well in California and the Southwest, but research has demonstrated that upstate New York is not yet ready for them. Fish-and-chips is doing well. Generally speaking, the item to be franchised should represent a general consensus of taste. A company that takes a gamble on something "ethnic," like Chinese egg rolls, pizza, or kosher delicatessen, usually finds that it must modify the product drastically—less garlic in the salami, process cheese in the pizza, no shrimp in the egg roll. Another consideration that works against the novel or unusual is that the franchised food has to be inexpensive, durable, and reasonably easy to manage. Beef bourguignonne or lobster New-burg would be absurd for those reasons. The few people who want something so eccentric for dinner don't usually care to eat standing up or in the car. They're difficult types, often insisting on candle-light, wine, waiters, dishes, linen, and other overhead-raising frip-peries. So, while the outlook for food franchising is still bright for the stock market investor and the franchisers, for ex-dentists and retired naval officers, it is somewhat dim for the hungry noncon-formist in search of an interesting meal.

[16] Although the business is only ten years old, the franchised chains of eleven or more units now purchase 25 percent of all goods—food as well as the extras—currently sold to commercial restaurants of any kind. Not even the horseless carriage caught on that quickly. There isn't much doubt that the chicken systems and the Mighty Macs are here to stay. Moreover, the transitional period of coexistence, during which we will have both "regular" restau-rants and the franchisers, just as we once had horses and autos, will be short. By February, 1969, those franchisers that had already become public companies were operating more than 8,000 outlets. The huge remainder remain truly uncountable, and there is no law to say that a franchiser has to go public and publish his figures. Most of them do not. One of the unique features of this particular business is that it can expand indefinitely without ever issuing stock for general sale. The smaller, privately held corporations, of course, will imitate their better known predecessors on the big board, capitalizing upon the established popularity of the same proved items. Multiplicity will not give us variety, but rather its direct opposite. In many medium-sized American cities and in most suburbs, hamburger, hot dog, pizza, and chicken stands are the only

restaurants. An entire generation of children has already grown up thinking that McDonald's is the word for hamburger the way Kleenex is the word for tissue and that "fried" always modifies "chicken."

[17]The automobile alone doesn't wholly explain the success of the franchising concept, although it's certainly central to it. Still, if it were just a case of getting into the car and going to eat or grabbing a quick bite once you *were* out driving, there would be no need for micromeasurements, secret formulas, tamper-proof safes for the spice blends, specially designed ovens, patented potato scoops, and endless guarantees of uniformity. Mere cheapness isn't the answer either, because by the time everybody has had the shake, the burger, and the appropriate "complementary" foods, the meal isn't really for pennies after all. Adults can never be satisfied with 1.6 ounces of hamburger in any case, so bare subsistence level is obviously two or three. The answer is not to be found in the swinging atmosphere, the soft lights, the jukebox, or the good-looking waitress with the long legs and the heart of gold because those things aren't presented. Change of scene can't be a factor because the franchise restaurant is the supreme example of "seen one, you've seen 'em all." Taste? There's no accounting for or disputing that, but it doesn't seem likely that a formula like the Kentucky Colonel's (devised to turn millions of different chickens into a single, archetypical chicken) can leave the consumer much to remember. And if the franchise dinner isn't cheap, fun, exciting, novel, tasty, or even especially convenient, where is its power?

[18]It seems clear that the American people yearn to be told what to eat, long to have that particular decision made for them. Only half a dozen options are available from these places, out of all the thousands of edibles that can be raised, grown, processed, and marketed in this huge, temperate, rich, and fertile country. We have narrowed the choices down to a nearly irreducible minimum. We, the most various collection of people ever assembled into a single nation, have agreed that we will be satisfied with these rigid limitations and that we all will stay satisfied from the time we can first be propped into a car seat until long after we're eligible for Medicare. If we have a widening generation gap, irreconcilable racial discord, or a new sense of individuality, no one would ever know it from the menu at the franchise shop. There the whole experience of eating has been completely drained of every last personal, social, and sensual aspect. You never have to give it a second thought.

COMMENT

Kendall builds to her thesis statement at the end of paragraph 1: the fast food companies have been "built on certain basic American attitudes toward food." Each of the paragraphs that follow deal with these attitudes, the topic sentences usually identifying or referring to them in some way. In paragraphs 3–6, which concern a typical fast food chain, Kendall moves from the more obvious practices that have made McDonald's a success to the less obvious ones. In paragraphs 7–8, she compares McDonald's with other chains before discussing other practices of McDonald's that have been widely imitated. After drawing a few preliminary conclusions about American attitudes (paragraphs 11–12), she turns to the fried chicken chains, which represent a different attitude toward fast food and different practices. The concluding paragraphs of the essay draw conclusions about the fast-food industry and American attitudes. In general, Kendall moves from specific examples to general ideas and uses her topic sentences to focus the discussion of each paragraph and to clarify her organization.

QUESTIONS FOR STUDY AND DISCUSSION

1. Paragraph 2 is transitional, connecting the thesis statement of paragraph 1 to the illustration that follows, and providing the topic sentence for paragraph 3. How does this topic sentence fit the examples of paragraph 3?

2. Which of the topic sentences in the remainder of the essay make direct reference to the concluding sentence of the preceding paragraph, as a means of transition?

3. How many opening sentences of Kendall's paragraphs state the central or controlling idea?

4. How does the whole essay illustrate "American historical inevitability at work"? What qualities of Americans is Kendall concerned with?

5. How are the various fast-food chains different from one another? What do they have in common? Are these similarities and differences equally important to the thesis of the essay?

6. Is Kendall merely illustrating a trait of American life, or is she seeking to persuade readers to change their attitude toward food and to change their eating habits?

7. Do you agree with Kendall's characterization of fast food and the reasons she gives for it? Do you and your friends prefer fast food to the home-cooked variety?

VOCABULARY STUDY

Complete the following sentences, using the italicized words in one of their dictionary meanings:

    a. The *triteness* of her statements is shown by
    b. The *prototype* for the sons of the family was
    c. There is no use in *depreciating*
    d. He made an *invidious* comparison between
    e. The *ambiguity* in the directions is shown by
    f. His *mercurial* temper is best revealed in
    g. The *innovations* in her design for the building were
    h. There is no reason to *jeopardize*
    i. The *antithesis* of democracy is
    j. The difference between an *ethnic* neighborhood and a mixed one is
    k. One *sensual* pleasure to be found in winter hikes is

SUGGESTIONS FOR WRITING

1. Describe your tastes in and attitude toward fast food. Use your description to state your agreement or disagreement with Kendall's ideas.

2. Compare your eating habits in different places—home, the school cafeteria, a fast-food store, for example. Use this comparison to state a thesis.

3. Discuss your agreement or disagreement with one of the following statements:
    a. "Multiplicity will not give us variety, but rather its direct opposite."
    b. "It seems clear that the American people yearn to be told what to eat, long to have that particular decision made for them."
    c. "We have narrowed the choices down to a nearly irreducible minimum."

order of ideas

One common order of ideas in essays is the *chronological*. In reporting an experience or describing a process we tend to present the facts or steps in the order they occur. In describing how to bake a cake, you would give the steps in the order you perform them, and you would list the ingredients before telling how to combine them. You would not explain to a person learning to drive how to turn corners until you had explained how to brake and control the steering wheel. We can change this chronological order somewhat— maybe starting with the final step to give the reader a sense of purpose. If we report the steps of a process or the facts of an experience out of chronological order, we must be certain that the reader understands the natural order.

The order of ideas in descriptive writing may be *spatial*—from background to foreground, from sky to earth, from north to south. Or they may be *temporal*—from past to present, from morning to evening. If we are giving reasons for supporting a political candidate, we can state them in the order of importance, or we can move from specific reasons (the candidate's voting record) to general ones (impressions of character). The principle of order usually will depend on the needs of clear exposition and on how much the reader knows about the subject. In describing the care of an automobile, we would probably discuss easy things before difficult ones—especially if our readers are people owning their first car. An automobile company, training mechanics in the repair of new engines, might proceed in the same way. Or it might proceed from the most common to the most unusual problems that the mechanics are likely to encounter.

We will shortly consider kinds of analysis—comparison and contrast, example, cause and effect—that provide important ways of ordering ideas in the whole essay as well as in the paragraph.

CONFESSIONS

Mrs. Kemper Campbell

Mrs. Kemper Campbell was born in 1886. After college and law school at the University of Southern California in Los Angeles, she practiced law with her husband for 35 years, retiring in 1953. During her long career of public service, she was a deputy district attorney (the first woman to hold such a position in California), taught medical jurisprudence, and wrote extensively about her life and the American scene in a series of books. She lives on a ranch in Victorville, California.

[1] There are two sound reasons for memorializing one's faults. Once you have admitted to them, friends are on notice and can avoid trouble. And when you have defined them, there is a hint of repentance.

[2] These traits or sins, depending on your side of the shield, are uniquely mine—not one of my children has inherited them, and my friends do not sympathize with them. First, I do not cut my flowers. I want to see them growing in the garden. It makes me sad to pick them and then find them fading as soon as my back is turned. And since I do not pick my flowers I do not want anyone else to pick them.

[3] Once I tended a peony with great care. It was the first peony I had raised on the desert. Finally it had one promising pink bud. On

a Thursday my cook phoned to tell me the awful truth. A guest had picked my peony. My anger was greater than her offense. She saw me when I came home for the weekend and threw the flower into the toilet and pulled the chain. I never even saw the flower in full bloom. But I forgave her when she wrote a penitent letter. She had looked all over Los Angeles for a replacement. Not one was to be found. She had mistaken the peony for a rose to wear in her hair.

[4]My next failing is harder to define. I do not like people to take my friends. People go shopping for friends as they would go to a dress shop. "I like this one," they say, and they extend uncalled-for kindnesses which cannot be ignored. I will divide my acquaintances with anyone—even strangers. But I am jealous of my intimate friends. I do not want many close friends; they are a blessing and an obligation. I find that I can only encircle a dozen or so with my love and protection. You are welcome to borrow my books, anyone can use my car, but I do not want to share my friends except with each other. My conduct is indefensible. It does not even endear me to the friends I have. I do not recommend this attitude.

[5]And last of all, I boast of my few generosities. I am never the "anonymous giver." In spite of what the Bible says about not letting your right hand know what your left hand does, I keep my right hand well-informed.

[6]There was a great woman who lived in Victorville. After she died it became known that she had helped many of our neighbors. She had paid to have a little boy's clubfeet corrected. She had buried a lone Indian widow beside her husband. She had kept a hard-working man from losing his home because his wife was ill. She had boasted of none of these things and she had sworn the recipients to secrecy while she lived. The village loved her and called a school by her name. They will never do this for me.

[7]I confess to these vices not to distinguish myself from all the other people I know but to warn them against the same failings. Let them discover their own faults and not copy mine. I wouldn't like that. I'm sure there is no danger. "There never was a hunchback by persuasion."

[8] I am not truly repentant. I am like a boy I grew up with so very long ago. He was engaged to a devout Christian girl. She persuaded him to attend a revival service. The minister asked those who wanted to be saved to stand up. The boy stood up and asked them to pray for him so that he would want to be saved. He said that so far he had no interest in salvation.

COMMENT

Mrs. Campbell outlines the essay in her first paragraph: she admits her failings, then mentions the "hint of repentance" she will discuss in paragraph 8: "I am not truly repentant." This discovery belongs at the end of the essay, not at the beginning. She tells us in paragraph 4 that she is presenting her first two failings in the order of their ease of definition: the second failing is "harder to define" than the first. She may have saved her third failing for last because boasting is the hardest for her to define or because she considers it her most serious failing. Perhaps both. Since her purpose is to warn her friends about faults that will affect them, she does not try to discuss all of them.

QUESTIONS FOR STUDY AND DISCUSSION

1. In what other ways might the three failings have been presented to the reader? What purpose might this different order serve?

2. What other traits of character can you predict about Mrs. Campbell, given the faults she discusses? Can you predict some of her virtues?

3. How does Mrs. Campbell identify the audience she has in mind, in the course of the essay?

4. Has she presented a thesis, or is the essay only a series of loosely connected confessions about her life?

5. Where in the essay does she present ideas chronologically, and why?

VOCABULARY STUDY

Look up the following words: *vice, failing, fault, sin, mistake, error*. Find a meaning for each word not shared by the others in this list and illustrate each of them in a sentence. In your dictionary, some of these words may be compared in a synonym list at the end of the definition. The synonym list for *vice*, for example, may refer you to *fault*. If your dictionary does not contain such synonym listings, you will have to compare the various definitions.

SUGGESTIONS FOR WRITING

1. Discuss several of your faults. State the purpose of your discussion in the opening paragraph, and remind your reader of it in your conclusion. Before writing, decide on the order of your ideas. Notice that if your purpose is to amuse your reader, you will probably want to present the most humorous of your faults last to avoid anticlimax.

2. Consider the various purposes and audiences that an analysis of one of your friend's virtues could serve. Write one paragraph analyzing these virtues for one of these purposes. Then rewrite the paragraph for another purpose, and revise the order of ideas to accord with it.

GROWING UP ON LONG ISLAND

Jim Brown

Jim Brown was born in 1936, and was raised in Georgia and New York. He attended Syracuse University, where he played football, and from 1957 to 1965 he played fullback with the Cleveland Browns. In 1958 and 1963, he was the Player of the Year. Brown is now a film actor. His autobiography, *Off My Chest,* from which the essay printed here is taken, was published in 1963.

[1] Psychologists, sociologists, and writers are fond of blaming juvenile delinquency and a variety of other disturbances on broken homes. I am not learned in such matters except for the fact that unlike many of the psychologists, sociologists, and writers, I happen to have come from a broken home. It's my opinion that the experts have given us poor children of misfortune a little too much sympathy.

[2] As a child, I liked movies. I was always a self-reliant kid, and consequently thought nothing of going to a movie alone. The upshot of this was that years later a national magazine writer searched into my past and came up with the verdict that I had been driven by pangs of insecurity to retreat into the darkness of theaters. Actually I just liked Cary Grant, Gary Cooper, and many of the other actors.

[3] I get a little weary of hearing broken homes blamed for 96.3 percent of American youth's difficulties. John Wooten, a big Cleveland lineman who opens up holes for me to run through, comes from

a broken home, and he and I have discussed the effect that such an environment has on children. We search our memories to recall when and how we suffered torment, but we find little to go on.

⁴My guess is that thanks to all the yakking about broken homes, a lot of kids have found a good excuse to get into trouble. The broken home is their crutch in Juvenile Court. I am not dogmatic about this. Looking back on my own boyhood, there were many times when I came perilously close to becoming a no-account. It took a kind word here and a guiding hand there to point me in the right direction. My teachers appealed to my better judgment. And so I submit that almost every kid at one time or another is given an opportunity to respond to similar kindnesses, but he is less likely to respond when he has learned in advance that he possesses a ready-made excuse—the broken home—for irresponsibility.

⁵By rough count, my mother and Sweet Sue reconciled four times during my youth but never for long. Sue worked at a variety of jobs—porter, caddy, waiter, etc.—but found himself unable to embrace the concept of permanent employment. He would earn a few dollars, then turn his attention to the gaming tables.

⁶I never came to know him well, or at least not nearly as well as other kids knew their fathers, but I liked Sue very much. Whenever he was around we were always running footraces. Not once did I beat him. He had a good heart and was what you might call a responsible gambler. He gambled with his own money, never with my mother's. And each time he left us, another reconciliation over, he would tell me: "Treat your mother good. You may not always like what she tells you to do, but understand she's telling you for your own good." Sue passed in and out of my life as if his coming and going were no more than the design by which we were to live. I did not miss having a father.

⁷When I first arrived in the North at the age of nine, my mother was employed by a Jewish family—the Brockmans—who lived in the well-to-do, all-white suburb of Great Neck, Long Island. They provided us with a small one-bedroom apartment off the kitchen. However, I had to attend school several miles away in Manhasset, a community that ranged from comfortably middle class to very poor. The poor lived in an area called "the Valley," which was ripe with slums that made the community fathers wince. Visible to motorists passing down Northern Boulevard through Manhasset, the slums were regarded as a bad advertisement for the town

and later were torn down and replaced by a park and a housing project.

[8]In Manhasset, Nate Brown became Jimmy Brown. At school I enrolled as James Nathaniel Brown, so the teachers called me James and the kids made it Jimmy. Many of the kids in my elementary school were from the poor Valley district, and I found out my first day in school that the student body was tough. I wasted no time fighting my way to the top.

[9]That first day, my mother dressed me neat-as-a-pin in a starched shirt and creased trousers; she brushed my hair and sent me off to school in a taxi. The student body took note of my arrival. At recess in the schoolyard, a Negro boy—no bigger nor smaller than I—addressed me. "You look real pretty, Sis," he said, and promptly shoved me back on my heels. "Well, good," I thought. Manhasset was going to be just as playful as St. Simons Island. I knocked him down and dove on top of him and began punching the daylights out of him. "Dirty fighter!" all the kids hollered. I stopped punching and looked up, mystified. Down on the island, this was the way we always fought. The purpose of knocking someone down was to sit on him and get in the best licks. Nobody back home called it dirty fighting.

[10]Anyhow, while I was trying to decide whether to go on, a man whom the kids called Bulldog Drummond strode into the schoolyard and yanked me off my new friend. Bulldog Drummond was the school principal, Mr. Hutchens. The kids had named him after the hero of the radio program because Mr. Hutchens had a square jaw and was old-fashioned tough.

[11]"I'll show you how we settle these things here," Mr. Hutchens told me. He marched us into the gym and handed us boxing gloves. I'd never seen a pair of boxing gloves. My opponent, having been marched to the gym by Mr. Hutchens on previous occasions, knew how to use the gloves. He gave me a licking. "These northerners have a funny way of doing things," I thought, but out of sight of Mr. Hutchens I managed to win all my fights and become known as a tough guy. My mother continued to send me off to school in a taxi, all starched and spotless.

[12]The Brockmans were wonderful people to live with. They bought me my first basketball and hung a basket for me in the yard. They did more things for me than I can remember, and even after they moved to Los Angeles several years later, they continued to

correspond with my mother and send her gifts. I would have liked to have lived with the Brockmans all my boyhood, but after perhaps two years there I was too old to live with my mother in a one-bedroom apartment. The Brockmans, with children of their own, had given us all the space they could, so my mother roomed me out with a Negro family in Manhasset.

[13]I wasn't happy in Manhasset. The lady of the house was very religious. She was, no doubt, a good woman but quite stern. Somehow, I felt like an intruder.

[14]Happily, I always saw my mother on weekends. I loved my mother as much as any son would, and yet I was never able to bring myself to call her mama. Mama was my great-grandmother, down on St. Simons. I didn't know what to call my mother. Once in a while I called her mother, but the word always sounded strange on my lips. I had known affection from my great-grandmother and had returned it, but was never able to demonstrate, overtly, my affection for my mother. This hurt her, I know. But in a way, I had two mothers, and mama had gotten there first.

[15]When the Brockmans moved to Los Angeles, my mother took a first-floor flat in Manhasset and brought me to live with her again, and I was happy once more. Her expenses were higher and she had trouble finding enough work, but with a lot of scraping she managed to keep me neatly dressed. My neatness had become a point of pride with me, and later, my high school football coach, Ed Walsh, came to realize this. "How'd you like to take a trip into Manhattan with me tomorrow?" he said to me one day. The next day I found myself standing in a Howard's store, where Ed Walsh had me fitted for a fine suit.

[16]My coaches and teachers were the big people in my life. The Lord knows, they had their work cut out for them in trying to make something of me, but they went at it.

[17]I had no interest in studies and, what's more, had become president and official warlord of a teen-age gang known as the Gaylords. We held dances and parties and with the ticket receipts decked ourselves out in reversible jackets—base black with orchid trim on one side and base orchid with black trim on the other. We had our gang name lettered across our backs and our own names in front. The jackets were a big deal.

[18]Many teen-age gangs roamed a string of communities across Long Island, picking up girls and attending rival gangs' parties

uninvited. Our Long Island gangs, however, were not of the zip gun variety known to Brooklyn. Our boys carried switchblade penknives but only to build up their own egos. They liked to stand on street corners clicking their knives, but they never used them in fights. Fights generally wound up with an enactment of the *West Side Story* bit—that is, warlord pitted against warlord, with everyone else forming a circle.

[19]As warlord of the Gaylords, I rarely had to fight, simply because my opponents almost always backed down. Since my first year on Long Island—the year I'd fought my way to the top of the class—I'd had a fairly formidable reputation. Still, I should have known that sooner or later I'd have to face a blade. One night in Hempstead I did.

[20]We had invited ourselves to a party being held by a rival gang. For a while, all was peaceful. I was just standing there, listening to the phonograph music and minding my own business. The rival warlord, however, had been drinking liquor and growing belligerent on it. He swayed with the music and snapped his fingers and then, pretending to be only releasing his feeling for the music, gave me a hard slap on the back. I knew he meant it as a challenge. I said nothing. He slapped me a second time, and I told him, "Look, don't slap me on the back." I moved a few steps away. "Oh, you think you're something big?" he said. "You guys come in here in your sharp jackets and think you're something." I said to myself, "Here it goes." I told him, "Look, we can settle this fast. Just come outside." He got loud. "Sure I'll come outside," he shouted for everyone to hear. "I'll wipe up the street with you." We went outside, and everyone crowded around us. Then, click! Out came his blade.

[21]I had no knife myself. I never carried one, because I never believed a knife would make me any bigger and I knew I could never cut anyone. Now I had to think fast. I reached into my pocket and held my hand there for a menacing moment. All I had in it was a ringful of keys. With a great show of purpose, I worked one key into position so that it pointed sharply against my trousers. Then I whipped my hand from my pocket. The instant I did, my opponent closed his knife and shoved it into his pocket. He smiled weakly. I opened the palm of my hand, revealing a fistful of keys, and then hauled off with my other hand—also open—and gave him a hard slap in the face. End of *West Side Story* bit. "Let's go home," I said to the Gaylords.

[22]Actually, I guess I never quite fit the image of a gang warlord. Though I never minded a fight, I never picked one and I disliked bullies. Kids sometimes teased me for not smoking or drinking liquor, but I couldn't see how a cigaret dangling from the corner of my mouth could make me any tougher. Then, too, I was coming to realize that my physical strength could be put to better use on a ball field than in fist fights.

[23]A succession of great men—men who were great simply because they cared—had come into my life:

[24]First, there was Jay Stranahan, coach of the basketball, lacrosse, and six-man football teams of Plandome Road Junior High. "Jimmy, you have tremendous athletic ability," he told me. "Don't waste it." There had been no such thing as football on St. Simons Island; the first game I'd seen in Manhasset had been on a corner lot that had been picked clean of rocks and broken glass. Now Jay Stranahan was telling me that I could play this game—and lacrosse and basketball, too—better than any kid in school, and he meant to give me no time to get into trouble.

[25]Then there was Jack Peploe, a cop. Patrolman Jack Peploe, today superintendent of parks and grounds for Nassau County, ran the Police Boys Club. He put me in charge of the Boys Club basketball team. He gave me the keys to the high school gym and appointed me the big shot to open the gym every night.

[26]There were others—people all around me who without hesitation went out of their way to make something of me. Mrs. Virginia Hansen, a speech teacher, observed that I was a quiet kid. She forced me to make two- and three-minute speeches in school and brought me to the point where I became a self-assured assembly speaker. Al Dawson, the high school track coach, worked tirelessly to develop my skills. Dr. Raymond L. Collins, superintendent of Manhasset schools, took me to the school gym Sunday afternoons to shoot baskets with him and his son. (Dr. Collins was an old-fashioned underhand set shooter but probably the deadliest shot of all school superintendents in the country.) In short, what I received from these adults around me was love. I was a poor kid from a broken home but I was not insecure, because where there is love there cannot be insecurity. Even when I was a little guy on St. Simons Island, mama and I never felt insecure because we loved one another and knew that come what may, we were not alone.

[27]At Manhasset High School there was a football coach

named Ed Walsh, and I will tell you about him because he was my idea of a saint. He was a slender, soft-spoken man but one whose actions made you realize that real strength was not physical strength but strength of character. I am convinced that Ed Walsh had not one iota of bigotry in him. Moreover, of all the football coaches I've played for, Ed, a mere high school coach, was the finest—the most expert. Even today, when I find it necessary to refresh my knowledge of fundamentals, I say to myself, "Let's see, how did Ed Walsh teach that move?" In the four years I played for him, his teams lost only two games—one by a touchdown and the other by a single point. Because he had movies made of his games, I've been able to go back to Manhasset from time to time and watch myself in action as a high school halfback. It's hard to believe, but I made better moves and cuts in high school than I've made in college and pro ball, and that's a fact.

²⁸More than a great teacher of football technique, Ed Walsh was a builder of character. He cared about his kids, and would reach into his own pocket to buy a needy student clothing. I had a childish spat with my mother once and told Ed I was going to leave home. "Come out and stay at my house a while," he told me, "until you've had a chance to think it over and you're sure you're doing the right thing." It was no phony gesture but a sincere invitation.

²⁹"You can be a professional football player," he told me on another occasion. "But you've got to go to college first, and you won't go to college unless you start taking your studies seriously." I began taking my studies seriously. In time I was nominated for student body president but said I wouldn't run, because I knew that if I were elected it would be only because of my popularity as an athlete. I felt one of the topmost students should be president. So I was elected chief justice of the student court, which though a lesser post was a step up from gang warlord.

³⁰"Okay, Jimmy," Ed Walsh barked at me one day in football scrimmage. "If you want to loaf get off the first team. Get over there on defense with the second team." I went over to the defense and did all I could to tear the first team apart. The next day I was back on the first team. The point is, I had to get back into Ed Walsh's good graces at all costs, not so much because I disliked being second-string but because I had let him down. Since that day I've never messed up on a coach of his stripe—that is, a coach I could talk to and reason with and who would give me the benefit of the doubt in a tough spot.

COMMENT

Brown describes his coming to Manhasset and his first experiences there in paragraphs 1–15, and in paragraph 16 he introduces the coaches and teachers who changed his life. In paragraph 15 he had mentioned Ed Walsh, the high school football coach, who took the place of his father in taking him to Manhattan to buy a suit. The transition to other coaches and teachers is thus a natural one; but Brown does not describe Walsh or discuss this man's effect on his life until he has explained why his coaches and teachers "had their work cut out for them in trying to make something of me." He presents this explanation through his experiences with the Gaylords. At the end of his narrative he finds a natural transition to a topic introduced earlier: "I was coming to realize that my physical strength could be put to better use on a ball field than in fist fights." In succeeding paragraphs, Brown builds to his discussion of Walsh; he reserves Walsh for last because of his great influence on Brown's career in football. He thus has introduced various experiences in the order necessary to explain his growth of character and development as an athlete. He could not have discussed his coaches and teachers without first describing his experiences with the Gaylords. The brief mention of the trip to Manhattan thus prepares the reader for the most important topic of the essay. Transitional statements of this kind, and transitional sentences and paragraphs—paragraph 23, for example—make the order of ideas clear to the reader.

QUESTIONS FOR STUDY AND DISCUSSION

1. Why does Brown provide more detail about his encounter with the rival ganglord than about his efforts to appear tough?

2. How important is the information about the Brockmans and his mother to our understanding of the influence of his coaches and teachers? What does the information about his great-grandmother contribute to the essay? Could this information come at the end?

3. Brown writes in the language of the adult, not in the language of a black boy from the South. What is gained by writing from the viewpoint of the adult? How would the essay differ if he had restricted his viewpoint to that of the boy?

4. Do you think Brown has a special audience in mind, or is he writing to the general reader?

5. What personal qualities of Brown the adult emerge in his telling of these experiences?

6. Is Brown trying to point out that his experiences on Long Island were typical of black youths in his situation at the time they occurred?

7. Do you agree with Brown's statements about irresponsibility and the importance of love in childhood?

VOCABULARY STUDY

Identify those words in the first two paragraphs that probably would not be used by an adolescent describing these same experiences. Indicate what words might be used instead.

SUGGESTIONS FOR WRITING

1. Rewrite one of the paragraphs from the viewpoint and in the language of a boy undergoing the experience instead of an adult remembering it. Then briefly explain the changes you made and the reasons you made them.

2. Describe several teachers who influenced your life. Show how their personal qualities influenced you. Decide on an order of ideas before writing.

3. Discuss your response to one of the following statements. You may want to draw on observations and personal experiences for your discussion:
   a. "My guess is that thanks to all the yakking about broken homes, a lot of kids have found a good excuse to get into trouble." (paragraph 4)
   b. "Looking back on my own boyhood, there were many times when I came perilously close to becoming a no-account. It took a kind word here and a guiding hand there to point me in the right direction." (paragraph 4)
   c. "I was a poor kid from a broken home but I was not insecure, because where there is love there cannot be insecurity." (paragraph 26)

unity

In conversation there is usually some disunity, for we move from one topic to another quickly, and we may return suddenly to a previous one. However, confusion seldom arises, at least with friends with whom we share assumptions and knowledge; but when it does occur we can clear it up easily through reminders of what we said and why. We can repeat ourselves in writing, too, but the more backtracking we do, the more reminders we have to give, and the harder the essay is to read.

By contrast, in a *unified* essay all ideas and details connect to the thesis or controlling idea. The reader sees their connection at every point, and experiences them as a unity, as in music where different sounds are heard together developing a single theme. To achieve unity when we write, we must decide on a single purpose, a controlling idea, and an order of ideas: we must be sure what ideas we want to begin with and why. We must also have a sense of what the reader knows about the subject and how soon the reader will be ready for the statement of the thesis or controlling idea. If we decide to digress from our main idea, we must be sure the reader knows that we are doing so. In general, unity means "one thing at a time," guided by a single purpose. Once an idea is introduced, it should be discussed fully and without interruption, unless there is good reason to digress.

ON SUMMER

Lorraine Hansberry

Lorraine Hansberry was born in Chicago in 1930, graduated from Englewood High School in 1948, and attended the University of Wisconsin for two years. After studying painting in Chicago and Mexico, she moved to New York City in 1950. Her play *Raisin in the Sun* opened in New York in 1959; a later play, *The Sign in Sidney Brustein's Window*, appeared in 1964. She died in 1965. The play *To Be Young, Gifted, and Black* (1969) is about her life and is drawn from her writings, including the essay printed here.

¹It has taken me a good number of years to come to any measure of respect for summer. I was, being May-born, literally an "infant of the spring" and, during the later childhood years, tended, for some reason or other, to rather worship the cold aloofness of winter. The adolescence, admittedly lingering still, brought the traditional passionate committment to melancholy autumn—and all that. For the longest kind of time I simply thought that *summer* was a mistake.

²In fact, my earliest memory of anything at all is of waking up in a darkened room where I had been put to bed for a nap on a summer's afternoon, and feeling very, very hot. I acutely disliked the feeling then and retained the bias for years. It had originally been a matter of the heat but, over the years, I came actively to associate displeasure with most of the usually celebrated natural features and social by-products of the season: the too-grainy texture of sand; the too-cold coldness of the various waters we constantly try to escape into, and the icky-perspiry feeling of bathing caps.

³It also seemed to me, esthetically speaking, that nature had got inexcusably carried away on the summer question and let the whole thing get to be rather much. By duration alone, for instance, a summer's day seemed maddeningly excessive; an utter overstatement. Except for those few hours at either end of it, objects always appeared in too sharp a relief against backgrounds; shadows too pronounced and light too blinding. It always gave me the feeling of

Reprinted by permission of Robert Nemiroff.

walking around in a motion picture which had been too artsily-craftsily exposed. Sound also had a way of coming to the ear without that muting influence, marvelously common to winter, across patios or beaches or through the woods. I suppose I found it too stark and yet too intimate a season.

[4] My childhood Southside summers were the ordinary city kind, full of the street games which other rememberers have turned into fine ballets these days and rhymes that anticipated what some people insist on calling modern poetry:

> Oh, Mary Mack, Mack, Mack
> With the silver buttons, buttons, buttons
> All down her back, back, back
> She asked her mother, mother, mother
> For fifteen cents, cents, cents
> To see the elephant, elephant, elephant
> Jump the fence, fence, fence
> Well, he jumped so high, high, high
> 'Til he touched the sky, sky, sky
> And he didn't come back, back, back
> 'Til the Fourth of Ju-ly, ly, ly!

[5] Evenings were spent mainly on the back porches where screen doors slammed in the darkness with those really very special summertime sounds. And, sometimes, when Chicago nights got too steamy, the whole family got into the car and went to the park and slept out in the open on blankets. Those were, of course, the best times of all because the grownups were invariably reminded of having been children in rural parts of the country and told the best stories then. And it was also cool and sweet to be on the grass and there was usually the scent of freshly cut lemons or melons in the air. And Daddy would lie on his back, as fathers must, and explain about how men thought the stars above us came to be and how far away they were. I never did learn to believe that anything could be as far away as *that*. Especially the stars.

[6] My mother first took us south to visit her Tennessee birth-place one summer when I was seven or eight, I think. I woke up on the back seat of the car while we were still driving through some place called Kentucky and my mother was pointing out to the beautiful hills on both sides of the highway and telling my brothers

and my sister about how her father had run away and hidden from his master in those very hills when he was a little boy. She said that his mother had wandered among the wooded slopes in the moonlight and left food for him in secret places. They were very beautiful hills and I looked out at them for miles and miles after that wondering who and what a *master* might be.

[7] I remember being startled when I first saw my grandmother rocking away on her porch. All my life I had heard that she was a great beauty and no one had ever remarked that they meant a half century before. The woman that I met was as wrinkled as a prune and could hardly hear and barely see and always seemed to be thinking of other times. But she could still rock and talk and even make wonderful cupcakes which were like cornbread, only sweet. She was captivated by automobiles and, even though it was well into the Thirties, I don't think she had ever been in one before we came down and took her driving. She was a little afraid of them and could not seem to negotiate the windows, but she loved driving. She died the next summer and that is all that I remember about her, except that she was born in slavery and had memories of it and they didn't sound anything like *Gone with the Wind*.

[8] Like everyone else, I have spent whole or bits of summers in many different kinds of places since then: camps and resorts in the Middle West and New York State; on an island; in a tiny Mexican village; Cape Cod, perched atop the Truro bluffs at Longnook Beach that Millay wrote about; or simply strolling the streets of Province-town before the hours when the cocktail parties begin.

[9] And, lastly, I do not think that I will forget days spent, a few summers ago, at a beautiful lodge built right into the rocky cliffs of a bay on the Maine coast. We met a woman there who had lived a purposeful and courageous life and who was then dying of cancer. She had, characteristically, just written a book and taken up painting. She had also been of radical viewpoint all her life; one of those people who energetically believe that the world *can* be changed for the better and spend their lives trying to do just that. And that was the way she thought of cancer; she absolutely refused to award it the stature of tragedy, a devastating instance of the brooding doom and inexplicability of the absurdity of human destiny, etc., etc. The kind of characterization given, lately, as we all know, to far less formidable foes in life than cancer.

¹⁰But for this remarkable woman it was a matter of nature in imperfection, implying, as always, work for man to do. It was an *enemy,* but a palpable one with shape and effect and source; and if it existed, it could be destroyed. She saluted it accordingly, without despondency, but with a lively, beautiful and delightfully ribald anger. There was one thing, she felt, which would prove equal to its relentless ravages and that was the genius of man. Not his mysticism, but man with tubes and slides and the stubborn human notion that the stars are very much within our reach.

¹¹The last time I saw her she was sitting surrounded by her paintings with her manuscript laid out for me to read, because, she said, she wanted to know what a *young person* would think of her thinking; one must always keep up with what *young people* thought about things because, after all, they were *change.*

¹²Every now and then her jaw set in anger as we spoke of things people should be angry about. And then, for relief, she would look out at the lovely bay at a mellow sunset settling on the water. Her face softened with love of all that beauty and, watching her, I wished with all my power what I knew that she was wishing: that she might live to see at least one more *summer.* Through her eyes I finally gained the sense of what it might mean; more than the coming autumn with its pretentious melancholy; more than an austere and silent winter which must shut dying people in for precious months; more even than the frivolous spring, too full of too many false promises, would be the gift of another summer with its stark and intimate assertion of neither birth nor death but life at the apex; with the gentlest nights and, above all, the longest days.

¹³I heard later that she did live to see another summer. And I have retained my respect for the noblest of the seasons.

COMMENT

Hansberry begins with a general observation about summer: "For the longest kind of time I simply thought that *summer* was a mistake." She explains why; then, without transition, she mentions a series of experiences associated with summer—childhood experiences in Chicago, a visit to her mother's birthplace in Tennessee and her first meeting with her grandmother, places visited in later years, her acquaintance with a woman dying of cancer. Unexpectedly she has returned to the idea she began with, for the dying woman taught her to look at summer in a new way. The essay seems to be unified only by its subject; we seem to be given a series of disconnected experiences and thoughts associated with summer. But a theme does connect these: happiness, and how we come to discover its meaning and value. We discover happiness at the point of losing something valuable: that is the author's controlling idea. She has moved from superficial reasons for disliking summer to deeper reasons for valuing it.

QUESTIONS FOR STUDY AND DISCUSSION

1. What reasons does the author give for disliking summer? What in the opening section tells us these are superficial reasons that she may later forget or overcome?

2. Could the sections on the summers in Chicago and the visit to Tennessee have been interchanged? Or is there an implied order of ideas?

3. What do the details about the grandmother contribute to the controlling idea of the essay?

4. Later in the essay Hansberry returns to the stars mentioned in the second section. Why does she? How does she return to attitudes introduced in the first section and for what purpose?

5. Hansberry observes the rule of unity—"one thing at a time." How does she do this while at the same time managing to return to earlier experiences and thoughts?

6. What personal qualities does the author reveal about herself through these thoughts about summer?

VOCABULARY STUDY

1. With the help of the dictionary explain the following phrases. Be ready to discuss how much your understanding of the phrase depends on the context—on its use in the sentence or paragraph: *cold aloofness* (paragraph 1); *esthetically speaking, muting influence* (paragraph 3); *negotiate the windows* (paragraph 7); *radical viewpoint, the stature of tragedy, inexplicability of the absurdity of human destiny* (paragraph 9); *without despondency* (paragraph 10); *pretentious melancholy, frivolous spring, life at the apex* (paragraph 12). Notice that some of these phrases are used to represent superficial or pretentious attitudes toward living and dying.

2. The author refers to the poetry of Edna St. Vincent Millay, who lived in

and wrote about New England. Read several of Millay's poems to discover how her language expresses the sounds and sights of New England and perhaps contributed to the author's view of that world.

SUGGESTIONS FOR WRITING

1. Write a series of paragraphs describing experiences associated with a season of the year. Make your final paragraph connect with your first, perhaps showing how your later experiences modified or changed earlier impressions and feelings.

2. Compare Hansberry's thoughts and experiences of summer with your own. You might discuss experiences similar to hers that led to similar or different feelings and thoughts.

3. Discuss what you learned about happiness through a relative or acquaintance who had overcome or was suffering hardship.

BASEBALL

Tom Wicker

Tom Wicker was born in Hamlet, North Carolina, in 1926, and studied journalism at the University of North Carolina, graduating in 1948. He worked as a journalist and editor for several Southern newspapers, including the *Nashville Tennessean,* and began working for the *New York Times* in 1960. He was chief of the *Times* Washington bureau from 1964 to 1968 and has been associate editor since 1968.

[1]One hot night in the summer of 1949, I climbed to my usual perch in the cramped press box above the wooden stands of the baseball park in Lumberton, North Carolina. As telegraph editor, general reporter and all-around handyman for the afternoon *Robesonian* of that city, I had appointed myself sports editor, also, and regularly covered the home games of the Lumberton Auctioneers, a

farm club of the Chicago Cubs playing in the Class D Tobacco State League. *The Robesonian* paid me not a cent more for spending my summer evenings keeping notes and score, but *The News and Observer* of Raleigh, the state-capital daily, paid me three dollars a game—as I recall it—for filing each night's box score by phone to its sports pages.

[2]The '49 Auctioneers were undistinguished by anything, including success, except a locally famous first baseman named Turkey Tyson. A stoop-shouldered slap hitter with a reputation for zaniness and getting on base, Tyson derived his nickname from a gobbler-like sound of derision he made when he pulled up at first after one of the frequent singles he poked through opposing infields. The Turkey had played with more minor-league teams than probably exist today and was at the end of the line in Class D; his future was ten seasons behind him and he was old enough to be the father of most of the post-high-school kids he played with and against.

[3]One exception—I recall only that his first name was Mike— was a burly, blue-bearded outfielder the Auks (as I labeled them in the headlines over my stories) had obtained somewhere in mid-season. He could play ball, or something resembling it, when infrequently sober, had traveled the minor leagues from coast to coast, and although younger than Tyson was also down and about to be out in Class D. (Neither got much closer to the majors than the Game of the Day on radio.) Mike had some difficulty handling the ball, except at the plate; he swung a bat the size of one of the telephone poles that held up the dim lights in the outfield. When he connected he could hit the ball over those lights. More often, he took three mighty swings and hurried back to the bench for a quick swig.

[4]I had noticed a little something about Mike and that morning in *The Robesonian* had unburdened myself of some inside dope for the avid readers, I liked to imagine. Mike, I told them, was a first-pitch swinger, and the other Tobacco State League clubs were onto him; if he'd lay off that first pitch, I suggested, and wait for *his* pitch, his average would go up and so would the Auks'.

[5]There was a good crowd on hand that night and in the first inning Turkey Tyson rewarded his fans with his specialty—a ground single about two inches out of reach of a flat-footed second baseman who was probably getting eighty dollars a month and meal money and might someday make it to the Piedmont League, Class B. *Gobble-gobble* went the Turkey triumphantly from first, and

Auks fans cheered. But that was nothing to the roar that went up when barrel-chested Mike, batting cleanup, strode to the plate, thumped his telephone pole twice upon it, then turned his back to the pitcher and pointed that huge bat straight up at the press box and me.

[6] I can only imagine what it was he yelled at me, but I learned one thing—those fans had read my article in *The Robesonian*. That roar told me everyone in the park knew Mike would defy my first-pitch edict. I prayed for the pitcher to throw him the deepest-breaking curve or the fanciest knuckle ball in the history of Abner Doubleday's cow-pasture creation. But somehow I knew, and the crowd knew—as Mike turned back to the plate, hunched over it, waved his war club menacingly, and waggled his rump at the world—exactly what was going to happen.

[7] It did. That pitcher came in with a fast ball that would have bounced off a windowpane. I can still see that mighty swing, hear the crack of the bat connecting, watch the ball soar into outer darkness. As one of the Auks said later, "Mike just disappeared it."

[8] I can still hear that crowd, too, roaring not just for Mike but *at* me, isolated as I was under the single light bulb in my press-box perch. In the open stands down the first- and third-base lines, they stood and pointed upward and howled with glee, as Mike show-boated around the bases behind Turkey Tyson and reached the plate again, jumped on it with both feet and bowed low to the press box. Cowering above him in that naked light, I did the only thing I could do; I stood up and bowed, too, and the crowd howled some more. I thought there must be for Mike, in that moment of defiance and triumph, a certain compensation for all those long bus rides through the minor leagues, that long decline of hope and youth down to the smelly locker rooms of Class D. And I *knew* I was never going to make a sportswriter.

[9] And I didn't, although I later did an unavoidable hitch in the sports department of the Winston-Salem *Journal* before I could escape to politics. I don't even see many baseball games these days.

[10] Some idle evenings, I may pick up an inning or two on television, but that's not really baseball on the screen—only part of a reasonable facsimile of the sport I've loved all my life. Maybe I'll get out to Shea Stadium two or three times a season, but somehow that doesn't seem like the real thing either.

[11] It's not just that the game, at least the way a fan sees it, has

changed. It has, but it's not fundamentally different from Turkey Tyson's game, or Babe Ruth's, for that matter. All the old symmetry is there—the innings and outs in their orderly multiples of threes, the foul lines radiating out to the stands, the diamond in its classic dimensions, the exact sixty feet and six inches between the pitching rubber and home plate. The ageless rituals seem never to change— the ball tossed around after an infield out, the coaches waggling and patting their impenetrable signals, the pitcher's sidewise stance with a man on first, the dash and whirl of the pregame infield practice, that solemn conclave of managers and umpires at the plate just before *The Star-Spangled Banner*.

[12] Astroturf, designated hitters, Disneyland scoreboards, salad-bowl stadiums, and Batting Glove Day can't change all that. Nothing seems really to change the game itself: the spectacular individual effort on which it depends; the lack of violence but the sense of menace in the thrown ball, the slashing spikes, the swinging bat; the sudden splendid bursts of action—a runner going from first to third, or even home, on a single, sliding in inches ahead of or behind a perfect peg; the suspense of pitcher vs. hitter in a late-inning rally, with the winning runs on base; all the straight-faced exchanges of "strategy" between managers pulling the same hoary maneuvers John McGraw did, or Connie Mack; the power and the glory of an overwhelming pitcher in his prime; the art and cunning of an experienced pitcher past his prime; the swagger of a big hitter at the plate.

[13] All that is still there for the seeing, even in stadiums like Shea or Chavez Ravine, where the players look like pygmies on a foreign field—even on Astroturf, which senselessly abolishes the clay crescent of the infield, which should be as much a part of the game as knee pants and billed caps.

[14] No, the reason I don't see much baseball today has little to do with the game itself. The problem is that all that's really left is the big leagues and the Little League, and I don't trace back to either. I go back to small-town baseball before television and the suburbs. I loved the game on the vacant lots of childhood, with pickup teams from the neighborhood, someone's dime-store ball coming apart at the seams, and—in the railroad town where I grew up—sometimes a brake stick for a bat.

[15] Later, in high school and the unending hot summer days of youth, baseball in the dust of skinned infields was life itself to me.

Catching for my high-school team, I took a throw from the outfield and put the tag on a runner coming in spikes up, but not before he ripped my thigh open for six inches above the knee. I lay on the ground by the plate while they poured iodine or something on me and it didn't hurt much, because I knew that runner was out and I hadn't ducked away from his spikes. And then I saw my father leaning over me, down from the stands to check on his little boy's wounds, and for the first time in my life I cursed him, told him to go away. I thought I was no kid to be fretted over. That was the spring of '44 and before the year was over one of my teammates was dead in the Battle of the Bulge.

[16]After school was out, we shifted annually to American Legion Junior Baseball, on the same skinned infields, before the same wooden grandstands, in the concession stands of which the ladies of the American Legion Auxiliary sold icy Cokes and peanuts and "bellywashers"—the local name for Royal Crown Cola. The first time I played baseball under lights it was with the Richmond County American Legion Juniors. We played a preseason game in Greensboro, a big city to Richmond County kids, and got stomped; I remember Coach Bill Haltiwanger taking out his fourth pitcher of the night, a rawboned left-hander out of the cotton mills, who had just given up something like five runs after striking out the first batter he faced.

[17]"Well, Lefty," Coach Haltiwanger said, taking the ball from him, "you almost had 'em."

[18]Later on, I tried out for college baseball and got cut the first day of practice. No arm. Even later, I tried to stage a comeback in the Peach Belt League, a semipro circuit in North Carolina, but I didn't last long. Still no arm, and that was a pretty fast league. I remember one elderly Peach Belt pitcher, about Turkey Tyson's vintage, who had been knocking around the semipro and mill-town leagues as long as I'd been living. He had one pitch, a jug-handle curve that came in from the general direction of third base, and he could throw it through a keyhole at about the speed of ice melting. I've seen husky young men who could have broken him in two break their backs instead, trying to hit that jug-handle. He would stand out there and spit tobacco juice, not infrequently on the ball, and throw it past them for nine innings, or as long as the game went on. And I'd have sold my soul just to be able to throw out a runner at second maybe once or twice a game.

[19] We were not, of course, unaware in those days of the major leagues, although we got a lot more news about the Charlotte Hornets of the Piedmont League, a Washington Senators farm club. I pored daily over the box scores from the big leagues, particularly the Dodgers and the Giants, and never missed a Game of the Day if I could help it. Other forms of life stopped during the World Series, while people huddled at the radio. In the main, however, the big leagues were far away and second fiddle to the American Legion Juniors—although I had seen a major-league game from the bleachers of old Griffith Stadium once when my family made a tourist trip to Washington. Dutch Leonard pitched and a good ole Georgia boy, Cecil Travis, got a couple of hits. Most of life has been downhill since that day.

[20] So baseball for a lot of people is the memory of Joe DiMaggio in center field, or the Gashouse Gang, or Lou Gehrig's farewell to Yankee Stadium, or all those Dodger-Yankee Series of the Fifties (those magic names! Gionfriddo, Podres, Mantle, the Duke, Berra, Robinson, Campanella, Ford). I remember all that, too. I remember Bobby Thomson's home run, and the first televised Series I saw—Durocher's Giants swept Cleveland. I remember Don Larsen's perfect game and Ernie Lombardi's swoon and I have a dim memory of my father boasting about somebody he called The Goose—Goslin, of course, of the Senators. I hit Hubbell's screwball in my dreams.

[21] But all that is secondhand to me, baseball once removed, the perfect baseball I never really saw or knew. Maybe it's age, maybe it's change, maybe it's wounds deeper than the one that left the scar I still bear on my thigh; but baseball to *me* is the skinned infield of my youth, the wooden grandstands, the despair of being washed up with no arm at age twenty-one, the recollection of a fast-ball pitcher who was throwing it past me until I choked the bat, stepped forward in the box and put it almost down his throat, just over second for a single. Baseball to me is the remembered taste of an ice-cold belly-washer sneaked between innings, against all rules. The railroad embankment was just beyond right field and the trains went by, whistling us on. It was always summer, and this season we were solid up the middle, we could win it all.

[22] I like to think that thirty years ago baseball in America was something we had to hold on to, to hold us together—solid, change-less, universal, at one and the same time peculiarly *ours* and yet part of the great world beyond us. You pulled off the double play the

same way for the Richmond County Juniors, the Auks or the White Sox. When I was in the press box in Lumberton or dying with shame when they stole second on me five times in Carthage, baseball was a common denominator; it had rules, symmetry, a beginning and an end, it challenged and rewarded, you could play or watch, it was the same one day as the next, in one town as in another.

[23] But now the minor leagues and the semipros and country baseball are all but gone, and in the suburbs they put kids of ten and twelve in expensive Little League uniforms to play on perfectly proportioned fields and in the smaller cities the old lopsided parks have been torn down for housing developments and shopping centers. If anything holds us together now, our hometown teams playing in surrounding leagues, those leagues part of the widening circle of all the leagues—if anything holds us together that way now, it isn't baseball, concentrated as it is in the major leagues, the Chavez Ravines of this amortized world, concerned as it is with tax shelters and reserve clauses and player strikes and antitrust, relying as it does on Bat Days and boom-boom superstars with salaries triple their batting averages. It isn't baseball that holds us together in 1976—not baseball in the Astrodome, on artificial grass, foreshortened by television, enlivened by organ music and computerized scoreboards that can simulate fireworks and joy.

[24] The game may be the same, but it's been taken away from the country and the towns and given to the accountants and the TV producers and the high rollers. Turkey Tyson and Mike, the home-run hitter of the Auks, couldn't find a place to play today. Class D doesn't exist. To me, Shea Stadium is a poor substitute.

COMMENT

In the course of the essay Wicker talks about his childhood and high school baseball experiences, his experiences in college and as a newspaperman, and those in later years, the changes in baseball, and the meaning of these changes for American life. But he does not talk about these topics in this order. Because he is writing to an audience unfamiliar with his world, he begins with what happened on a hot night in 1949. This extended episode not only immerses the reader in the actions and feelings of a different world, but also introduces the personality and feelings of the author. Thus we discover what baseball was like through people like Turkey Tyson and Mike. So thorough is the detail that Wicker is able to make a brief comment about the changes in baseball (paragraphs 11 and 12), then turn to a short account of his earlier and later experiences. These later paragraphs lead to a review of these experiences and, finally, a longer comment on these changes. The order of ideas is determined by Wicker's assumptions about his readers and by the guiding purpose of clear exposition. The essay is unified through its thesis and also its order of ideas—an order determined by what the reader needs to know in order to understand what follows.

QUESTIONS FOR STUDY AND DISCUSSION

1. How do the episode on the hot night in 1949 and the personality and actions of Tyson and Mike suggest the qualities of baseball as Wicker knew it and characterizes it later in the essay?

2. Does Wicker single out one essential change that came about, or is he concerned with many changes that together changed baseball?

3. Consider paragraphs 22–24 carefully. Is Wicker saying—and does he show—that the rules and "symmetry" of baseball have changed? What does he mean by "symmetry"?

4. Does Wicker consider the change in baseball typical of changes in American life? Is he commenting on American life generally? If you agree, do you think that his criticism of baseball today is also true of other sports?

5. Wicker informs the reader of unfamiliar details and experiences. What details and experiences does he assume the reader will understand or recognize?

6. Does Wicker want merely to inform the reader of his experiences and ideas, or is he trying also to persuade the reader of these ideas?

VOCABULARY STUDY

1. Consult your dictionary and also a dictionary of American slang, in the reference section of your library, on the meaning and currency of the following: *slap hitter, inside dope, batting cleanup, knuckle ball, billed caps, screwball.*

2. Write sentences using each of the following words and phrases that clarify or explain their meaning: *zaniness, gobbler-like sound, thumped his telephone pole, showboated around the bases, the dust of skinned infields, jug-handle curve, amortized world.*

SUGGESTIONS FOR WRITING

1. Write a characterization of Tom Wicker on the basis of qualities he reveals, directly and indirectly, through statements about himself and his feelings and ideas about baseball.

2. Discuss the changes you have witnessed in a favorite sport. In the course of your discussion, suggest an explanation and relate it to the changes you are describing.

3. Describe in detail an experience in playing a sport, or watching one, that reveals something important about the sport and your attitude toward it. Keep in mind the knowledge of your audience.

transitions

Formal connectives, or *transitions,* are often necessary to clarify the relation of ideas when natural transitions such as pronoun reference are absent or insufficient. If the steps of a process are presented chronologically and each requires much detail, we may introduce the words *first, second,* and *third* to keep the steps distinct. We may have to add *less important, just as important, more important* to show that the ideas are being presented in the order of their importance. The connectives *specifically* and *generally* show that we are proceeding from the specific to the general; *least of all* and *most of all,* from the least to the most frequent or common. Connectives like *thus, however, moreover, therefore,* and *furthermore* are sometimes used to show the logical relation of ideas. *Thus* and *therefore* show that the second idea is the consequence of the first, or that certain conclusions may be drawn from the evidence. *However* shows that the second idea qualifies the first or contradicts it. *Moreover* and *furthermore* show that something additional is to be said.

GAMES OF YESTERYEAR

Harry Golden

Born in New York City in 1903, Harry Golden was educated at the City College of New York, and later was a newspaper reporter in New York City and Charlotte, North Carolina. In 1942 he began publishing and doing most of the writing for *The Carolina Israelite,* a personal newspaper which comments on

Southern and Jewish life, and the American scene generally. Much of his writing describes his early life in New York City. His many books include *Only in America* (1958), *For 2¢ Plain* (1959), *Enjoy, Enjoy!* (1960), and his autobiography, *The Right Time* (1969).

[1]In the course of writing my autobiography, I took the time to describe some of the games we played as boys on the Lower East Side of New York. We played "Johnny-on-the-pony," in which one side bent against the wall and the other side leaped on their backs and tried to shout "Johnny on the pony" three times without being shaken off. "Puss-n-cat" was played with a sawed-off broom handle and a piece of wood. The regular rules of baseball applied except we touched only two bases. Boxball was played in the squares of the sidewalk.

[2]I had to describe these games and others more specifically in the book because my editor said, "There are people forty years old who never heard of these." One of my sons contributed a photographic essay to a national magazine on the games *he* played which are no longer in vogue: tag, leapfrog, hide and seek, and kick the can.

[3]What games do kids play now? I know they have a soapbox derby sponsored by several organizations in town. I know this because in Charlotte, the speedway, so-called, goes down Elizabeth Avenue, right past my front door, where the soapbox derby officials station themselves. Every year these fellows give me a pith helmet made of plastic.

[4]And towns also sponsor football and baseball leagues. I haven't seen a pick-up game with the kids choosing sides for years and years. I know they play basketball unattended by coaching adults because I see the hoops fastened to the garages. In fact, I drove up to a friend's house one afternoon as he poked his head out the window to yell at his oldest son, "If you don't learn to dribble that basketball, I'm going to take it away from you." Quite right, I thought. Quite right.

[5]I never see a punching bag or boxing gloves. When I was first a father, boxing was popular. I always encouraged it not because I

From *So Long as You're Healthy* by Harry Golden. Copyright © 1962, 1963, 1964, 1965, 1966, 1967, 1968, 1969, 1970 by Harry Golden. Reprinted by permission of G. P. Putnam's Sons.

thought they should learn to defend themselves but to learn a hard one in the nose doesn't hurt all that much.

[6]I never see kids on roller skates, and I never see kids playing marbles. Roller-skate hockey became the rage in New York when the city covered over the cobblestones with asphalt or macadam. It was easier then because there were not as many cars to interrupt the game. When the Board of Education covered over the playground with asphalt to create more tennis courts, they dealt marbles a death blow. You could always tell a marble champ because he had a hole worn in his thumbnail, and the knuckles and joints on his shooting hand were oversized.

[7]The kids are more attracted to organized sports today not because organizations are more fun or more sophisticated but because the parents insist they are. The parents want the kids in organized activities so that they have time for their own organized recreation.

COMMENT

Golden focuses on changes in childhood sports—more specifically, on his discovery of these changes. The first or second sentence of each paragraph re-establishes this focus—through personal references like "I knew," "I haven't seen," and "I never see," and through repetition of key words like "games" and "kids." These are the main transitions of the essay. Golden's writing is clear and direct, his details brief and informative. He speaks to us simply and informally.

QUESTIONS FOR STUDY AND DISCUSSION

1. The first sentence of paragraph 3 is transitional, and it also states the topic idea of the paragraph. How is the transition different from that of the first sentence in paragraph 4?

2. The overuse of "I" can make sentences monotonous. How has Golden varied his sentence openings to avoid monotony?

3. Does Golden say or imply that the changes he describes are typical of American life?

4. Are the games you played in childhood different from games today? If they are the same, what do you think explains this fact? Are you

convinced that changes you observe in games, or in other activities, reflect changes everywhere in the United States?

VOCABULARY STUDY

Identify those words you would expect to find in informal speech rather than in a formal essay. Examine the classification of those words that your dictionary contains. Some of these may be listed as *colloquial,* others as *slang.* Be ready to discuss the difference between these two kinds of words.

SUGGESTIONS FOR WRITING

1. Discuss changes in games or other amusements you have observed. In the course of your discussion, or at the end, suggest an explanation that your details support.

2. Compare the conclusions Wicker and Golden reach about sports in America and the ways they reach these conclusions. State the similarities as well as the differences. Such transitions as *similarly, by contrast,* and *likewise* are appropriate in comparing and contrasting ideas.

THE PLAYGROUND

John Updike

> John Updike was born in Shillington, Pennsylvania, in 1932, and graduated from Harvard in 1954. He attended the Ruskin School of Drawing and Fine Art in Oxford, England, and later wrote for *The New Yorker,* where many of his sketches and stories have appeared. His novels include *The Poorhouse Fair* (1959), *The Centaur* (1963), *Rabbit, Run* (1964), and *Couples* (1968). (In the essay here, his reference to "the Nightingale" is to one of three groups in his school music class—the Nightingales, Robins, and Crows.)

[1]The periphery I have traced; the center of my boyhood held a calm collection of kind places that are almost impossible to describe, because they are so fundamental to me, they enclosed so many of my hours, that they have the neutral color of my own soul, which I have always imagined as a pale oblong just under my ribs. In the town where I now live, and where I am writing this, seagulls weep overhead on a rainy day. No seagulls found their way inland to Shillington; there were sparrows, and starlings, and cowbirds, and robins, and occasionally a buzzard floating high overhead on immobile wings like a kite on a string too high to be seen.

[2]The playground: up from the hardball diamond, on a plateau bounded on three sides by cornfields, a pavilion contained some tables and a shed for equipment. I spent my summer weekdays there from the age when I was so small that the dust stirred by the feet of roof-ball players got into my eyes. Roof ball was the favorite game. It was played with a red rubber ball smaller than a basketball. The object was to hit it back up on the roof of the pavilion, the whole line of children in succession. Those who failed dropped out. When there was just one person left, a new game began with the cry *Noo*-oo *gay*-ame," and we lined up in the order in which we had gone out, so that the lines began with the strongest and tallest and ended with the weakest and youngest. But there was never any doubt that everybody could play; it was perfect democracy. Often the line contained as many as thirty pairs of legs, arranged chronologically. By the time we moved away, I had become a regular front-runner; I knew how to flick the ball to give it spin, how to leap up and send the ball skimming the length of the roof edge, how to plump it with my knuckles when there was a high bounce. Somehow the game never palled. The sight of the ball bouncing along the tarpaper of the foreshortened roof was always important. Many days I was at the playground from nine o'clock, when they ran up the American flag, until four, when they called the equipment in, and played nothing else.

[3]If you hit the ball too hard, and it went over the peak of the roof, you were out, and you had to retrieve the ball, going down a steep bank into a field where the poorhouse men had stopped planting corn because it all got mashed down. If the person ahead of you

hit the ball into the air without touching the roof, or missed it entirely, you had the option of "saving," by hitting the ball onto the roof before it struck the ground; this created complex opportunities for strategy and gallantry. I would always try to save the Nightingale, for instance, and there was a girl who came from Louisiana with a French name whom everybody wanted to save. At twelve, she seemed already mature, and I can remember standing with a pack of other boys under the swings looking up at the undersides of her long tense dark-skinned legs as she kicked into the air to give herself more height, the tendons on the underside of her smooth knees jumping, her sneakered feet pointing like a ballerina's shoes.

[4]The walls of the pavilion shed were scribbled all over with dirty drawings and words and detailed slanders on the prettier girls. After hours, when the supervisors were gone, if you were tall enough you could grab hold of a crossbeam and get on top of the shed, where there was an intimate wedge of space under the slanting roof; here no adult ever bothered to scrub away the pencillings, and the wood fairly breathed of the forbidden. The very silence of the pavilion, after the daylong click of checkers and *pokabok* of ping-pong, was like a love-choked hush.

[5]Reality seemed more intense at the playground. There was a dust, a daring. It was a children's world; nowhere else did we gather in such numbers with so few adults over us. The playground occupied a platform of earth; we were exposed, it seems now, to the sun and sky. Looking up, one might see a buzzard or witness a portent.

COMMENT

Updike has been describing the scenes and experiences of his childhood. In this section of his memoir, he makes his transition through a direct reference to the previous section: "The periphery I have traced." At the start of paragraph 2 he makes a transition through a short phrase: "The playground." Like Golden, Updike depends on key words like "playground" and "pavilion," and on personal reference. He also depends on parallel structure as a means of transition in the paragraph: "If you hit the ball too hard," "If the person ahead of you hit the ball into the air." Punctuation can be a means of transition: the colon shows that what follows is an explanation or amplification of what precedes, as in this sentence. One use of the semicolon is to join closely related details and ideas; this, too, is a kind of transition. Semicolons are more common in long paragraphs than in short ones that contain one or two ideas and few or no details. Updike uses the semicolon to connect closely related ideas: "But there was never any doubt that everybody could play; it was perfect democracy."

QUESTIONS FOR STUDY AND DISCUSSION

1. Where else in the essay does Updike use semicolons to join closely related ideas? What use does he make of the colon in paragraph 2?

2. How many formal transitions do you find in the essay? Where does Updike make transitions through reference to details or ideas of the preceding paragraph?

3. Updike evokes the playground through a few carefully chosen details—details evoked by the adult remembering his childhood. How different would these details be if Updike were showing the playground as the child sees it?

4. Does the essay have a controlling idea, or has Updike presented a series of random impressions?

5. Does Updike explain why the playground was a "more intense" reality? Is the answer merely that games are often intense?

6. What exactly were the special interests or appeals of "roof ball," and how does Updike illustrate these?

7. How different from Updike's memories are yours of childhood playgrounds?

VOCABULARY STUDY

1. Many words have a wide range of meanings. This range is limited by the context of the word—by its use in a particular sentence or passage. State the general meaning of the italicized words in the following sentences. Then write a sentence of your own for each word, using it in the sense that Updike uses it:
   a. "The *center* of my boyhood held a *calm* collection of *kind* places that are almost impossible to describe. . . ."
   b. "But there was never any doubt that everybody could play; it was perfect *democracy.*"
   c. "The playground occupied a *platform* of earth; we were exposed, it seems now, to the sun and sky."
   d. "Somehow the game never *palled.*"

2. Though he uses adjectives to help describe the games of the play-ground, Updike depends on exact details. Show how words like *skimming* and *bouncing* contribute to the exactness of the description.

SUGGESTIONS FOR WRITING

1. Rewrite several sentences in the language of a child, not of an adult remembering childhood. Then explain the changes you made.

2. Develop the following statement from your own childhood experiences: "Reality seemed more intense at the playground."

climax

When ideas are stated in the order of their importance, they are said to be in the order of *climax:*

He could not find his cap.

He discovered that someone had driven his car away.

He felt a ground tremor and saw houses start to shake.

The steel and glass buildings were buckling; the street was cracking open.

If these events happened simultaneously, we would expect the more important ones to be given proper emphasis. The reader knows that something is wrong with the following sentence:

As he felt a ground tremor and watched the street crack open and houses begin to crumple, he discovered that someone had driven his car away, and that he had lost his cap.

The sentence conveys anticlimax. It is, of course, possible to arrange ideas in the order of their importance without conveying a sense of high climax. How much climax is conveyed depends on the force of the statements and the vividness of the details. Where the inherent drama or force of the experience is not immediately evident, transitional words *(more important, most important)* may be added to clarify the relation of ideas.

THE DECLINE OF SPORT
(A Preposterous Parable)

E. B. White

E. B. White is a distinguished essayist, humorist, and editor. He was born in Mount Vernon, New York, in 1899, and graduated from Cornell in 1921. He has long been associated with *The New Yorker* as writer and editor and has also written for *Harper's Magazine* and other publications. His books include *Charlotte's Web* (1952) and *Stuart Little* (1945), both for children, and *One Man's Meat* (1943), *The Second Tree from the Corner* (1954), and *The Points of My Compass* (1962), collections of his essays.

[1] In the third decade of the supersonic age, sport gripped the nation in an ever-tightening grip. The horse tracks, the ballparks, the fight rings, the gridirons, all drew crowds in steadily increasing numbers. Every time a game was played, an attendance record was broken. Usually some other sort of record was broken, too—such as the record for the number of consecutive doubles hit by left-handed batters in a Series game, or some such thing as that. Records fell like ripe apples on a windy day. Customs and manners changed, and the five-day business week was reduced to four days, then to three, to give everyone a better chance to memorize the scores.

[2] Not only did sport proliferate but the demands it made on the spectator became greater. Nobody was content to take in one event at a time, and thanks to the magic of radio and television nobody had to. A Yale alumnus, class of 1962, returning to the Bowl with 197,000 others to see the Yale-Cornell football game would take along his pocket radio and pick up the Yankee Stadium, so that while his eye might be following a fumble on the Cornell twenty-two-yard line, his ear would be following a man going down to second in the top of the fifth, seventy miles away. High in the blue sky above the Bowl, skywriters would be at work writing the scores

of other major and minor sporting contests, weaving an interminable record of victory and defeat, and using the new high-visibility pink news-smoke perfected by Pepsi-Cola engineers. And in the frames of the giant video sets, just behind the goalposts, this same alumnus could watch Dejected win the Futurity before a record-breaking crowd of 349,872 at Belmont, each of whom was tuned to the Yale Bowl and following the World Series game in the video and searching the sky for further news of events either under way or just completed. The effect of this vast cyclorama of sport was to divide the spectator's attention, over-subtilize his appreciation, and deaden his passion. As the fourth supersonic decade was ushered in, the picture changed and sport began to wane.

[3] A good many factors contributed to the decline of sport. Substitutions in football had increased to such an extent that there were very few fans in the United States capable of holding the players in mind during play. Each play that was called saw two entirely new elevens lined up, and the players whose names and faces you had familiarized yourself with in the first period were seldom seen or heard of again. The spectacle became as diffuse as the main concourse in Grand Central at the commuting hour.

[4] Express motor highways leading to the parks and stadia had become so wide, so unobstructed, so devoid of all life except automobiles and trees that sport fans had got into the habit of travelling enormous distances to attend events. The normal driving speed had been stepped up to ninety-five miles an hour, and the distance between cars had been decreased to fifteen feet. This put an extraordinary strain on the sport lover's nervous system, and he arrived home from a Saturday game, after a road trip of three hundred and fifty miles, glassy-eyed, dazed, and spent. He hadn't really had any relaxation and he had failed to see Czlika (who had gone in for Trusky) take the pass from Bkeeo (who had gone in for Bjallo) in the third period, because at that moment a youngster named Lavagetto had been put in to pinch-hit for Art Gurlack in the bottom of the ninth with the tying run on second, and the skywriter who was attempting to write "Princeton 0–Lafayette 43" had banked the wrong way, muffed the "3," and distracted everyone's attention from the fact that Lavagetto had been whiffed.

[5] Cheering, of course, lost its stimulating effect on players, because cheers were no longer associated necessarily with the immediate scene but might as easily apply to something that was

happening somewhere else. This was enough to infuriate even the steadiest performer. A football star, hearing the stands break into a roar before the ball was snapped, would realize that their minds were not on him, and would become dispirited and grumpy. Two or three of the big coaches worried so about this that they considered equipping all players with tiny ear sets, so that they, too, could keep abreast of other sporting events while playing, but the idea was abandoned as impractical, and the coaches put it aside in tickler files, to bring up again later.

[6] I think the event that marked the turning point in sport and started it downhill was the Midwest's classic Dust Bowl game of 1975, when Eastern Reserve's great right end, Ed Pistachio, was shot by a spectator. This man, the one who did the shooting, was seated well down in the stands near the forty-yard line on a bleak October afternoon and was so saturated with sport and with the disappointments of sport that he had clearly become deranged. With a minute and fifteen seconds to play and the score tied, the Eastern Reserve quarterback had whipped a long pass over Army's heads into Pistachio's waiting arms. There was no other player anywhere near him, and all Pistachio had to do was catch the ball and run it across the line. He dropped it. At exactly this moment, the spectator—a man named Homer T. Parkinson, of 35 Edgemere Drive, Toledo, O.—suffered at least three other major disappointments in the realm of sport. His horse, Hiccough, on which he had a five-hundred-dollar bet, fell while getting away from the starting gate at Pimlico and broke his leg (clearly visible in the video); his favorite shortstop, Lucky Frimstitch, struck out and let three men die on base in the final game of the Series (to which Parkinson was tuned); and the Governor Dummer soccer team, on which Parkinson's youngest son played goalie, lost to Kent, 4–3, as recorded in the sky overhead. Before anyone could stop him, he drew a gun and drilled Pistachio, before 954,000 persons, the largest crowd that had ever attended a football game and the *second*-largest crowd that had ever assembled for any sporting event in any month except July.

[7] This tragedy, by itself, wouldn't have caused sport to decline, I suppose, but it set in motion a chain of other tragedies, the cumulative effect of which was terrific. Almost as soon as the shot was fired, the news flash was picked up by one of the skywriters directly above the field. He glanced down to see whether he could spot the trouble below, and in doing so failed to see another skywriter approaching.

The two planes collided and fell, wings locked, leaving a confusing trail of smoke, which some observers tried to interpret as a late sports score. The planes struck in the middle of the nearby east-bound coast-to-coast Sunlight Parkway, and a motorist driving a convertible coupé stopped so short, to avoid hitting them, that he was bumped from behind. The pileup of cars that ensued involved 1,482 vehicles, a record for eastbound parkways. A total of more than three thousand persons lost their lives in the highway accident, including the two pilots, and when panic broke out in the stadium, it cost another 872 in dead and injured. News of the disaster spread quickly to other sports arenas, and started other panics among the crowds trying to get to the exits, where they could buy a paper and study a list of the dead. All in all, the afternoon of sport cost 20,003 lives, a record. And nobody had much to show for it except one small Midwestern boy who hung around the smoking wrecks of the planes, captured some aero news-smoke in a milk bottle, and took it home as a souvenir.

[8] From that day on, sport waned. Through long, noncompetitive Saturday afternoons, the stadia slumbered. Even the parkways fell into disuse as motorists rediscovered the charms of old, twisty roads that led through main streets and past barnyards, with their mild congestions and pleasant smells.

COMMENT

White depends on climax to make his satirical points. The opening sentence of paragraph 2 states that he is building to a more important idea: "*Not only* did sport proliferate *but* the demands it made on the spectator became greater." The transitional sentence that concludes paragraph 2 might suggest a turn to less important ideas; in fact, the following paragraphs present the reasons for the decline of sport in the order of their importance. White builds to the Dust Bowl game and the climactic accident on the Sunlight Parkway. At first glance, the brief concluding paragraph may seem anticlimactic; it is not, however, for the reader feels the importance to White of the old winding roads "that led through main streets and past barnyards, with their mild congestions and pleasant smells." The satirical force of the essay depends, then, on the sense of climax, achieved in many ways in the various paragraphs. That sense of climax is important to White's ironic comment on the American obsession with sports. We are being ironic when we imply more than we say; we do this sometimes through a smile or wink of the eye when we speak, or, in writing and in speech, through understatement or exaggeration.

QUESTIONS FOR STUDY AND DISCUSSION

1. What attitudes or habits is White satirizing in the America of late 1947, when this essay first appeared? Do you think he is on target about attitudes toward sport and the behavior of sports fans in the seventies?

2. Are the targets of White's satire limited to attitudes and habits relating to sport, or does he have general attitudes and habits in mind too?

3. What is a "parable"? And what does the subtitle "A Preposterous Parable" show about White's intention?

4. Names like *Dejected* and *Futurity* can be satirical as well as humorous. Are they? Do you find other humorous names in the essay, and are they used satirically?

5. Where has White used overstatement for humor? Does he also use understatement?

6. White refers to the "high visibility pink news-smoke perfected by Pepsi-Cola engineers." Why "Pepsi-Cola" rather than "U. S. Steel" or "Dow Chemical"?

VOCABULARY STUDY

Write a paraphrase of paragraph 2 or paragraph 6—a sentence-for-sentence rendering in your own words. Be sure to find substitutes for *proliferate, interminable,* and *oversubtilize* (paragraph 2), and *deranged, whipped,* and *drilled* (paragraph 6). Try to retain the tone of White's original paragraph in your rendering.

SUGGESTIONS FOR WRITING

1. Discuss the extent to which White's predictions have come true. Cite events and attitudes in the seventies that support his predictions or show him to be mistaken.

2. Identify the targets of White's satire and explain how you discover them in the essay. Then compare his view of sport and ways of expressing it with Wicker's.

3. A writer sometimes can be characterized through his sense of humor. Discuss the qualities you believe the essay reveals about E. B. White. Comment also on his probable interests and attitudes.

THE AMERICAN CAUSE

John Dos Passos

John Dos Passos was born in Chicago in 1896. After graduating from Harvard in 1916 he went to Spain to study architecture, but soon joined the French ambulance corps and, later, the Red Cross ambulance corps in Italy and the United States Army Medical Corps. After the World War, he worked as a journalist and began writing novels. His first major work, *Manhattan Transfer,* was published in 1925. His great trilogy, *U.S.A.* (1936), experimented with cinematic and stream-of-consciousness techniques. In later years Dos Passos wrote extensively about American history and democratic values. He died in 1970.

[1] Not long ago I received a letter from some German students asking me to explain to them in three hundred words why they should admire the United States. "Young people in Germany," they wrote "as in other places in the world are disillusioned, weary of pronouncements on the slogan level. They are not satisfied with negations, they have been told over and over again what to hate and what to fight. . . . They want to know what to be and what to do."

[2] This is what I didn't tell them: I didn't tell them that they should admire the United States for the victories of our armed forces

From *The Theme Is Freedom* by John Dos Passos (Dodd, Mead, 1956). Reprinted by permission of Mrs. John Dos Passos.

or because we had first developed the atomic bomb or the hydrogen bomb, or because we had shinier automobiles or more washing machines and deep freeze or more televisions or ran up more passenger miles of airplane travel a year than any other people in the world. I didn't tell them to admire us for getting more productive work done with less backbreaking than any other people in the world or for our high wages, or our social security system. I didn't tell them to admire us because our popular leaders had the sweetest smiles before the television cameras or because we lived on a magnificent continent that offered an unbelievable variety of climates, mountains, plains, rivers, estuaries, seashores. Some of these are very good things but they are not things that would help them "to know what to be and what to do."

[3] This is what I told them: I told them they should admire the United States not for what we were but for what we might become. Selfgoverning democracy was not an established creed, but a program for growth. I reminded them that industrial society was a new thing in the world and that although we Americans had gone further than any people in spreading out its material benefits we were just beginning, amid crimes, illusions, mistakes and false starts, to get to work on how to spread out what people needed much more: the sense of belonging, the faith in human dignity, the confidence of each man in the greatness of his own soul without which life is a meaningless servitude. I told them to admire our failures because they might contain the seeds of great victories to come, not of the victories that come through massacring men, women and children, but of the victories that come through overcoming the evil inherent in mankind through urgent and warmhearted use of our best brains. I told them to admire us for our foolish trust in other peoples, for our failure to create an empire when empire building was easy. I told them to admire us for our still unstratified society, where every man has the chance, if he has the will and the wit, to invent his own thoughts and to make his own way. I told them to admire us for the hope we still have that there is enough goodness in man to use the omnipotence science has given him to ennoble his life on earth instead of degrading it. Selfgovernment, through dangers and distortions and failures, is the American cause. Faith in selfgovernment, when all is said and done, is faith in the eventual goodness of man.

COMMENT

Dos Passos might have begun with what he did tell the German students (in 1955, when he wrote the essay), not with what he didn't. If he had, these ideas probably would seem less important than they do in the essay. In a whole essay as in a sentence, ideas that come last usually carry the most weight. One explanation for this effect is that ideas seem most important that take longest to develop or build to a conclusion. In this essay paragraph 3 carries the greatest weight, not only because it is the concluding paragraph but also because its ideas are in the order of climax. In paragraph 2, on the other hand, some but not all the ideas are in the order of importance. The carefully balanced sentences, the arrangement of sentence parts of equal length and structure—more usual in formal writing and speech—increase the sense of climax in the whole essay.

QUESTIONS FOR STUDY AND DISCUSSION

1. What ideas in paragraph 2 are in climactic order? What was gained in the whole essay by not arranging all the ideas in the order of importance?

2. The longer the phrases, the longer the sentences, the greater the sense of climax in paragraphs. Does Dos Passos depend on formal transitions to mark the build in importance of ideas?

3. The following sentence balances the two italicized phrases:

   > I told them they should admire the United States
   > *not for what we were*
   > *but for what we might become.*

   In what other sentences are phrases balanced in this way?

4. Do you agree that a country (and people) should be judged for its idealism and potential for growth rather than for its accomplishments to date?

VOCABULARY STUDY

The diction of this essay is highly abstract, particularly in paragraph 3. Identify those words you would not expect to find in ordinary conversation and look for informal equivalents for them. Rewrite two sentences of the essay in informal language and sentence structure.

SUGGESTIONS FOR WRITING
Discuss how true you believe the statements of the essay are of America in the late seventies. You might wish to write a statement of your own, directed to German students who have asked about America today.

THE PRINCESS AND THE TIN BOX

James Thurber

James Thurber was born in Columbus, Ohio, in 1894. He attended Ohio State University for three years, and later worked for the U.S. State Department as a code clerk. From 1920 to 1925 he worked as a journalist on the *Columbus Dispatch* and *Chicago Tribune*. His long association with *The New Yorker* began in 1925, the year it began publication, and most of his stories, sketches, and cartoons appeared in that magazine. Thurber was a humorist and a satirist of many aspects of American life, in particular the relations of the sexes. His many books include *My Life and Hard Times* (1933), *Fables for Our Time* (1943), *The Thurber Carnival* (1945), and *Thurber Country* (1953). He died in 1961.

[1] Once upon a time, in a far country, there lived a king whose daughter was the prettiest princess in the world. Her eyes were like the cornflower, her hair was sweeter than the hyacinth, and her throat made the swan look dusty.

[2] From the time she was a year old, the princess had been showered with presents. Her nursery looked like Cartier's window. Her toys were all made of gold or platinum or diamonds or emeralds. She was not permitted to have wooden blocks or china dolls or rubber dogs or linen books, because such materials were considered cheap for the daughter of a king.

[3] When she was seven, she was allowed to attend the wedding of her brother and throw real pearls at the bride instead of rice. Only the nightingale, with his lyre of gold, was permitted to sing for the princess. The common blackbird, with his boxwood flute, was kept out of the palace grounds. She walked in silver-and-samite slippers to a sapphire-and-topaz bathroom and slept in an ivory bed inlaid with rubies.

[4] On the day the princess was eighteen, the king sent a royal ambassador to the courts of five neighboring kingdoms to announce that he would give his daughter's hand in marriage to the prince who brought her the gift she liked the most.

[5] The first prince to arrive at the palace rode a swift white stallion and laid at the feet of the princess an enormous apple made of solid gold which he had taken from a dragon who had guarded it for a thousand years. It was placed on a long ebony table set up to hold the gifts of the princess's suitors. The second prince, who came on a gray charger, brought her a nightingale made of a thousand diamonds, and it was placed beside the golden apple. The third prince, riding on a black horse, carried a great jewel box made of platinum and sapphires, and it was placed next to the diamond nightingale. The fourth prince, astride a fiery yellow horse, gave the princess a gigantic heart made of rubies and pierced by an emerald arrow. It was placed next to the platinum-and-sapphire jewel box.

[6] Now the fifth prince was the strongest and handsomest of all the five suitors, but he was the son of a poor king whose realm had been overrun by mice and locusts and wizards and mining engineers so that there was nothing much of value left in it. He came plodding up to the palace of the princess on a plow horse and he brought her a small tin box filled with mica and feldspar and hornblende which he had picked up on the way.

[7] The other princes roared with disdainful laughter when they saw the tawdry gift the fifth prince had brought to the princess. But she examined it with great interest and squealed with delight, for all her life she had been glutted with precious stones and priceless metals, but she had never seen tin before or mica or feldspar or hornblende. The tin box was placed next to the ruby heart pierced with an emerald arrow.

[8]"Now," the king said to his daughter, "you must select the gift you like best and marry the prince that brought it."

[9] The princess smiled and walked up to the table and picked up

the present she liked the most. It was the platinum-and-sapphire jewel box, the gift of the third prince.

[10]"The way I figure it," she said, "is this. It is a very large and expensive box, and when I am married, I will meet many admirers who will give me precious gems with which to fill it to the top. Therefore, it is the most valuable of all the gifts my suitors have brought me and I like it the best."

[11]The princess married the third prince that very day in the midst of great merriment and high revelry. More than a hundred thousand pearls were thrown at her and she loved it.

[12]*Moral: All those who thought the princess was going to select the tin box filled with worthless stones instead of one of the other gifts will kindly stay after class and write one hundred times on the blackboard "I would rather have a hunk of aluminum silicate than a diamond necklace."*

COMMENT

Thurber's humor derives through what for the reader will probably be anticlimax—but clearly is not anticlimax for the princess. This disparity between what we expect to happen and what does happen is at *our* expense, as the moral shows. Much of the humor also arises from incongruity—a kingdom that contains wizards and mining engineers—and from the disparity between the setting and the language of this very modern girl. Disparities of this sort are a major source of irony. Many authors allow the irony to make its point without commenting on it. One delight in reading Thurber is in the discovery of those little deceptions that keep us feeling confident and pleased with ourselves.

QUESTIONS FOR STUDY AND DISCUSSION

1. How do the details of the first six paragraphs lead us to believe that the princess will choose the fifth prince?

2. At what point does the reader discover the real character of the princess?

3. Thurber, in his moral, talks to us in a language different from that of the story. What exactly is this difference, and what humor arises from it?

4. What human frailties is Thurber satirizing? Is he satirizing the princess or the reader of the essay or possibly both?

VOCABULARY STUDY

Look up the following words: *parable, fairy tale, fable, allegory.* How closely does "The Princess and the Tin Box" fit the definitions you found?

SUGGESTIONS FOR WRITING

1. Compare Thurber's ways of satirizing attitudes and values with E. B. White's. You might wish to compare the kinds of humor they use.
2. Write a fairy tale or fable or parable of your own which uses the order of climax.

point
of
view

In describing a person, a scene, or an event, we may specify the place of observation, the time we make it, or the angle of vision (the window of an upstairs apartment). These comprise the *physical point of view*. Not all of them need be stated directly; how much information we provide depends on our purpose in writing and on the needs of the reader. If we are describing an event of the past, the physical point of view may be indefinite.

Usually our feelings and ideas about people and events color our description. One viewer will notice details that a second viewer will miss completely. Neither viewer may be aware of having mentioned certain details and ignored others. This stated or implied *psychological point of view* is another type.

A piece of writing can exhibit both kinds of point of view. Here are two passages from George Orwell's description of Marrakech, a city in Morocco:

> As the corpse went past the flies left the restaurant table in a cloud and rushed after it, but they came back a few minutes later.

> Most of Morocco is so desolate that no wild animal bigger than a hare can live on it. Huge areas which were once covered with forest have turned into a treeless waste where the soil is exactly like broken-up brick. Nevertheless a good deal of it is cultivated, with frightful labor.

The point of view of the first passage is limited to a particular time and place; the point of view of the second is indefinite about both. Orwell saw the flies leave the table at the moment the corpse passed the restaurant; he observed most of the country over a period of time that need not be specified. In both passages attitudes are implied: the foreign visitor may notice and report the swarm of flies because he is not used to seeing them in his own country; a native of Marrakech might take no notice of them at all. Most of Morocco is desolate in comparison with southern England. To a person not used to hard manual labor, the work required to cultivate the rocky Moroccan ground is "frightful." Whether we realize it or not, we identify with a point of view as we read and perhaps absorb the attitudes of the writer revealed in his description.

I'LL MEET YOU AT THE Y

John Craig

John Craig was born in Peterborough, Canada, in 1921. He attended the University of Manitoba and the University of Toronto, served in the Canadian Navy, and worked for twenty years in public opinion and marketing research. In addition to writing for Canadian television, he is the author of a number of books, including *Wagons West* (1955), *The Pro* (1966), *No Word for Good-bye* (1969), and *Zach* (1972).

[1] The Y.M.C.A. in our town, like Y.M.C.A.s of that period the world over, was a red brick, military-looking building, with Gothic towers at the corners. You had the feeling that, with a moat around its stone base, it could have repelled legions of infidels almost indefinitely. It stood on the main street, just on the northern fringe of the business section, and immediately south of the park where the World War I memorial stood.

From *How Far Back Can You Get?*, copyright © 1974 by John Craig. Reprinted by permission of Doubleday & Co., Inc.

[2] During the '30s the Y was a combined community centre, soup kitchen, rest home, and meeting place as well as the hang-out for most of the town's athletes. The baseball and football teams used to dress there, walking back and forth over the hill and across the cement bridge to the ball park in their uniforms.

[3] It's hard to understand now how the place managed to keep open through those lean years, but it must have been subsidized through some central organization, no doubt supported by the churches. There was a businessmen's group, mostly fat, older guys in knee-length white shorts, who did calisthenics on Tuesday evenings and played volleyball Saturday afternoons, and presumably they paid their annual fees. Hardly any of the rest of us did, though, even if it *was* the best bargain in the world at fifteen dollars a year.

[4] The Y was managed by a man who emerges in retrospect as a somewhat unlikely, and at the time completely unsung, hero of the long, bitter fight against the Depression. "G. H.", as we called him—among ourselves, though not to his face—was a fairly tall, slim man with trim whitish-grey hair. To us, at the time, he seemed to have a somewhat stern countenance and a cold manner, but in reality he was undoubtedly a very kind man of substantial understanding and almost infinite patience.

[5] Every year the pattern was the same. Each September we would scrape up a dollar or two with which to make a token payment on that year's membership. It never occurred to us to be grateful that the balance of the previous year's fees was waived at that point; after all, that was ancient history. The initial instalment would be enough to get you your membership card for the up-coming season. As of that moment, you were a member in good standing (no matter how much you might owe in back dues), entitled to use the gym and the shower room, the bowling alley and the pool table, and all the other facilities the Y had to offer. From then on, it became a matter of stretching that first, token payment as far as possible; the man who eventually had to adjudicate its elasticity was, of course, G.H.

[6] He presided behind a circular desk off the lobby to the right. That desk was the nerve centre of the Y; it was there that you took out the snooker balls for the pool table, picked up your towels for the pool or the shower room, had your card stamped if you wanted to take part in any of the hobby classes, and so on. And it was from

there that the buzzer was controlled which unlocked the door giving you access to the downstairs locker rooms, showers, pool, and gym. That all important door was about twenty feet to the left of G.H.'s desk and it was as critical, in its way, as the Khyber Pass or the Franco-German frontier. Each time it remained locked to you, you knew that you were finally due again for a little chat with G.H.

[7] You could cross that lobby a dozen times, or thirty or fifty times, and always the buzzer would sound as you approached the door so that you knew it would open when you got to it. And then one day, without warning, you would saunter in for a shower, or, worse still, for an important basketball game, and as you moved towards the door the ominous silence would continue. As you drew nearer, step by increasingly resigned step, you would carefully avoid any glance towards the desk. Finally there would remain no recourse but to reach out and try the door, which, of course, would not open. And then you would hear the quiet voice of reckoning from behind the desk.

[8] "Hmmmm, hmmmm . . . Pete [or John, or Sam, or Jimmy] . . . hmmmm . . . hmmmm . . . can I see you a minute?"

[9] You would go over to the desk with your head down, conscious of the snooker players watching you as you walked towards your confrontation. G.H. would fidget with the blotter on the desk, straighten and restraighten the towels on the shelf under the counter, and do everything he could to avoid looking at you. We didn't realize then how much he must have hated having to do it, and he would always speak in a low voice so that nobody else around the lobby could hear.

[10] "Hmmmm . . . hmmmm . . . haven't had a chance to talk with you in a while, Pete. How's it going?"

[11] "Not bad."

[12] "Well, hmmmm . . . the year's getting on, Pete. What would you think about making a small payment on your fees?"

[13] You'd study your shoelaces and mutter something about "bringing in something next week," and both you and G.H. would know that there was no way in the world you were going to pay any more until the initial instalment the following September.

[14] "That's fine, Pete . . . hmmmm . . . appreciate that. Nice talking to you, Pete."

[15] And then he'd press the button and let you go down for your shower or basketball game, and you would know that you were a

member in good standing, and that the sound of the ever-loving buzzer was assured, for another few weeks.

[16]The Y was like a home away from home. You could play table tennis there, shoot pool, bowl, have a swim, play volleyball or basketball, read the papers and magazines in the reading room, go to the dances on Saturday nights. Even on Sunday nights, when it was officially closed, there was a way to get in and make use of some of the facilities. The Y had a few boarders, more or less impoverished bachelors, who used to come and go by a side door to which each of them had a key. You could hide in the shadows in the lane, slip out after a boarder entered, and quickly insert a foot so that the door wouldn't close. Then you waited until the boarder's footsteps receded up the stairs, opened the door and went in.

[17]There was a ghostly atmosphere about the place on Sunday nights. You couldn't turn on any lights, of course, and the faint glow from the street lights outside the windows would transform the familiar shapes in subtle and mysterious ways. Sometimes, if the snooker balls had been left out, you could shoot a game of pool in the pale, bluish light, wincing with each click of the ivory balls for fear somebody might hear. We didn't dare bowl because of the noise. There were always some lights left on in the gym and sometimes we would go in and shoot some baskets, but dribbling was strictly forbidden.

[18]There was a cafeteria on the second floor where they served meals to the boarders, and provided occasional banquets for various Y groups. The door to the kitchen led off a back hall, and the bolt could be slipped quite easily with a piece of cardboard. Once inside, it was often possible to pilfer a pie or a plate of doughnuts, which could do a lot to brighten up a cold, dark winter night. The trouble was that, if the caretaker happened to come by while you were in the kitchen, the only way out was through a window and onto a ledge which ran around one of the corner towers. It was a pretty precarious perch, if you had to outwait the caretaker for any length of time on a bitter-cold Sunday night in January. Once Gus Gunsolus was out there for almost an hour and when we finally got him in, he looked like a survivor (just barely) from a seal-hunting disaster on the Labrador ice floes. There were icicles hanging from his hair, eyebrows and nose, and he was shaking like the last, dried maple leaf in a November gale. It was a long time before he came around enough to talk coherently.

[19]The worst part of it was that all the kitchen staff had left out that Sunday night was a big pot full of tired old carrots, soaking in water.

COMMENT

The physical point of view is stated immediately: we are seeing the Y as Craig saw it in the thirties, and as he remembers it in later years. His memories reveal an attitude, a controlling impression, composed of many feelings—ranging from security to mystery and excitement. The view we are given of the Y would be incomplete without a statement of these feelings. And so Craig shows us the Y at various times and on various days. The proportion of details in the whole essay is important to the impression we receive: we are told more about G.H. than we are about the businessmen who used the Y. That is because we are seeing the Y mainly as Craig the boy saw it, and G.H. was more important to his experience than the businessmen. The description would be different in many ways if we were seeing the Y through the eyes of one of these people or of an impoverished boarder.

QUESTIONS FOR STUDY AND DISCUSSION

1. What is the controlling impression of the Y in the whole essay? Is Craig developing a thesis through it?

2. What do the details about G.H. contribute to our impression of the Y? How does Craig indicate that we are seeing G.H. from the point of view of a boy rather than of a businessman or boarder?

3. What features of life at the Y might have been stressed by the businessman or boarder?

4. In what order are the various impressions presented? Is Craig moving from morning to evening, or through the days of the week, or from less to more exciting experiences? Is he possibly employing two or more principles of order?

5. Does Craig imply rather than state certain feelings or attitudes? In other words, does he let his details and impressions reveal what he felt and thought?

6. Do you know people like G.H. who reveal one self on the job and another self off? What do you think explains this difference in these instances?

VOCABULARY STUDY

Use reference books like *The Columbia Encyclopedia, Facts on File, New York Times Index,* and *Encyclopedia of World History* to gain information on the following. Then write an explanation of the allusion to each in the essay:

    a. Khyber Pass

    b. the Franco-German frontier in the thirties (Maginot Line)

    c. Gothic towers

    d. seal-hunting on Labrador ice floes

SUGGESTIONS FOR WRITING

1. Describe the Y in your hometown, or the gymnasium of your high school, or a general recreation area in your town or city—at various times and on various days. You need not specify your feelings about the place: carefully chosen details will reveal these to your reader.

2. Describe a room in your house in the same way. In the course of your description, contrast your view of the room with that of a stranger in the house.

3. Describe the main street of your hometown or city in the same way— from the point of view of an inhabitant and that of a visitor.

A WHOLE SOCIETY
OF LONERS AND DREAMERS

William Allen

> William Allen teaches creative writing at Ohio State University and is the editor of *The Ohio Journal*. His fiction and nonfiction have appeared in numerous periodicals including *The Antioch Review, Saturday Review,* and the *New York Times.* His book *Starkweather: The Story of a Mass Murderer* was published in 1976.

[1]On Sunday afternoons here, if you're tired of taking walks in the country and fighting off the green-bellied hogflies, your next best choice is thumbing magazines at the downtown drugstore. One Sunday not long ago, when I ran out of anything else to thumb, I started looking through one of those magazines geared toward helping new writers achieve success. I used to pore over them a lot when I was a teenager, and the first thing I noticed now was that the ads haven't changed much over the past fifteen years:

[2]"IMAGINE MAKING $5,000 A YEAR WRITING IN YOUR SPARE TIME! Fantastic? Not at all . . . . Hundreds of People Make That Much or More Every Year—and Have Fun Doing It!"

[3]"TO PEOPLE WHO WANT TO WRITE FOR PROFIT BUT CAN'T GET STARTED. Have You Natural Writing Ability? Now a Chance to Test Yourself—FREE!"

[4]"I FIRE WRITERS . . . with enthusiasm for developing God-given talent. You'll 'get fired' too with my 48-lesson home study course. Over-the-shoulder coaching . . . personalized critiques! Amazing sales opportunity the first week. Write for my FREE STARTER KIT."

[5]The ad that struck me the most showed a picture of a handsome and darkly serious young man sitting on a hill, picking his teeth with a weed, and gazing out over the countryside. The caption read: DO YOU HAVE THE "FAULTS" THAT COULD MEAN YOU WERE MEANT TO BE A WRITER? The ad went on to list the outstanding characteristics of writers. They are dreamers, loners, bookworms. They are too impractical, too intense, too idealistic.

[6]When I was fourteen and had just started trying to write, I saw an ad much like this and was overwhelmed by it. That fellow on the hill was just like me, I thought. It was a tremendous feeling to discover that I might not be alone—that there was a whole society of loners and dreamers, that they were called writers, and that by sending off for a free writing IQ test I could find out by return mail if I qualified to climb the hill and chew straw with them.

[7]I took that test and blew the top off it. The writing school said I demonstrated a rare creative potential unlike anything they had seen in years. They did wonder, though, if I had what it took to stick

with them through long months of arduous training to develop my raw talent. If I really did have that kind of fortitude, the next step would be to send in some actual samples of my writing.

[8]Spurred, I sent off everything I had ever written—two stories of about 200 words each. One was about some unidentified creatures who lived in dread of an unidentified monster who came around every week or so to slaughter as many of them as he could. Some of the persecuted creatures had the option of running, hopping, scurrying, or crawling to safety, but the others, for some unexplained reason, couldn't move and had just to stand there and take it. There was a description of the monster's roaring approach. Then the last line hit the reader like a left hook: "The lawn mower ran swiftly over. . . ."

[9]The other story I have preserved these many years:

THE RACE

Two gleaming hot rods stand side by side, poised and tensed—eager to scream down the hot asphalt track, each secretly confident that he will be the supreme victor. The time is drawing close now; in just a few minutes the race will be on.

There is a last minute check of both cars . . . everything is ready. A yell rings out for everyone to clear the track. The flagman raises the starting flag above his head, pauses for a second, and with a downward thrust of the flag, he sends the cars leaping forward with frightening speed.

They fly down the track, side by side, neither able to take the lead. They are gaining speed with every second. Faster and faster they go, approaching the half-way mark with incredible momentum. . . .

Wait! Something is wrong—one of the cars is going out of control and skidding toward the other car! The rending sound of ripping metal and sliding tires cuts through the air as the two autos collide and spin crazily off the track.

For a moment the tragic panorama is hidden by a self-made curtain of dust, but it isn't a second before the curtain is pulled away by the wind, revealing the horrible sight. There are the two hot rods, one turned over, both broken and smashed. All is quiet. . . .

Two small children, a boy and a girl, get up from the curb

where they have been sitting. They eye each other accusingly as
they walk slowly across the street where the two broken toy cars
lay silent . . . . "Woman driver," grumbles the little boy.

THE END

[10]The correspondence school's copy desk quickly replied that
the writing samples confirmed my aptitude test results and that
they looked forward to working with me to the point of publication
and beyond. I couldn't imagine what could be beyond publication
but finally figured out they meant to handle my work later as agent-
representative. They praised my choice of subject matter, sense of
drama, and powerful surprise endings—all of which they said indicated I could sell to the sci-fi market. This made sense, because
science fiction was all I had ever read voluntarily except for *Comic
Classics* and, as a child, *Uncle Wiggily*. The school was particularly
impressed by my style, which they said was practically poetry, in
places. They made reference to my use of alliteration ("rending
sound of ripping metal") and of metaphor ("self-made curtain of dust
. . . pulled away by the wind").

[11]They were quick to make clear, however, that what I had
here were only germs of stories. They needed to be expanded to
publishable lengths and had to have better character development—particularly the one about the bugs and grass being slaugh-
tered by the lawn mower. They said a good writer could give even an
insect an interesting personality.

[12]The next step was to send them $10 for each of the two
stories—the standard fee for detailed, over-the-shoulder copy-desk
criticism. Then after these stories had been redone and rushed off
for publication, I should enroll in their thirty-six-lesson course, in
which I would be taught the ins and outs of plotting, characterization, point of view, theme, tone, and setting. The fee was $10 a
lesson, and after my successful completion of the course they would
then handle my literary properties, protect my legal rights, etc., for
the regular 10 per cent.

[13]At this point I began to wonder if I might be going in over my
head. I was getting only a dollar a week from my folks and didn't
understand half of what the writing school was talking about. In
English class I had heard of such terms as "alliteration," "tone," and
"point of view" but had no clear idea what they meant. Also I felt

like an imposter. I had given my age as twenty-one. Of course, I was strutting because at fourteen I was doing better than anybody they had worked with in years, but I wondered if I could keep it up. "Rending sound of ripping metal" was genius, but could I crank out lines like that on a daily basis? I decided to try.

[14] First I wrote them that I was a little short of cash this month and asked if just to get started, it would be all right to work on one story for $10 instead of two for $20. They replied that that would be fine—just send in the ten bucks so they could get rolling.

[15] Meanwhile I hadn't been able to get even that much money together. I approached my family and was turned down flat because my father thought there was something unhealthy about people who wanted to write. He was bothered by the school's remark that my writing was like poetry. "If you were a girl, it might be different," he said, and showed me a copy of *Men's Adventure*. "Look here, why don't you get one of these two ninety-eight worm ranches? Or one of these small-game boomerangs?"

[16] After a few days of trying to drum up work around the neighborhood, I realized I wasn't going to be able to pull it off and decided just not to write back. But in a week I got a curt note saying they wanted to help me, were trying to be patient, but I was going to have to be more responsible. They said that writing was 1 per cent inspiration and 99 per cent perspiration and wondered if in my case the figures might be reversed.

[17] This both goaded and scared me. I wrote back that on account of unexpected medical expenses I could afford to give them only $5 at first. Could they possibly let me have a cut rate? They replied that it was strictly against their policy, but in view of my undeniably vast potential the copy-desk team had voted to go along with me just this once—send the $5.

[18] By mowing lawns and selling bottles, I had by this time scraped together $3, but there my earning potential dropped sharply. Another week went by, and I made only 48 cents more. Then a letter arrived stamped in red, front and back: URGENT! IMPORTANT! DO NOT DISCARD! It said I had violated an agreement based on mutual trust and had exactly twenty-four hours to send in the $5. Without exactly spelling it out, they gave the impression that legal action might be taken. The letter ended: "Frankly, Mr. Allen, we're about at our wits' end with you."

[19] I was hurt as well as shaken. I felt that I just didn't have

what it takes. If there ever had been a chance of my climbing that hill and sitting with that elite group of loners and dreamers, it was gone now. I had my mother write them that I had suddenly been struck down with polio and was unable even to write my name, much less take their course. I hung onto the little money I had in case I had to give it to them to avoid a lawsuit, but I didn't hear from them after that. In a few weeks I relaxed and mailed off for the $2.98 worm ranch.

COMMENT

Allen implies more than he actually states. That "whole society of loners and dreamers" probably includes all adolescents. But everyone has been intimidated by clerks and salesmen and dunning letters. The point of view, in other words, is one shared by adolescent and adult, as Allen's opening paragraphs show. The point of view also shapes the reader's response in one important way. Allen is not developing a thesis, and therefore we need not be on our intellectual guard, as we are in active if silent debate with a writer. We give more of ourselves imaginatively to the essay, maybe identifying with the experience through one of our own. One of the important means to this identification is the lively detail. We are not merely told about the stories Allen wrote: we are given passages from them, and also his responses to the ad and to the letters that followed, and the response of his father to his interest in writing. Another important means to identification is the careful focus and consistent point of view. Once he has introduced himself and mentioned his experience in the drugstore, Allen does not stray from the point of view he establishes.

QUESTIONS FOR STUDY AND DISCUSSION

1. What qualities does Allen reveal about himself as a boy and a man? What are the qualities of "dreamers, loners, bookworms"?

2. What personal qualities do Allen's stories reveal?

3. What information about or view of himself as a boy—information or a view that the boy could not have possessed—does Allen share with the reader? What humor arises through this information or view?

4. What does Allen show about adolescence in general? What in your

experience illustrates these same qualities? Do you find his comments generally true of people you know?

VOCABULARY STUDY

1. Study current advertisements in magazines for writers and compare their language with that cited by Allen. How similar are the vocabulary and the appeals? Do you find exaggerated claims? Take notes on your findings for class discussion.

2. Look up *metaphor* and *alliteration* and write sentences containing both that could be added to one of the stories Allen wrote.

SUGGESTIONS FOR WRITING

1. Develop the topic "A Whole Society of Loners and Dreamers," from your point of view and experience. Contrast your awareness of the world today with your awareness of it as a boy or girl.

2. Develop the topic "Magazine Advertisements" from your point of view and experience. You might contrast advertisements for different products and for the same product. Use your discussion to reach a conclusion about the use of language and the appeals you found.

THE REVOLT OF THE EVIL FAIRIES

Ted Poston

Ted Poston (1907–1974) was born and raised in Hopkinsville, Kentucky, and graduated from Tennessee Agricultural and Industrial College in 1928. He worked in politics, then as a freelance journalist, and later as a reporter for the *New York Amsterdam News* and the *New York Post*. Poston was one of the first black journalists to work for a major New York newspaper. The essay printed here is one of many that he wrote about his Kentucky boyhood.

¹The grand dramatic offering of the Booker T. Washington Colored Grammar School was the biggest event of the year in our social life in Hopkinsville, Kentucky. It was the one occasion on which they let us use the old Cooper Opera House, and even some of the white folks came out yearly to applaud our presentation. The first two rows of the orchestra were always reserved for our white friends, and our leading colored citizens sat right behind them—with an empty row intervening, of course.

²Mr. Ed Smith, our local undertaker, invariably occupied a box to the left of the house and wore his cutaway coat and striped breeches. This distinctive garb was usually reserved for those rare occasions when he officiated at the funerals of our most prominent colored citizens. Mr. Thaddeus Long, our colored mailman, once rented a tuxedo and bought a box too. But nobody paid him much mind. We knew he was just showing off.

³The title of our play never varied. It was always "Prince Charming and the Sleeping Beauty," but no two presentations were ever the same. Miss H. Belle LaPrade, our sixth-grade teacher, rewrote the script every season, and it was never like anything you read in the story books.

⁴Miss LaPrade called it "a modern morality play of conflict between the forces of good and evil." And the forces of evil, of course, always came off second best.

⁵The Booker T. Washington Colored Grammar School was in a state of ferment from Christmas until February, for this was the period when parts were assigned. First there was the selection of the Good Fairies and the Evil Fairies. This was very important, because the Good Fairies wore white costumes and the Evil Fairies black. And strangely enough most of the Good Fairies usually turned out to be extremely light in complexion, with straight hair and white folks' features. On rare occasions a dark-skinned girl might be lucky enough to be a Good Fairy, but not one with a speaking part.

⁶There never was any doubt about Prince Charming and the Sleeping Beauty. They were *always* light-skinned. And though nobody ever discussed those things openly, it was an accepted fact that a lack of pigmentation was a decided advantage in the Prince Charming and Sleeping Beauty sweepstakes.

⁷And therein lay my personal tragedy. I made the best grades

Reprinted by permission of Henry Lee Moon.

in my class, I was the leading debater, and the scion of a respected family in the community. But I could never be Prince Charming, because I was black.

[8] In fact, every year when they started casting our grand dramatic offering my family started pricing black cheesecloth at Franklin's Department Store. For they knew that I would be leading the forces of darkness and skulking back in the shadows—waiting to be vanquished in the third act. Mamma had experience with this sort of thing. All my brothers had finished Booker T. before me.

[9] Not that I was alone in my disappointment. Many of my classmates felt it too. I probably just took it more to heart. Rat Joiner, for instance, could rationalize the situation. Rat was not only black; he lived on Billy Goat Hill. But Rat summed it up like this:

[10]"If you black, you black."

[11] I should have been able to regard the matter calmly too. For our grand dramatic offering was only a reflection of our daily community life in Hopkinsville. The yallers had the best of everything. They held most of the teaching jobs in Booker T. Washington Colored Grammar School. They were the Negro doctors, the lawyers, the insurance men. They even had a "Blue Vein Society," and if your dark skin obscured your throbbing pulse you were hardly a member of the élite.

[12] Yet I was inconsolable the first time they turned me down for Prince Charming. That was the year they picked Roger Jackson. Roger was not only dumb; he stuttered. But he was light enough to pass for white, and that was apparently sufficient.

[13] In all fairness, however, it must be admitted that Roger had other qualifications. His father owned the only colored saloon in town and was quite a power in local politics. In fact, Mr. Clinton Jackson had a lot to say about just who taught in the Booker T. Washington Colored Grammar School. So it was understandable that Roger should have been picked for Prince Charming.

[14]My real heartbreak, however, came the year they picked Sarah Williams for Sleeping Beauty. I had been in love with Sarah since kindergarten. She had soft light hair, bluish gray eyes, and a dimple which stayed in her left cheek whether she was smiling or not.

[15]Of course Sarah never encouraged me much. She never answered any of my fervent love letters and Rat was very scornful of

my one-sided love affair. "As long as she don't call you a black baboon," he sneered, "you'll keep on hanging around."

[16] After Sarah was chosen for Sleeping Beauty, I went out for the Prince Charming role with all my heart. If I had declaimed boldly in previous contests, I was matchless now. If I had bothered Mamma with rehearsals at home before, I pestered her to death this time. Yes, and I purloined my sister's can of Palmer's Skin Success.

[17] I knew the Prince's role from start to finish, having played the Head Evil Fairy opposite it for two seasons. And Prince Charming was one character whose lines Miss LaPrade never varied much in her many versions. But although I never admitted it, even to myself, I knew I was doomed from the start. They gave the part to Leonardius Wright. Leonardius, of course, was yaller.

[18] The teachers sensed my resentment. They were almost apologetic. They pointed out that I had been such a splendid Head Evil Fairy for two seasons that it would be a crime to let anybody else try the role. They reminded me that Mamma wouldn't have to buy any more cheesecloth because I could use my same old costume. They insisted that the Head Evil Fairy was even more important than Prince Charming because he was the one who cast the spell on Sleeping Beauty. So what could I do but accept?

[19] I had never liked Leonardius Wright. He was a goody-goody, and even Mamma was always throwing him up to me. But above all, he too was in love with Sarah Williams. And now he got a chance to kiss Sarah every day in rehearsing the awakening scene.

[20] Well, the show must go on, even for little black boys. So I threw my soul into my part and made the Head Evil Fairy a character to be remembered. When I drew back from the couch of Sleeping Beauty and slunk away into the shadows at the approach of Prince Charming, my facial expression was indeed something to behold. When I was vanquished by the shining sword of Prince Charming in the last act, I was a little hammy perhaps—but terrific!

[21] The attendance at our grand dramatic offering that year was the best in its history. Even the white folks overflowed the two rows reserved for them and a few were forced to sit in the intervening one. This created a delicate situation, but everybody tactfully ignored it.

[22] When the curtain went up on the last act, the audience was in

fine fettle. Everything had gone well for me too—except for one spot in the second act. That was where Leonardius unexpectedly rapped me over the head with his sword as I slunk off into the shadows. That was not in the script, but Miss LaPrade quieted me down by saying it made a nice touch anyway. Rat said Leonardius did it on purpose.

[23]The third act went on smoothly though until we came to the vanquishing scene. That was where I slunk from the shadows for the last time and challenged Prince Charming to mortal combat. The hero reached for his shining sword—a bit unsportsmanlike I always thought, since Miss LaPrade consistently left the Head Evil Fairy unarmed—and then it happened!

[24]Later, I protested loudly—but in vain—that it was a case of self-defense. I pointed out that Leonardius had a mean look in his eye. I cited the impromptu rapping he had given my head in the second act. But nobody would listen. They just wouldn't believe that Leonardius really intended to brain me when he reached for his sword.

[25]Anyway he didn't succeed. For the minute I saw that evil gleam in his eye—or was it my own?—I cut loose with a right to the chin, and Prince Charming dropped his shining sword and staggered back. His astonishment lasted only a minute though, for he lowered his head and came charging in, fists flailing. There was nothing yellow about Leonardius but his skin.

[26]The audience thought the scrap was something new Miss LaPrade had written in. They might have kept on thinking so if Miss LaPrade hadn't been screaming so hysterically from the sidelines. And if Rat Joiner hadn't decided that this was as good a time as any to settle old scores. So he turned around and took a sock at the male Good Fairy nearest him.

[27]When the curtain rang down, the forces of Good and Evil were locked in combat. And Sleeping Beauty was wide awake, and streaking for the wings.

[28]They rang the curtain back up fifteen minutes later, and we finished the play. I lay down and expired according to specifications, but Prince Charming will probably remember my sneering corpse to his dying day. They wouldn't let me appear in the grand dramatic offering at all the next year. But I didn't care. I couldn't have been Prince Charming anyway.

COMMENT

Like William Allen, Ted Poston does not argue a thesis, and the response of his reader to the experience would be different if he had. The humor of the essay is to be enjoyed for its own sake. It is humor, however, that arises from keen observation of a world whose attitudes and contradictions are still with us. We laugh at what we see to be true; knowing this, Poston presses the implied similarities between the world he is describing and his present world. As in Allen, it is the careful selection of details that makes the writing successful. Poston is not satisfied to report the outlines of the experience: he allows us to see and feel the black world of Hopkinsville, Kentucky. Superimposed on the point of view of the black boy destined to play the Head Evil Fairy is that of the adult remembering and savoring the revolt—and revealing the frustrations and pain of a black boy in a black world.

QUESTIONS FOR STUDY AND DISCUSSION

1. How do the details of the adult black world of Hopkinsville help the reader to understand the attitude of the black boys toward the lighter-skinned children in the grammar school?

2. Poston finds irony in the conception of the play—"a modern morality play of conflict between the forces of good and evil"—and the circumstances of its performance. The irony arises from the contradiction, the disparity between what should be and what is—between how adults should behave and set an example and how they do. How does Poston explore that irony?

3. The attitudes that made it impossible for Poston to play Prince Charming are not shown to be vicious. What exactly is the attitude Poston expresses toward them?

4. If Poston had wished to comment on contemporary social values directly, how might the organization and selection of details have been different?

5. What examples would you use to comment on the same social values?

VOCABULARY STUDY

Decide how the connotations of the following words are determined by their use in the essay: *skulking, yallers, hammy, slunk off.* Then write sentences of your own, using these words to reveal these meanings.

SUGGESTIONS FOR WRITING

1. Write a characterization of the author on the basis of what he reveals about himself—through his choice of incident and the details he selects to narrate it.

2. Narrate a similar incident in your school experience that reveals the effect of social values on the feelings and attitudes of children and grownups. Let the details reveal the effect. Don't state it directly.

3. Rewrite a paragraph of the essay from the point of view of Leonardius Wright. Change the details or the presentation of the original details of the paragraph to accord with how you think he may have felt about the Head Evil Fairy and the play itself.

tone

We know the meaning of a statement when we know the attitude or feeling it expresses—its *tone*. The statement

What a tragedy!

expresses pain—but the speaker may also be expressing anger or sarcasm. The statement

What a lucky boy!

can express wonder, delight, amazement, or even jealousy or sarcasm. Hearing a statement rather than reading it on a page, we usually can tell from the speaker's face or inflection of voice what attitude he or she is expressing; but in reading the statement, we may have to look for details or other statements that clarify the speaker's attitude. Dickens is usually plain in his anger and sarcasm, as in this comment on the birth of Oliver Twist in an early nineteenth-century workhouse:

> Oliver cried lustily. If he could have known that he was an orphan, left to the tender mercies of churchwardens and overseers, perhaps he would have cried the louder.

We cannot be quite sure of the tone of Jane Austen, in her opening statement in *Pride and Prejudice:*

> It is a truth universally acknowledged, that a single man in possession of a good fortune must be in want of a wife.

Jane Austen is certainly not angry, but is she serious? Does she believe the statement herself? Her next statement clarifies her attitude and therefore the tone of her opening statement:

> However little known the feelings or views of such a man may be on his first entering a neighborhood, this truth is so well fixed in

the minds of the surrounding families, that he is considered as the rightful property of someone or other of their daughters.

We know what Jane Austen means: it is a truth generally believed by families with marriageable daughters. She is being ironic, and her irony expresses amusement over small-town attitudes and values. Compare her opening sentences with this description of Mrs. Bennet, who has marriageable daughters:

> She was a woman of mean understanding, little information, and uncertain temper. When she was discontented, she fancied herself nervous. The business of her life was to get her daughters married; its solace was visiting and news.

We are in no doubt about Jane Austen's tone because she is plain about her view of Mrs. Bennet.

The tone of a statement like the above may express several feelings and attitudes simultaneously. And so may an essay. The longer the essay, the greater the opportunity for changes in and development of tone. Because statements can express so many feelings and attitudes, we must be aware when we write of how our words may be interpreted: we must look carefully at what we write, and revise statements that may say more than we intend or that are not consistent with the general tone we have in mind.

GUARANTEEING THE VALUE OF MONEY

William Raspberry

William Raspberry is a columnist for the *Washington Post,* and is syndicated widely in the United States. He has written on a wide range of subjects including Washington politics, urban problems, and black education in America. His recent columns urging an examination of attitudes toward black education have been much discussed.

[1] Years of economic stagnation, high unemployment and, above all, inflation may have succeeded in doing what the lectures and legislation of the economic theorists were unable to do.

[2] We may have gotten over our notion that it is the God-given right of man to be paid more this year than last.

[3] Don't expect workers to start turning down pay raises or to stop seeking them. The demands for higher and higher wages are, quite obviously, still with us. But more and more, it seems to me, the wage demands are based not on the expectation of increased purchasing power but on the hope of staying even.

[4] If this really is so—even if it is so only for those who have achieved middle class or higher—it represents a profound change in the American psychology, which has led us to suppose not only that more is better but also that more is natural and inevitable.

[5] The psychology had its origins, I suppose, in the early days of the country, when the encouragement of the appetite for more led to the development of a continent. It also led to the growth of smaller enterprises into larger ones, and it resulted in ever-higher levels of productivity. And for a long time, no one took notice of the fact that it depended for its success on virtually unlimited natural resources, a growing population and an expanding economy.

[6] But if that's how it started, it wound up with the in-grade syndrome: the idea that it is unnatural, if not immoral, not to earn more this year than last, whether there has been a corresponding growth in productivity or not. The newspaper columnist, no less than the GS-7 in government, considers it natural and right that he should get a pay raise simply because a year has elapsed since the last pay raise.

[7] What government has institutionalized with its in-grade pay hikes, the rest of us have to scrounge for, through our unions if we are organized or through whatever arguments we can muster if we are not.

[8] All of us have come to expect more. Not just the apprentice whose pay (and presumably productivity) increases as he moves along the ladder to journeyman, but also the fully experienced worker who, whether his skills and productivity have improved or not, expects an improvement in his paycheck.

[9] Well, we have finally learned that the increases don't mean

anything. For a time the pay raises looked like economic progress, but then it dawned on us that blowing more air into a tire doesn't increase the amount of rubber.

[10]By now, every worker in the country knows what every economist has been telling him: that baseless pay increases don't improve living standards; they only feed inflation.

[11]He knows it, but what does he do about it? He can wish that the merry-go-round would stop so that his dollars would stop losing their value, forcing him to demand that his employer supply more of them. But he can't stop demanding more dollars until they stop losing their value, which means they don't stop losing their value.

[12]How can they not keep losing value, when the manufacturer whose products he buys is having to pay his workers inflated wages to produce those products?

[13]That is the inflationary spiral that everybody talks about. What I am saying now is that the psychological impetus for that spiral seems to have subsided, thanks to a sustained period of economic bad times. The impetus that remains is supplied by our efforts not to get ahead but to stay even.

[14]If that is so, wouldn't most American workers forgo pay raises if they could be guaranteed that what they already earn will be protected from inflation?

[15]So-called cost-of-living clauses are commonplace in labor union contracts.

[16]But what if there were a national policy, endorsed by organized labor but not limited to union members, to the effect that cost-of-living increases would be the only nonproductivity pay increases workers would receive for, say, two or three years. If every worker were guaranteed against loss of purchasing power, wouldn't that remove the remaining impetus for the inflationary spiral?

[17]My guess is that it would and also that after the first year or so, it wouldn't even cost very much.

COMMENT

Raspberry is talking to readers who, with him and the workers Raspberry describes, have suffered from the "inflationary spiral." He is mainly concerned with the long-held assumption "that more is better but also that more is natural and inevitable." Present negotiations suggest to Raspberry that some or all of his readers may have changed their thinking about economic gain without realizing they have, and need to be shown that they have. They also need perhaps to realize what must be given up to prevent the spiral of inflation. Notice how Raspberry identifies basic assumptions in his thinking and at the same time focuses on a specific issue that, as he shows, concerns everyone.

QUESTIONS FOR STUDY AND DISCUSSION

1. What changes in tone do you find in the whole essay? Does Raspberry express anger or exasperation at any point? Or is he trying to sound objective, though concerned with the issue of inflation?

2. Judging from what he says about our attitude toward money, what would Raspberry's attitude be toward money in the general scheme of values?

3. Writers often address a limited audience; they deal with problems and select examples from one area of experience or work. Is Raspberry addressing a general or specific audience?

4. Are you convinced by Raspberry's argument? Would you give up a pay raise for the reason he suggests?

VOCABULARY STUDY

Write sentences using each of the italicized words in the sense that Raspberry uses them in the essay:
   a. "a corresponding growth in *productivity*"
   b. "What government has *institutionalized*"
   c. "whatever arguments we can *muster*"
   d. "as he moves along the ladder to *journeyman*"
   e. "psychological *impetus*"

SUGGESTIONS FOR WRITING

1. Use Raspberry's argument to analyze your own attitude toward money and economic gain, in particular to define its place in your scheme of values.

2. Show how economic hardship or changes you have had to make in how you live have changed your attitude toward money or toward the assumptions Raspberry discusses. Decide on your dominant tone before writing.

3. The American sociologist Thorstein Veblen suggested in a famous book, *The Theory of the Leisure Class,* that certain articles are valued

for their cost—that we buy one make of automobile rather than another because it costs more money. His phrase for this attitude is "conspicuous consumption." Discuss the extent to which advertisements for automobiles today appeal to this attitude. Then compare these advertisements with those in a national magazine ten or twenty years ago and discuss your findings. Comment in particular on the tone of these advertisements.

4. Show how two letters to the editor of a newspaper, concerning the same issue, are different in tone. Discuss the extent to which the differences are to be explained by differences in background and experience.

WORKING OUT A DEAL

Calvin Trillin

Calvin Trillin was born in Kansas City, Missouri, in 1935. He has been a staff member of *The New Yorker* since 1963. His books include *An Education in Georgia* (1964), *Barnett Frummer Is an Unbloomed Flower* (1969), and *U.S. Journal* (1970), a collection of essays on life in the United States drawn from his column in *The New Yorker*.

[1] The merchandising method of Reedman's, the world's largest car dealer, seems to be based on the theory that a lot of Americans have bought so many new cars that they consider themselves experts at the art. Respecting the fact that a man of experience will have gone beyond loyalty to any one make of car, Reedman salesmen are equally helpful about selling him a new Chevrolet or a new Plymouth or a new almost anything else; Reedman's has fourteen new-car franchises. Reedman salesmen will reassure a customer that the small Plymouth station wagon and the small Dodge station wagon, both of which Reedman's handles, are virtually the same

car—the slight difference in headlights and the different names being merely a way to make one car do for two different dealers. Good hard shoptalk is expected among experts. Included in the Reedman display of the Plymouth Duster and the American Motors' Hornet is the competing car not handled by Reedman's, the Ford Maverick—its roof decorated with a sign drawing attention to the relative puniness of its wheelbase, its trunk open to reveal a sign that says "The Exposed Gas Tank Is in the Trunk Floor." Since the customer will be sophisticated enough to know precisely what he wants in a car—whether, for example, he can do without air-conditioning but must have vinyl bucket seats—Reedman's has an inventory of some five thousand cars, and a computer that will instantly find out if a particular model is available and will then type out a precise description of it before the customer's eyes. An enormous selection being a great advantage in dealing with expert car purchasers, some people in the trade say that Reedman's sells so many cars because it has so many to sell—a merchandising adaptation of Mies van der Rohe's "Less is More" dictum that comes out "More is More."

[2]The Reedman newspaper advertisement invites customers to a hundred-and-fifty-acre, one-stop car center that has a ten-million-dollar selection of cars—and then, adding the note of exclusivity that is considered necessary in advertising even the world's largest, it says, "Private Sale Now Going On." The premises on which the private sale is held look like the average citizen's vision of the supply depot at Cam Ranh Bay. Behind a series of showrooms on Route 1, just down the road from the Greenwood Dairies, the five thousand cars are lined up on acres and acres of asphalt—the neat rows interrupted by occasional watchtowers and the entire area surrounded by a heavy, iron, electronically monitored fence. On a busy Saturday, attendants direct streams of traffic in and out of the customers' parking lot. Hostesses with the dress and manner of airline stewardesses circulate in the showrooms offering to call a salesman for anybody who feels the need of one. Muzak, which reaches the most remote line of hardtops, is interrupted every two or three bars by calls for salesman.

[3]The opportunity to perfect a veteran car buyer's style is so great at Reedman's—the opportunity to shrug off a computer's offer of a Dodge Coronet with fourteen extras, to exchange jargon about engines and wheelbases, to take a new model for a few spins around

the Reedman test track and make some observations to the family about how she handles on the curves—that some people seem to make Saturday at Reedman's a kind of outing. A lot of them, of course, find themselves buying a car, with vinyl bucket seats and air-conditioning. The route back to the customers' parking lot leads through a small building where the customer is greeted by a man even more helpful than the hostesses. "How'd you make out, sir?" the man asks. "What kind of car were you looking at? What was your trade-in? Who was your salesman? Of course you want to think about it, but why wait?" There is no reason for an experienced car buyer to concern himself with the fact that his most recent experience was so recent that he has yet to pay for the car he has; the first sign on the Reedman lot begins, "If you still have payments on your present car, truck, etc., we will pay off the balance and work out a deal."

[4]Although selling at Reedman's is based on working out a deal rather than on glamour or showmanship, a car dealer cannot afford to create an atmosphere of pure, unglamorous functionalism. If anyone is going to be totally practical, why should he spend his money on an overlarge, gas-eating, non-functional, instantly depreciating new car? Although the Chevrolet section of the Reedman showrooms is crowded with as many models as can be crammed in, the decor includes huge crystal chandeliers and wallpaper of raised-velvet fleur-de-lis patterns on ersatz gold leaf. On one wall of the showroom, a picture display of Reedman service facilities describes one of the three waiting rooms available for service customers as having "fifteen stereophonic speakers mounted in the acoustical ceiling," as well as "embossed vinyl covered walls, plus carpeting, velvet draperies, a crystal chandelier, and living-room type furniture." Any car buyer of experience recognizes that as a description of something that, with the addition of some heavy-duty whitewall tires, could provide great transportation until next year's models come out.

COMMENT

Since tone expresses the writer's attitude toward reader as well as subject, we must ask what Trillin is assuming about his reader's preference in cars and in ways they are sold. The reader may agree that "Good hard shoptalk is expected among experts," and at the same time be amused or disgusted or, instead, admiring of people who know how to work out a deal. The answer to this question depends on what we hear as we read Trillin's words. In writing, we can substitute turns of phrase for the inflections of voice that convey tone in speech. We can also reveal our attitude implicitly through our selection of details and the emphasis we give them.

QUESTIONS FOR STUDY AND DISCUSSION

1. Is Trillin merely reporting in paragraph 2 what the first sign on the car lot says, or is he expressing approval or disapproval through this detail?

2. What details in the essay reveal the attitude at Reedman's toward buying and selling cars? What interests Trillin most about Reedman's, and how do you know?

3. Examine paragraph 4 carefully. Is Trillin stating his own preference for cars in the opening sentences? Does he seem to assume that these sentences express the preference of his reader?

4. Would you describe the overall tone of the essay as sarcastic, amused, passionate, serious, objective, or perhaps a combination of these? What is the chief way Trillin establishes his tone?

5. Has Trillin described your preference in cars in paragraph 4? What is your preference in ways of buying and selling them? If you were describing the scene at Reedman's, would you describe it in the same tone and emphasize the same details?

6. What is the subject of the essay—"the world's largest car dealer," or a way of selling cars, or American attitudes toward consumption, or perhaps another topic?

VOCABULARY STUDY

1. State how the italicized words convey tone through their connotative meanings:
   a. "the relative *puniness* of its wheelbase"
   b. "to make Saturday at Reedman's a kind of *outing*"
   c. "*ersatz* gold leaf"

2. Find other words and phrases in the essay that contribute to the overall tone through their connotative meaning and descriptive power.

3. Rewrite one of the paragraphs in a different tone. Select new words and phrases appropriate to this tone.

SUGGESTIONS FOR WRITING

1. Analyze the structure and details of the final paragraph to specify its tone. Then discuss what the paragraph contributes to the overall tone of the essay.

2. On the basis of what he says or implies in his description of Reedman's, discuss the extent to which Trillin would agree with Raspberry's stated or implied attitude toward money and the role it should play in our lives.

3. Describe a place of business—a grocery store, a clothing store, a motorcycle shop—and through your selection of details show the attitude of the proprietor toward his or her customers. Do not specify this attitude: let your details establish it.

BEAUTY AND EVERLASTING FAITH— LOCAL LEVEL

Frank Deford

Frank Deford was born in 1938, and was educated at Princeton, where he edited *The Daily Princetonian* and the humor magazine *The Tiger*. A senior writer for *Sports Illustrated,* he has written on tennis, basketball, roller derbies, and the Miss America pageant. In the essay printed here (a section from a chapter of his book *There She Is,* 1971), he is describing the preliminary contest in Wilson, North Carolina, for the state title.

[1]The judging formally begins with the Saturday luncheon at the Heart of Wilson Motel. Dr. Vincent Thomas, the head of the judges' committee, welcomes all the judges, and is himself thereafter always introduced as "Dr. Vincent," by Jerry Ball, the well-known "dean of beauty-pageant judges." Jerry has sent two state

queens on to become Miss America, and judged in states as far away as Alaska. Jerry is joined on the jury by Mrs. Judy Cross, who was Most Photogenic at Miss North Carolina a few years ago, and by Mrs. Marilyn Hull, a former Miss New Jersey. She is married, as so many beauty queens are, to an athlete. Her husband is Bill Hull, a former Kansas City Chief. The other two judges are Jim Church, chairman of the board of the North Carolina Jaycees, and Bob Logan, Charlotte sales manager for Fabergé, the beauty products concern. It is a hot-shot panel for any local Pageant.

²The eight contestants keep a wary eye out as they sit down to lunch and make sure to reach for the correct implements. The judges, however, show no interest whatsoever in what eating tools are being utilized. They are genial and pleasant; the girls could be dispensing peas with a knife for all they seem to care about such formalities.

³Doris's hat tumbles off. She does not realize it has gone, which is not surprising, since hats are as foreign to these girls as bustles or U.S.-Army fatigues would be. Judi has a hat on for exactly the second time in her life. The first time was when she was in another beauty pageant. There are speeches and everyone in attendance is introduced. Then the room is cleared, and a table set up for the judges at the far end. It is time for the serious interviewing. Officially, the girls in any *Miss America* Pageant are not graded on their interviews. Actually, it is the underside of the iceberg that determines the winner.

⁴The girls are directed to another room where, one by one, they will be funneled toward the judges. Following an interview, the contestant will proceed on to another room for a sort of debriefing. The judges arrange themselves and pour coffee. The men must concentrate to do their best, for the South Carolina–Duke basketball game is just starting on TV, and their hearts all lie there. Jerry Ball presides in the middle, like a Chief Justice, a leader among equals, and everyone agrees that there will be no set order to the questioning, just "catch as catch can."

⁵Dr. Thomas sits at the other end of the room with a stop watch. Jerry says, "All right, Dr. Vincent, bring in the first young lady." The girls have been assigned an order in which they will present their talents in the show; they visit the judges in the same order. Rita Deans is first. Like all the others, she has her little hat on and carries a handbag, and she walks, as she has been taught, in

the proper manner. This is an unfamiliar gait for all the girls and makes them resemble the little dogs on the Ed Sullivan Show, who have outfits on, are balanced precariously on their hind feet, and take desperate little steps to keep from pitching forward.

[6] Rita, seated, is straightforward and demure. She assures the panel that her fourteen-year Sunday-School record is not in any danger of being jeopardized by a victory tonight. The judges spring what is considered as a controversial question: what does Rita think of coed college dormitories? Rita thinks awhile. "Well, I haven't formed an opinion about that," she finally says. Mrs. Butner has instructed the girls to answer that way whenever they feel that they are unsure of an answer. The judges nod and agree that Rita would be unwise, indeed, to venture into unknown philosophical territory.

[7] Sharon Shackleford is next. Talkative anyway, she seems especially garrulous when juxtaposed to Rita. "You've got to pull the plug on her," a judge says upon her departure. Wendy Formo, the third contestant, makes the best approach of all. Over six feet tall, she cannot help walking like a normal person. Also, she shuffles a question about Vice President Agnew beautifully, and the panel is obviously impressed. "It reminds you," Jim Church says. "I always liked that Jeanne Swanner."

[8] Bob Logan asks, "What time is it?"

[9] Jerry answers, "About the end of the first quarter."

[10] Peggy Murphy, recovered from the flu, is next, and for her, the judges reach back for a classic old standard of a question: what kind of person do you think you are yourself? There is one stock answer to this question, which every girl ever in a beauty pageant has always provided. In so many words, it is: that I am naturally a shy, thoughtful person, but I love a good time on occasion. Also, I am nuts about people. Peggy is close enough.

[11] The interviewing is now halfway through, so the judges stand and reach for some coffee. Doris comes in. She is in yellow, with a matching handbag that she sets on the rug by the side of her chair. She banters back the usual polite preliminaries, and then one of the judges asks her if she believes there is a generation gap. "Yes, I definitely believe there is one," Doris replies firmly. All the judges sit up and cock their heads. The regular answer to this question is that there certainly isn't one around my house, where everyone works to understand each other better. Doris proceeds. "Ours is the first generation brought up with the threat of the hydrogen and

atom bombs, and the first generation to have grown up with television as a major force in our lives. I really don't even believe it is surprising that there is a gap. Maybe we should only be surprised that there is not more of one."

[12]The judges nod sagely, and to test her further, pull another old chestnut out of the fire. All right, what about coed dorms? Doris backs down here; she comes out with the company line. "It may be fine for other people," she says, "but I can certainly see enough of the opposite sex on dates and other things." Doris has inserted a proper amount of righteous indignation in her voice by the end of her speech. The judges draw a breath, relieved not to have a genuine revolutionary on their hands. They are spent, though, so they ask her if she has any questions for them.

[13]Gay Butner has informed the girls that they may be faced with this request, and to have a question on stand-by. "Yes," Doris says, "I'd like to know why you're still interested in judging. Does it keep you closer to our generation and help close the gap for you?" Yes, the judges agree, yes, it certainly works that way for them.

[14]Time is up; the panel smiles and thanks her; and Doris is hardly out of the door when Jerry slams his hand down. "She came through like 'Gangbusters,' " he exclaims. "She took everything we threw at her and came right back."

[15]"A live cookie," Jim Church says.

[16]Vince Thomas goes to fetch Judi. She comes in, smiling broadly, wearing her aunt's bright orange sleeveless dress. She talks enthusiastically, almost conversationally, from the moment she deposits herself in the chair before the judges. It is as if she has been doing this all her life. Judi is restrained only by what she keeps reminding herself, to keep her hands anchored in her lap and not to say "you know." She is bright and cheery and carries the judges along with her. "Learn to gain control over the interview," Gay has told all the girls. "Give a brief answer, then lead into another area that you particularly like to talk about."

[17]That advice was like giving Judi a license to steal. She and all the other modern Southern belles are born and bred in this briar patch. In Atlantic City a few months later, Phyllis George, Judi's temperamental and verbal kin, babbled on with such dazzle about her pet crab and her dog that the most serious thing that the judges found time to ask her was whether or not she liked beer—and Phyllis even side-stepped that one, and went rambling right on, absolutely stunning the judges from start to finish of the interview.

Judi's footwork is proportionately as good at the Heart of Wilson Motel, but she slows down and twice permits the judges time to reach into their portfolio of controversial questions.

[18]First, they want to know if Judi endorses drugs. Well, she doesn't. Then Marilyn Hull remembers Doris. "Do you think there is a generation gap?" she asks. Judi pauses but for a second, then replies: "I don't think there's any more gap now than there's ever been." The judges nod, and then they want to know if she might have a question for them.

[19]Judi has come loaded for that bear. "What is your idea of a Miss Wilson?" she rips back at them.

[20]A girl with poise, the judges solemnly agree.

[21]"Now, do you have any other question you would like to ask us?" Jerry asks. This is a formality, like drop-over-some-time-and-see-us, but Judi tears into it at face value. "Do you think there is a generation gap?" she asks. Marilyn fields the answer, uneasily, and this time Jerry does not ask Judi if she has another question to ask. "I'm afraid Dr. Vincent is signaling that our time is up," he informs her. Judi thanks everyone and leaves. As soon as she is out of the room, the judges start marveling about her performance. "Imagine," one says, "we asked if she had another question, and she did." There is a first time for everything.

[22]They are still chuckling at Judi's effervescence as Rose Thorne comes in. She expresses a solid opposition to coed dorms, and then Connie Whisenant finishes up by voicing displeasure at those college students who had participated in the Vietnam Moratorium.

[23]Outside the room Doris and Judi are already comparing notes. It is immediately obvious to each that her rival was not disappointed; at the least, neither felt she had done poorly. Judi is stunned to learn, though, that Doris has actually said that there is a generation gap. Was she right? Was that the correct answer that the judges were fishing for? Anyway, it only reinforces Judi's growing opinion. By the time she goes home to put her hair up in curlers, and to affix false eyelashes for the first time in her life, Judi Brewer is absolutely convinced that Doris Smith is the only thing that stands between her and Miss Wilson 1970.

COMMENT

In this early section of his book on Miss America, Frank Deford describes the preliminary interview in the local Miss America contest in Wilson,

North Carolina. In succeeding sections he describes the events that followed. The judges of the local contest are old hands and have long memories; one of them mentions Jeanne Swanner, Miss North Carolina of 1963, who sometimes emcees local contests. The chapter from which this section is taken focuses on Doris Smith and Judi Brewer, who became finalists for first and second place.

Deford's attitude toward Miss America is suggested by his opening comment in the book: "Maligned by one segment of America, adored by another, misunderstood by about all of it, Miss America still flows like the Mississippi, drifts like amber waves of grain, sounds like the crack of a bat on a baseball, tastes like Mom's apple pie, and smells like dollar bills." He is obviously concerned with the values the contest represents. In the section printed here, he is direct about how the contest affects the participants. "Over six feet tall," he says about Wendy Formo, "she cannot help walking like a normal person." And he has similar things to say about how the girls act on the advice of Mrs. Butner, a woman from Rocky Mount who has been tutoring them. Another important indication of tone is the incongruity he stresses: the girls are forced to walk and sit in uncomfortable ways; their answers to questions are also forced. Deford need not comment directly on their situations. His sympathy for them shapes his attitude and therefore his tone; so does his complex attitude toward the contest and the idea of "Miss America." Tone is revealed unmistakably in exaggeration as in understatement—if the author prefers not to state his or her attitude directly. The details selected for emphasis can be equally revealing.

QUESTIONS FOR STUDY AND DISCUSSION

1. How does Deford stress the incongruous in other details? How do his comparisons to Army fatigues, bustles, and little dogs make the incongruities vivid to us?

2. Does he express or imply the same attitude toward all the girls in the contest? To what extent is his sympathy toward them qualified by his attitude toward the values represented by or implied in the contest?

3. What are those values, and what details best reveal them?

4. How sympathetic is Deford toward the judges? Is it his view that the panel is "hot-shot," or is he giving someone's opinion of it?

5. What does Deford mean by the statement that "it is the underside of the iceberg that determines the winner"? How does he illustrate the statement?

6. Does Deford resort to understatement or irony, or does he depend on the details solely to create tone?

7. How does he establish and maintain a consistent point of view in the whole essay? What is the order of ideas?

8. What are your feelings toward the contestants and the judges? How much were they shaped for you by Deford?

VOCABULARY STUDY

Identify words and phrases that you would classify as slang (such as "hot-shot") and determine their use in the essay, in particular their contribution to the overall tone. If these slang words and phrases are no longer current, suggest how the statements might be reworded to convey the same tone.

SUGGESTIONS FOR WRITING

1. Describe a contest in which you were a participant. Focus on the behavior and attitude of the judges or the participants, and use your discussion to reveal your attitude toward the contest. Make your details vivid and choose those that best reveal the values represented by or implied in the contest.

2. Discuss what you think Deford is saying or implying about the contest. Consider his details about the judges as well as about the contestants.

3. Rewrite a part of this essay from the point of view of one of the contestants. Allow her attitude toward the judges and the contest itself to emerge in the details she selects and the feelings she expresses.

definition

There are many ways to define a word, each depending on our purpose in writing and on the knowledge of our readers. In talking to a child, it may be enough to define a cow by pointing to one in a pasture or picture book. To an older child we may do more, and point to a cow through words: first by relating it to the class *animal,* then stating the *specific differences* between the cow and all other animals: "the mature female of domestic cattle (genus *Bos*)" *(Webster's New World Dictionary).* We could state also that *cow* can refer to the female elephant or whale and other female animals.

These definitions are called *denotative* because they point to the object or single it out from all other objects. *Connotative* definitions by contrast refer to ideas and feelings associated to the word. Denotative definitions are the same for everyone; connotative definitions are not. To some people *cow* suggests laziness, sloppiness, even stupidity—connotations that explain phrases like "dumb as an ox"; others may associate a cow with feelings of contentment. These connotations are sometimes called *subjective*. Connotations may, however, express intrinsic, *objective* properties: the cow is a passive animal, compared to the bull.

If we want to explain the origin or derivation of a word, perhaps for the purpose of explaining current meanings, we may state its etymology. The word *coward* derives from the idea of an animal whose tail hangs between its legs. The etymology illuminates one or more connotations of coward. We may, if we wish, propose or stipulate a new word for an idea or discovery. In the thirties Congressman Maury Maverick proposed the word *gobbledygook* as a description for pretentious, involved official writing. Such definitions may gain general acceptance. Some definitions remain in use for years, only to fall into disuse as new discoveries are made and new ideas appear, and better terms are invented to describe them.

These are formal kinds of definition. There are also informal kinds, fitted to different needs in exposition. For one kind of reader it may not be necessary to point to or single out an object: the writer will assume that the reader knows what the object is, and needs only to be told how it works. Parts of the object (the blade casing of a manual lawn mower) may be defined fully in the course of describing how to care for or fix it; other parts may not be defined because they are unimportant to the process. Another kind of informal definition may fit an object to a class without giving the specific difference: it may be enough to tell readers of novels written about the twenties that the Pierce-Arrow is an expensive automobile. And still another may list some or all of its properties: we may give one or two distinctive qualities of the Pierce-Arrow to explain an allusion to it.

SHLEMIEL

Leo Rosten

Leo Rosten was born in Lodz, Poland, in 1908, and was raised and educated in the United States. He received his Ph.D from the University of Chicago in 1937, and studied also at the London School of Economics. He served in various government posts, taught at Yale, the University of California at Berkeley, and Columbia, and is the author of numerous books, including the Hyman Kaplan stories and *The Joys of Yiddish* (1968), from which the essay printed here has been excerpted.

1. A foolish person; a simpleton. "He has the brains of a *shlemiel*."
2. A consistently unlucky or unfortunate person; a "fall guy"; a hard-luck type; a born loser; a submissive and uncomplaining victim. "That poor *shlemiel* always gets the short end of the stick." A Yiddish proverb goes: "The *shlemiel* falls on his back and breaks his nose."
3. A clumsy, butterfingered, all-thumbs, gauche type. "Why does a *shlemiel* like that ever try to fix anything?"
4. A social misfit, congenitally maladjusted. "Don't invite that *shlemiel* to the party."
5. A pipsqueak, a Caspar Milquetoast. "He throws as much weight as a *shlemiel*." "No one pays attention to that *shlemiel*."
6. A naive, trusting, gullible customer. This usage is common among furniture dealers, especially those who sell the gaudy, gimcrack stuff called "borax."
7. Anyone who makes a foolish bargain, or wagers a foolish bet. This usage is wide in Europe; it probably comes from Chamisso's tale, *Peter Schlemihl's Wunderbare Geschichte,* a fable in which the protagonist sold his shadow and, like Faust, sold his soul to Satan.

[1] It is important to observe that *shlemiel,* like *nebech,* carries a distinctive note of pity. In fact, a *shlemiel* is often the *nebech*'s twin brother. The classic definition goes: "A *shlemiel* is always knocking things off a table; the *nebech* always picks them up."

[2] *Shlemiel* is said to come from the name Shlumiel, the son of a leader of the tribe of Simeon (Numbers, 2). Whereas the other generals in Zion often triumphed on the field of war, poor Shlumiel was always losing.

[3] Another theory about the origin of *shlemiel* runs that it is a variation of *shlimazl* or *shlemozzl.* I can't quite see how *shlimazl* gave birth to *shlemiel;* the words are as different as "hard luck" is from "that jerk."

[4] The classic attempt to discriminate between the two types runs: "A *shlemiel* is a man who is always spilling hot soup—down the neck of a *shlimazl.*" Or, to make a triple distinction: "The *shlemiel* trips, and knocks down the *shlimazl;* and the *nebech* repairs the *shlimazl*'s glasses."

[5]I suppose that *shlemiels* often are *shlimazls*—but that need not be. A *shlemiel* can make a fortune through sheer luck; a *shlimazl* can't: He loses a fortune, through bad luck.

[6]Nor is every *shlimazl* a *shlemiel:* e.g., a gifted, able, talented man is no *shlemiel,* but he may run into such bad luck that he is a *shlimazl:* thus, Gregor Mendel and Thomas Alva Edison, both of whom encountered strings of perverse fortune in their experiments; one might have called them *shlimazls,* but surely never *shlemiels.*

[7]Can a brilliant or learned man be a *shlemiel?* Of course he can; many a savant is: the absentminded professor, the impractical genius, are paradigms of *shlemielkeit* (*shlemiel*-ness).

COMMENT

Though Rosten gives a denotative definition of *shlemiel* ("a foolish person"), his definitions of the word are mainly connotative, as in his statement that *shlemiel* "carries a distinctive note of pity." Rosten means that the word carries this meaning for most people: this is an *objective connotation.* If Rosten had given the personal associations *shlemiel* has for him but not necessarily for others, he would be giving its *subjective connotations.* He also gives the etymology of the word, and reports a theory about its origin—connecting it to *shlimazl.* Like other definitions in his book on Yiddish, his discussion reveals cultural attitudes expressed by a much used but little understood word.

QUESTIONS FOR STUDY AND DISCUSSION

1. What in Rosten's listing shows that *shlemiel* is really several words with different etymologies? What use does Rosten make of etymological definition in the essay?

2. Are there words in ordinary English that express the qualities of *shlemiel* and *shlimazl?* What words do you use?

3. Could Rosten have explained the various meanings of *shlemiel* without providing the context of these meanings?

4. In one of the examples omitted from this excerpt, Rosten writes, "A *shlemiel* takes a bath, and forgets to wash his face." What examples can you provide from your observations of people?

5. Can you think of related types of people—that is, "bad luck" types? Do you have special names for these types?

VOCABULARY STUDY

1. Look up the following words, then illustrate each of them from your own experience with words of each type: *slang, jargon, argot.*

2. Look up the following words, and explain how they differ from *slang* and *jargon: dialect, cant, vernacular.*

3. Later in this definition, Rosten refers to the following synonyms of *shlemiel: nebech, shlump, shlepper, shlimazl, shmo, yold.* Consult his book *The Joys of Yiddish* for the meaning of these words. Check an unabridged dictionary to find out how many have been absorbed into English.

SUGGESTIONS FOR WRITING

1. Write an essay on the denotative and connotative meanings of a word like *shlemiel* in your vocabulary (a word like *patsy, fink, piker*).

2. Families often share a private language—words, phrases, gestures— that they create themselves or derive from a second language spoken by older members of the family, and sometimes the younger members. Describe and define the private language you share with your family or with friends.

3. In many families two languages are spoken (for example, English and Italian, English and Yiddish, English and Polish). If your family speaks two languages, discuss the situations in which they do so. Or describe the differences between the language you use at home and the language you use on the street or at school.

THE WOOLEN SARAPE

Robert Ramirez

Robert Ramirez was born in Edinburg, Texas, in 1950. He graduated from Pan American College, where he later taught freshman composition. He also taught elementary school and he is now a photographer, reporter, and announcer for a television news department in Texas.

[1] The train, its metal wheels squealing as they spin along the silvery tracks, rolls slower now. Through the gaps between the cars blinks a streetlamp, and this pulsing light on a barrio streetcorner beats slower, like a weary heartbeat, until the train shudders to a halt, the light goes out, and the barrio is deep asleep.

[2] Throughout Aztlán (the Nahuatl term meaning "land to the north"), trains grumble along the edges of a sleeping people. From Lower California, through the blistering Southwest, down the Rio Grande to the muddy Gulf, the darkness and mystery of dreams engulf communities fenced off by railroads, canals, and expressways. Paradoxical communities, isolated from the rest of the town by concrete columned monuments of progress, and yet stranded in the past. They are surrounded by change. It eludes their reach, in their own backyards, and the people, unable and unwilling to see the future, or even touch the present, perpetuate the past.

[3] Leaning from the expressway or jolting across the tracks, one enters a different physical world permeated by a different attitude. The physical dimensions are impressive. It is a large section of town which extends for fifteen blocks north and south along the tracks, and then advances eastward, thinning into nothingness beyond the city limits. Within the invisible (yet sensible) walls of the barrio, are many, many people living in too few houses. The homes, however, are much more numerous than on the outside.

[4] Members of the barrio describe the entire area as their home. It is a home, but it is more than this. The barrio is a refuge from the harshness and the coldness of the Anglo world. It is a forced refuge. The leprous people are isolated from the rest of the community and contained in their section of town. The stoical pariahs of the barrio accept their fate, and from the angry seeds of rejection grow the flowers of closeness between outcasts, not the thorns of bitterness and the mad desire to flee. There is no want to escape, for the feeling of the barrio is known only to its inhabitants, and the material needs of life can also be found here.

[5] The *tortillería* fires up its machinery three times a day, producing steaming, round, flat slices of barrio bread. In the winter, the warmth of the tortilla factory is a wool *sarape* in the chilly morning hours, but in the summer, it unbearably toasts every noontime customer.

Reprinted by permission of Robert Ramirez.

[6] The *panadería* sends its sweet messenger aroma down the dimly lit street, announcing the arrival of fresh, hot sugary *pan dulce*.

[7] The small corner grocery serves the meal-to-meal needs of customers, and the owner, a part of the neighborhood, willingly gives credit to people unable to pay cash for foodstuffs.

[8] The barbershop is a living room with hydraulic chairs, radio, and television, where old friends meet and speak of life as their salted hair falls aimlessly about them.

[9] The pool hall is a junior level country club where 'chucos, strangers in their own land, get together to shoot pool and rap, while veterans, unaware of the cracking, popping balls on the green felt, complacently play dominoes beneath rudely hung *Playboy* foldouts.

[10] The *cantina* is the night spot of the barrio. It is the country club and the den where the rites of puberty are enacted. Here the young become men. It is in the taverns that a young dude shows his *machismo* through the quantity of beer he can hold, the stories of *rucas* he has had, and his willingness and ability to defend his image against hardened and scarred old lions.

[11] No, there is no frantic wish to flee. It would be absurd to leave the familiar and nervously step into the strange and cold Anglo community when the needs of the Chicano can be met in the barrio.

[12] The barrio is closeness. From the family living unit, familial relationships stretch out to immediate neighbors, down the block, around the corner, and to all parts of the barrio. The feeling of family, a rare and treasurable sentiment, pervades and accounts for the inability of the people to leave. The barrio is this attitude manifested on the countenances of the people, on the faces of their homes, and in the gaiety of their gardens.

[13] The color-splashed homes arrest your eyes, arouse your curiosity, and make you wonder what life scenes are being played out in them. The flimsy, brightly colored, wood-frame houses ignore no neon-brilliant color. Houses trimmed in orange, chartreuse, lime-green, yellow, and mixtures of these and other hues beckon the beholder to reflect on the peculiarity of each home. Passing through this land is refreshing like Brubeck, not narcoticizing like revolting rows of similar houses, which neither offend nor please.

[14] In the evenings, the porches and front yards are occupied with men calmly talking over the noise of children playing baseball in the unpaved extension of the living room, while the women cook

supper or gossip with female neighbors as they water the *jardines.* The gardens mutely echo the expressive verses of the colorful houses. The denseness of multicolored plants and trees gives the house the appearance of an oasis or a tropical island hideaway, sheltered from the rest of the world.

[15] Fences are common in the barrio, but they are fences and not the walls of the Anglo community. On the western side of town, the high wooden fences between houses are thick, impenetrable walls, built to keep the neighbors at bay. In the barrio, the fences may be rusty, wire contraptions or thick green shrubs. In either case you can see through them and feel no sense of intrusion when you cross them.

[16] Many lower-income families of the barrio manage to maintain a comfortable standard of living through the communal action of family members who contribute their wages to the head of the family. Economic need creates interdependence and closeness. Small barefooted boys sell papers on cool, dark Sunday mornings, deny themselves pleasantries, and give their earnings to *mamá.* The older the child, the greater the responsibility to help the head of the household provide for the rest of the family.

[17] There are those, too, who for a number of reasons have not achieved a relative sense of financial security. Perhaps it results from too many children too soon, but it is the homes of these people and their situation that numbs rather than charms. Their houses, aged and bent, oozing children, are fissures in the horn of plenty. Their wooden homes may have brick-pattern asbestos tile on the outer walls, but the tile is not convincing.

[18] Unable to pay city taxes or incapable of influencing the city to live up to its duty to serve all the citizens, the poorer barrio families remain trapped in the nineteenth century and survive as best they can. The backyards have well-worn paths to the outhouses, which sit near the alley. Running water is considered a luxury in some parts of the barrio. Decent drainage is usually unknown, and when it rains, the water stands for days, an incubator of health hazards and an avoidable nuisance. Streets, costly to pave, remain rough, rocky trails. Tires do not last long, and the constant rattling and shaking grind away a car's life and spread dust through screen windows.

[19] The houses and their *jardines,* the jollity of the people in an adverse world, the brightly feathered alarm clock pecking away at

supper and cautiously eyeing the children playing nearby, produce a mystifying sensation at finding the noble savage alive in the twentieth century. It is easy to look at the positive qualities of life in the barrio, and look at them with a distantly envious feeling. One wishes to experience the feelings of the barrio and not the hardships. Remembering the illness, the hunger, the feeling of time running out on you, the walls, both real and imagined, reflecting on living in the past, one finds his envy becoming more elusive, until it has vanished altogether.

[20]Back now beyond the tracks, the train creaks and groans, the cars jostle each other down the track, and as the light begins its pulsing, the barrio, with all its meanings, greets a new dawn with yawns and restless stretchings.

COMMENT

The word *barrio* is Spanish in origin; in Spanish-speaking countries it refers to a neighborhood, district, or suburb. Ramirez goes beyond this simple denotative definition to objective connotations of the word—the associations the barrio has for its inhabitants. We know that Ramirez considers these connotations objective, for he states that he is describing barrios in the southwestern United States. The word also has subjective connotations for him; he suggests these toward the beginning and at the end of the essay. Through his definition Ramirez defines not only a place but a culture. His details reveal the quality of life that distinguishes the barrio from other cultural worlds in the United States.

QUESTIONS FOR STUDY AND DISCUSSION

1. What statements and details show that Ramirez is writing to an audience unfamiliar with the barrio?

2. What qualities do the people of the barrio share? Does Ramirez show qualities or attitudes that mark them as individuals—as separate people living in the same neighborhood?

3. Is Ramirez saying that the barrio culture is a protest against the "Anglo" world outside the barrio?

4. What are the objective connotations of the barrio for Ramirez? What subjective connotations does the barrio hold for him?

5. In what order are the details of the barrio presented? What is the physical and personal point of view of the essay?

6. Do you find an overall tone in the essay—or several tones?

7. What details of barrio life do you recognize in your own neighborhood or town or city? In general, what similarities and differences are there between the barrio and your own world?

VOCABULARY STUDY

1. Look up the following words in a Spanish-English dictionary and state their use in the essay: *tortillería, sarape, panadería, pan dulce, cantina, machismo, jardines, rucas.*

2. Write sentences of your own, using the following words to reveal their dictionary meanings: *paradoxical, permeated, stoical, pariahs, mutely, adverse.*

SUGGESTIONS FOR WRITING

1. Discuss how the title of the essay contributes to the overall tone and point of view. Then analyze the order of ideas and development of the thesis.

2. Describe the prevailing culture, or variety of cultures, in a neighborhood or community you know well. Include the extent to which people of the neighborhood share a common language, perhaps a slang that protects them from the world outside. Give particular attention to their feelings and attitudes toward that outside world. Note that you will be defining through a listing of properties.

THE WOOD STOVE

The Foxfire Book

Eliot Wigginton was born in Wheeling, West Virginia, in 1942. In 1966 he came to Rabun Gap, Georgia, a small town in the Appalachians, to teach English and journalism at Rabun Gap-Nacoochee School. In the following year, with his help, the students of the school began publication of *Foxfire*, a magazine that described their world and ways of doing things. The contents of the magazine—and of *The Foxfire Book* (1972)—are the work of these students.

[1] Wood stoves were considered to be an improvement over fireplaces for cooking, but they still required a lot of attention. As with the fireplace, dry kindling and green wood had to be cut to fit the firebox and kept on hand, and the fire had to be watched so that it didn't go out or get too hot.

[2] The fire was built in the firebox located on the left-hand side of the stove right under the cooking surface. To save time, people often used coals right from the fireplace to start the fire.

[3] At the bottom of the firebox is a coarse iron grate through which the ashes fall into the ash box. The soot which rises into the flue later falls back down into the soot tray which is directly underneath the oven. Both the ash box and soot tray are drawers that must be cleaned out once a week if the stove is used regularly.

[4] The cooking surface of a wood stove usually has six eyes (round openings with iron lids). Sometimes they are all the same size, sometimes of varying sizes. The one at the center in the back of the stove is the hottest, the two over the woodbox are middling, and the other three are the cooler ones. The heat under the eyes cannot be regulated individually, so pots have to be moved from one to the other according to how much heat is required. Sometimes, when people wanted to heat something in a hurry, they would remove an eye and place the pot directly over the flames in the firebox.

[5] Most of the stoves were fairly simple, though some of them got quite elaborate. One larger variety even had a flat griddle on top for frying things like pancakes, eggs, and bacon.

[6] The oven is usually located on the right-hand side of the stove and is heated from the left and top by the circulation of heat from the firebox. The heat flows from the firebox through a four-inch high air space directly under the cooking surface to the other side. It heats more evenly than one might imagine, but if something tends to cook more on one side than the other, it has to be turned around at regular intervals. The main problem with the oven is that it is difficult to keep the temperature constant. Many varieties have a temperature gauge on the door, but this acts as a warning signal rather than as a regulator. If the oven gets too cool, more wood has to be added; and if it gets too hot, the only thing that can be done is to open the door slightly or put a pan of cold water on one of the

racks. For something that takes an hour to bake, the fire has to be tended three or four times to maintain the temperature.

[7]When cooking biscuits and cornbread, early cooks often started them on the lower rack of the oven to brown the bottom and then placed them on the higher rack to brown the top. Cakes, pies and roasts were usually kept on the bottom rack all the time. When broiling meat or toasting bread, the top rack was used.

[8]About two feet above the cooking surface, most wood stoves have two warming closets. These are metal boxes about six inches deep with a door on each, and they are used to keep food warm until it is ready to be served. The stoves also have a damper that seals off the right side of the firebox and greatly cuts the circulation of heat. It doesn't put out the fire, but it cools the rest of the stove so that it can be left unattended fairly safely. When the damper is closed, the coals will remain hot for several hours. It has to be left open when the stove is in use.

[9]We asked Margaret Norton, a real chef on a wood stove, what some of the advantages and disadvantages of using one are. Here's what she told us—

[10]"I've always used a wood stove because we live up here in the woods and there's always plenty of wood. They're good in the wintertime because they sure do warm up the kitchen. In the summer it gets uncomfortable hot in here; 'course we can go out on the porch every few minutes. But we're used to it. With this you have to build a fire and wait till it's ready, but by the time you make up your cornbread or peel your potatoes, it's hot.

[11]"Sometimes wind'll blow down the pipe hard and smoke the house, and the soot flies out all over the place and you have to wipe off everything. And you have to clean it out every so often and watch that sparks don't fall out on the floor.

[12]"And of course you have to gather your wood, and that's a disadvantage when you're out of it. But if the electricity goes off or the gas gives out, you're alright if you've got wood."

COMMENT

If the object under discussion is well known, the writer may dispense with a formal definition of it, or may provide only the specific difference between it and other objects in the same class. The author here dispenses with part of the definition, assuming that the reader has a general idea of the wood stove, and states only a few of its specific differences from fireplaces and other stoves. The purpose of the essay is to explain the use of wood stoves, and the author accordingly discusses those properties basic to cooking.

QUESTIONS FOR STUDY AND DISCUSSION

1. In what order are the properties of the wood stove presented? Would you present these in the same order in teaching a person how to cook on a wood stove?

2. What are the disadvantages mentioned? Would you mention them in the order the author does in teaching a person how to avoid them?

3. What does the description suggest about the life and values of people who cook on wood stoves?

4. Can you think of advantages and disadvantages of the wood stove not mentioned by the author but implied in the description?

VOCABULARY STUDY

1. Write a formal definition of *wood stove* on the basis of the information provided in the essay and your knowledge of other stoves, including the fireplace.

2. The class of a denotative dictionary definition may be exceedingly broad *(tool)* or relatively narrow *(saw).* A saw might be defined as a tool or cutting instrument that is different from other tools or cutting instruments in specific ways; a hacksaw would be defined as a saw that is different from all other saws in specific ways. Examine the class in the dictionary definitions of the following objects, and decide how broad or narrow you think it is: *woodbox, griddle, temperature gauge, pan, damper, rack.*

3. The following words are mainly connotative in their meanings. Write definitions for two of them, distinguishing their objective from their subjective connotations—that is, the general associations everyone makes and the special associations you make to the words: *cute, cool, flip, crazy, silly.*

SUGGESTIONS FOR WRITING

1. Define an object in the kitchen or workshop by listing its properties and various uses. Decide on a principle of order for your details before you begin writing.

2. Describe the advantages and disadvantages of an automobile or other vehicle that you drive or use. You may wish to compare the vehicle with another of the same kind.

division

Division

To *divide* is to arrange in constituent groups or parts. The grouping depends on the basis or principle of division. For example, apples can be divided in a number of ways:

> *by color:* red apples, green apples, yellow apples, etc.
> *by use:* eating apples, cooking apples, etc.
> *by variety:* Winesap, Jonathan, Golden Delicious, etc.
> *by taste:* sweet, tart, winy, etc.

The principle of division depends on the purpose of the analysis. In instructing people what apples to buy for eating raw, cooking, or canning, we would group or divide apples according to use, variety, and taste at least. Color would not be so important. The division need be only as complete as our purpose requires, but we should state whether the division is an exhaustive one—that is, whether we have listed all the uses or varieties or tastes. If more than one division is made in the course of an essay (that is, a division according to color, use, and variety), each should be distinguished for the reader.

Division is, like definition, an important method of analysis in exposition and argument. Before we discuss the effects of insecticides on orchard fruits, we may wish to identify the uses of these fruits in order to explain how these effects would come about; division according to *use* would be essential in this particular analysis.

WOODS FOR CARVING

Florence H. Pettit

Florence H. Pettit attended Northwestern University and the School of the Art Institute of Chicago. A fabric designer and sculptor in cast metals, her works have been shown in Smithsonian Institute traveling exhibits. She is a founding member of the Connecticut State Commission on the Arts, and the author of many books on fabric design and crafts.

[1]*Hard,* in terms of wood, really means *harder* to cut, but most hardwoods are also fine and even-grained. They are not apt to split, and they take polish well. For these reasons they are generally better for small wood carvings than the softwoods; most sculptors prefer to use hardwoods for large pieces, too. All the fruitwoods, like cherry, apple, pear, and orange, are hard, and so are oak, mahogany, walnut, birch, holly, and maple. Hardwoods range in color from the almost white of holly to the almost black of walnut. Oak and mahogany are the most open-grained, and therefore more apt to split. They are probably less good for small carvings than the other kinds.

[2]Soft and medium woods can be used for larger carvings, because the wood shaves off more easily and in larger pieces. Not so much strength is required to use the tools. The most common softwoods are balsa, basswood, sugar pine, white pine, buckeye, poplar, and butternut. Balsa is unique because it is so soft you can dent it with your finger. It is used for model-making and for small preliminary studies for larger works, but it is not much good for anything else. The two other softest woods are basswood and sugar pine; they will not take a good polish, but are fine for things that are to be painted or do not need a high finish. The rest of the softwoods will take almost as good a finish as the hardwoods. White pine must be of what is called "clear-select" or best quality, for the hard, dark streaks and knots in the other grades would spoil the appearance of most projects and be a nuisance to the carver.

[3]The medium woods—fir and redwood—are also better for larger carvings because they are open-grained and rather apt to split.

[4]All of the above are domestic woods from trees that grow in various parts of the United States. Most of them can be bought from wood specialty firms. There are a number of tropical and exotic foreign woods that are fine to carve, but they are not commonly available. Only seasoned wood should be used for carving, that is, wood that has been dried and aged, because green wood is apt to warp and split as it dries. The wood used by Peter Schimmel in Pennsylvania over a century ago is described as *driftwood,* which means that it was wood he picked up along rivers and streams where it had been aged by being alternately heated by the sun and wet by the waters. It is interesting, however, to note that the rule about using seasoned wood has been purposely broken by some Oriental craftsmen who *like* to have their bowls warp into odd shapes!

[5]Before they are ready to be carved, logs cut from green trees require a long period of drying in a protected, ventilated place until the sap has entirely left the wood. Before you buy any wood, search your own basement and garage. You may find some nice old boards.

COMMENT

The author divides woods on the basis of ease in cutting—her principle of division. Hardwoods, she tells us, are the hardest to cut; soft and medium are easier. She provides additional information about these woods but she does not stray from her original principle of division. Notice that if she had divided according to the place of origin, she would have discussed not only domestic woods but also foreign woods.

QUESTIONS FOR STUDY AND DISCUSSION

1. What purpose would a division between domestic and foreign woods have served? By what other principles could *wood* be divided?

2. How does the information about color (paragraph 1) serve the analysis?

3. Are the details on soft woods presented in the same order as the

details on hardwoods? If not, how do you explain the difference in their arrangement?

4. What are the possible principles of division for *teachers, students, classes?* To what uses could these divisions be put?

VOCABULARY STUDY
Look up the following words and phrases, and write a sentence for each—explaining how their meanings contribute to your understanding of ideas in the essay: *even-grained, open-grained, dent, knot, exotic, warp.*

SUGGESTIONS FOR WRITING
1. Write an essay on a holiday experience or family gathering. In the course of the essay choose a principle of division for your friends or family as a way of developing your main idea.

2. List several principles of division for one of the following subjects. Then write two paragraphs—using one of the principles to divide the subject in the first, and another of the principles to divide it in the second. Use your division to make a point about the subject:
> high school textbooks   women's clothing advertisements
> television crime shows   men's clothing advertisements

THE VIOLENT GANG

Lewis Yablonsky

Lewis Yablonsky was born in 1924 in Irvington, New Jersey. He studied at Rutgers and New York University, where he received his Ph.D. in 1957. He has taught at several universities, including the University of Massachusetts and the University of California at Los Angeles, and he is now professor of sociology at California State University in Northridge. He has written much about juvenile crime. This essay was first published in 1960.

[1] It is a truism that criminal organizations and criminal activities tend to reflect social conditions. Just as surely as the Bowery gang mirrored aspects of the 1900's, the Capone mob aspects of the twenties, and the youth gangs of the depression elements of the thirties, so do the delinquent gangs that have developed since the 1940's in the United States reflect certain patterns of our own society.

[2] The following quotations indicate the tone and ethos of a representative gang of today, the so-called Egyptian Kings, whose members beat and stabbed to death a fifteen-year-old boy named Michael Farmer in a New York City park not long ago. Michael Farmer, who had been crippled by polio, was not known to the Kings before the killing, nor had be been acquainted with any members of the gang.

> He couldn't run any way, 'cause we were all around him. So then I said, "You're a Jester," and he said "Yeah," and I punched him in the face. And then somebody hit him with a bat over the head. And then I kept punchin' him. Some of them were too scared to do anything. They were just standin' there, lookin'.

> I was watchin' him. I didn't wanna hit him, at first. Then I kicked him twice. He was layin' on the ground, lookin' up at us. I kicked him on the jaw, or some place; then I kicked him in the stomach. That was the least I could do, was kick 'im.

> I was aimin' to hit him, but I didn't get a chance to hit him. There was so many guys on him—I got scared when I saw the knife go into the guy, and I ran right there. After everybody ran, this guy stayed, and started hittin' him with a machete.

> Somebody yelled out, "Grab him. He's a Jester." So then they grabbed him. Magician grabbed him, he turned around and stabbed him in the back. I was ... I was stunned. I couldn't do nuthin'. And then Magician—he went like that and he pulled ... he had a switch blade and he said, "You're gonna hit him with the bat or I'll stab you." So I just hit him lightly with the bat.

> Magician stabbed him and the guy he ... like hunched over. He's standin' up and I knock him down. Then he was down on the ground, everybody was kickin' him, stompin' him, punchin' him,

stabbin' him so he tried to get back up and I knock him down
again. Then the guy stabbed him in the back with a bread knife.

The attitudes toward homicide and violence that emerge from these
statements led to eleven gang killings last summer and can be
expected to produce an even greater number from now on.

[3] One important difference between the gangs of the past and
those that now operate on our city streets is the prevalence of the
psychopathic element in the latter. The violent gangs of the twenties contained psychopaths, but they were used to further the profit-
making goal of the gang, and were themselves paid for their violence. Here, for example, is how Abe "Kid Twist" Reles—who
informed on Murder, Inc., and confessed to having committed over
eighteen murders himself—described the activities of the Crime
Trust to a writer in the *Nation:*

> The Crime Trust, Reles insists, never commits murders out of
> passion, excitement, jealousy, personal revenge, or any of the
> usual motives which prompt private unorganized murders. It kills
> impersonally and solely for business considerations. No gangster
> may kill on his own initiative; every murder must be ordered by
> the leaders at the top, and it must serve the welfare of the
> organization. . . . Any member of the mob who would dare kill on
> his own initiative or for his own profit would be executed. . . . The
> Crime Trust insists that murder must be a business matter orga-
> nized by the chiefs in conference and carried out in a disciplined
> way.

[4] Frederic Thrasher's famous analysis of Chicago gangs in the
mid-twenties describes another group that bears only a limited
resemblance to the violent gangs of today. Thrasher's gangs

> . . . broke into box cars and "robbed" bacon and other merchan-
> dise. They cut out wire cables to sell as junk. They broke open
> telephone boxes. They took autos for joy-riding. They purloined
> several quarts of whiskey from a brewery to drink in their
> shack. . . .

[5] Nor do the gangs of the thirties and early forties described by
W. F. Whyte in *Street Corner Society* bear much resemblance to the
violent gang of today. The difference becomes strikingly evident
when we compare the following comments by two Egyptian Kings
with those of Doc, the leader of Whyte's Norton Street gang.

I just went like that, and I stabbed him with the bread knife. You know I was drunk so I stabbed him. [*Laughs*] He was screamin' like a dog. He was screamin' there. And then I took the knife out and told the other guys to run. . . .

The guy that stabbed him in the back with the bread knife, he told me that when he took the knife out o' his back, he said, "Thank you."

Now Doc, leader of the Norton Street gang:

Nutsy was a cocky kid before I beat him up. . . . After that, he seemed to lose his pride. I would talk to him and try to get him to buck up. . . . I walloped every kid in my gang at some time. We had one Sicilian kid on my street. When I walloped him, he told his father and the father came out looking for me. I hid up on a roof, and Nutsy told me when the father had gone. When I saw the kid next, I walloped him again—for telling his father on me. . . . But I wasn't such a tough kid, Bill. I was always sorry after I walloped him.

[6]Doc's comments about beating up Nutsy—"I would talk to him and try to buck him up"—or about fighting the other kids—"I was always sorry after I walloped them"—are in sharp contrast to the post-assault comments of the Egyptian Kings. Here is how one of the Kings who stabbed Farmer replied to my questions about his part in the homicide. The interview took place in a reformatory.

KING: "I stab him with the butcher—I mean the bread-knife and then I took it out."
QUESTION: "What were you thinking about at the time, right then?"
KING: "What was I thinking? [*Laughs*] I was thinking whether to do it again."
QUESTION: "Are you sorry about what happened?"
KING: "Am I sorry? Are you nuts; of course, I'm sorry. You think I like being locked up?"

The element of friendship and camaraderie—one might almost call it cooperativeness—that was central to the Norton Street gang and others like it during the depression is entirely absent from the violent gang of today. To be sure, "candy store" or corner hang-out groups similar to those described by Whyte still exist, but it is not such groups who are responsible for the killings and assaults that have caused so much concern in our major cities in recent years.

[7]Today's violent gang is, above all, characterized by flux. It lacks all the features of an organized group, having neither a definite number of members, nor specific membership roles, nor a consensus of expected norms, nor a leader who supplies directive for action. It is a moblike collectivity which forms around violence in a spontaneous fashion, moving into action—often on the spur of an evening's boredom—in search of "kicks." Violence ranks extremely high in the loose scheme of values on which such gangs are based. To some boys it acts as a kind of existential validation, proving (since they are not sure) that they are alive. Others, clinging to membership in this marginal and amorphous organization, employ violence to demonstrate they are "somebody." But most members of the gang use violence to acquire prestige or to raise their "rep."

I didn't want to be like ... you know, different from the other guys. Like they hit him, I hit him. In other words, I didn't want to show myself as a punk. You know, ya always talkin', "Oh, man, when I catch a guy, I'll beat him up," and all of that, you know. And after you go out and you catch a guy, and you don't do nothin' they say, "Oh man, he can't belong to no gang, because he ain't gonna do nothin'."

Momentarily I started to thinking about it inside: I have my mind made up I'm not going to be in no gang. Then I go on inside. Something comes up, den here come all my friends coming to me. Like I said before, I'm intelligent and so forth. They be coming to me—then they talk to me about what they gonna do. Like, "Man, we'll go out here and kill this cat." I say, "Yeah." They kept on talkin'. I said, "Man, I just gotta go with you." Myself, I don't want to go, but when they start talkin' about what they gonna do, I say, "So, he isn't gonna take over my rep. I ain't gonna let him be known more than me." And I go ahead just for selfishness.

If I would of got the knife, I would have stabbed him. That would have gave me more of a build-up. People would have respected me for what I've done and things like that. They would say, "There goes a cold killer."

It makes you feel like a big shot. You know some guys think they're big shots and all that. They think, like you know, they got the power to do everything they feel like doing. They say, like, "I wanna stab a guy," and then the other guy says, "Oh, I wouldn't dare to do that." You know, he thinks I'm acting like a big shot. That's the way he feels. He probably thinks in his mind, "Oh, he probably won't do that." Then, when we go to fight, you know, he finds out what I do.

[8]The structure of the violent gang can be analyzed into three different levels. At the center, on the first level, are the leaders, who—contrary to the popular idea that they could become "captains of industry if only their energies were redirected"—are the most psychologically disturbed of all the members. These youths (who are usually between eighteen and twenty-five years old) need the gang more than anyone else, and it is they who provide it with whatever cohesive force it has. In a gang of some thirty boys there may be five or six such leaders who desperately rely on the gang to build and maintain a "rep," and they are always working to keep the gang together and in action. They enlist new members (by force), plot, and talk gang warfare most of their waking hours.

[9]At the second level, there are youths who claim affiliation to the gang but only participate in it sporadically. For example, one of the Egyptian Kings told me that if his father had not given him a "bad time" and kicked him out of the house the night of the homicide, he would not have gone to the corner and become involved in the Michael Farmer killing. The gang was for this boy, on that night, a vehicle for acting out aggressions related to another area of his life. Such a "temporal" gang need, however, is a common phenomenon.

[10]At the third level are boys who occasionally join in with gang activity but seldom identify themselves as members of the gang at any other time. One boy, for instance, went along with the Egyptian Kings and participated in the Farmer killing, as he put it, "for old time's sake." He never really "belonged" to the gang: he just happened to be around that night and had nothing else to do.

[11]The "size" of violent gangs is often impossible to determine. If a leader feels particularly hemmed in at a given moment, he will say—and believe—that his gang is very large. But when he is feeling more secure, he will include in his account of the gang's size only those members he actually knows personally. In the course of a one-hour interview, for example, a gang leader variously estimated the size, affiliations, and territory of his gang as follows: membership jumped from one hundred to four thousand, affiliation from five brother gangs or alliances to sixty, and territorial control from about ten square blocks to jurisdiction over the boroughs of New

York City, New Jersey, and part of Philadelphia. To be sure, gangs will often contact one another to discuss alliances, and during the street-corner "negotiations," the leaders will brag of their ability to mobilize vast forces in case of a fight. On a rare occasion, these forces will actually be produced, but they generally appear quite spontaneously—the youths who participate in such alliances have very little understanding of what they are doing.

[12]The meaning of gang membership also changes according to a boy's needs of the moment. A youth will belong one day and quit the next without necessarily telling any other member. To ask certain gang boys from day to day whether they are Dragons or Kings is comparable to asking them, "How do you feel today?" So, too, with the question of role. Some boys say that the gang is organized for protection and that one role of a gang member is to fight—how, when, whom, and for what reason he is to fight are seldom clear, and answers vary from member to member. One gang boy may define himself more specifically as a protector of the younger boys in the neighborhood. Another will define his role in the gang by the statement, "We are going to get all those guys who call us Spics." Still others say their participation in the gang was forced upon them against their will.

[13]Despite these differences, however, all gang members believe that through their participation they will acquire prestige and status; and it is quite clear, furthermore, that the vagueness which surrounds various aspects of gang life and organization only enables the gang to stimulate such expectations and, in some respects, actually helps it to fulfill them. Similarly, if qualifications for membership were more exact, then most gang members would not be able to participate, for they lack the ability to assume the responsibilities of more structured organizations.

[14]The background out of which the violent gang has emerged is fairly easy to sketch. In contemporary American society, youth is constantly bombarded by images—from the media, schools, and parents—of a life of ownership and consumption, but for the great majority of young people in this country, and especially for those from depressed social and economic backgrounds, the means of acquiring such objectives are slim. Yet something more definite than class position or the inadequate relation between means and ends disturbs young people. It is the very fact of their youth which places them at an immediate disadvantage; objects and goals that

adults take for granted are, for them, clearly unattainable. As a consequence, many young people step beyond the accepted social boundaries in an attempt to find through deviant means a dramatic short-cut to an immediate feeling of success.*

[15]Drugs and alcohol are two possible short cuts; another characteristic deviant path is the search for thrills or "kicks." The violent gang, especially because it is both flexibly organized and amenable to the distortions of fantasy, is an obvious vehicle for acting out the desire for ownership and status. In the gang, a youth can be "president" and control vast domains, while the members can reinforce one another's fantasies of power—"Don't call my bluff and I won't call yours." In the gang, it is only necessary to talk big and support the talk with some violent action in order to become a "success," the possessor of power and status: "We would talk a lot and like that, but I never thought it would be like this. Me here in jail. It was just like fun and kidding around and acting big."

[16]The choice of violence as a means toward achieving "social" success seems to be the result in part of the past two decades of war as well as the international unrest that filters down to the gang boy and gives him the same feelings of uneasiness that the average citizen experiences. At this level of analysis, direct casual relations are by *no means* precise; yet a number of connections do seem apparent.

[17]A considerable amount of explicit data indicates that recent wars and current international machinations serve as models for gang warfare. For example, one form of gang battle is called a "Jap": "a quick stomp where a group of guys go into an enemy's territory, beat up some of their guys and get out fast. The thing is not to get caught." "Drafting" members is another common gang practice. The boys themselves freely use such terms as "drafting," "allies" (brother gangs), "war counselor," "peace treaty," etc., and they often refer, both directly and indirectly, to more complex patterns of conflict and structure. Here is one Egyptian King talking about a territorial dispute:

> You have a certain piece of land, so another club wants to take over your land, in order to have more space, and so forth. They'll

*This statement is a gross oversimplification of conceptual developments of Emile Durkheim, Robert Merton, and others, who have examined the means-goal dislocation.

fight you for it. If you win, you got your land; if you don't win, then they get your land. The person that loses is gonna get up another group, to help out, and then it starts all over again. Fight for the land again.

Here is another discussing gang organization:

> First, there's the president. He got the whole gang; then there comes the vice president, he's second in command; then there's the war counselor, war lord, whatever you're gonna call it—that's the one that starts the fights; then there's the prime minister—you know, he goes along with the war counselor to see when they're gonna fight, where they're gonna fight. And after that, just club members.

Murder, Inc., Thrasher's gangs, and Whyte's Norton Street gang did not have the "divisions," "war lords," and "allies" typical of the contemporary violent gang.

[18] In addition to this international model, it is important to note that many weapons now used by gangs were brought to this country by veterans of recent wars. Where in former years, gang wars were more likely to be fought with sticks, stones, and fists, today abandoned World War II weapons such as machetes (one was used in the Michael Farmer killing) and Lugers consistently turn up. The returning soldiers also brought back stories of violence to accompany the weapons. War and violence dominated not only the front pages of the press, but everyday family discussion, and often it was a father, an uncle, or an older brother whose violent exploits were extolled.

[19] Another aspect of international events which gang youths may have absorbed, and which they certainly now emulate, is the authoritarian-dictatorial concept of leadership. Earlier gangs sometimes utilized democratic processes in appointing leaders. But, today, in the violent gang, the leader is usually supreme and gang members tend to follow him slavishly. In recent years, in fact, there have been many abortive attempts—several on the Upper West Side of New York City—to pattern gangs specifically upon the model of Hitler and the Nazi party.

[20] What finally confronts the youth of today is the possibility of total destruction by atomic power—everyone is aware of this on some level of consciousness—and the possibility of induction into the army at a point when he might be establishing himself in the

labor force. In short, the recent history of international violence, the consequences of the past war, and the chance of total annihilation, establish a framework which may not only stimulate the formation of gangs but in some respects may determine its mode of behavior—in other words, its violence.

[21]But such background factors, however much they create an atmosphere that gives implicit social approval to the use of violence, cannot actually explain how violence functions for the gang boy. As I have already indicated, gang youths feel extremely helpless in their relations to the "outside" world. The gang boy considers himself incapable of functioning in any group other than the gang, and is afraid to attempt anything beyond the minimal demands of gang life. One interesting indication of this is the way gang boys respond to flattery. They invariably become flustered and confused if they are complimented, for the suggestion that they are capable of more constructive activity upsets their conviction of being unfit for the hazards of a life outside the protective circle of the gang.

[22]Given this low self-estimate, the gang boy has carved out a world and a system of values which entail only the kind of demands he can easily meet. Inverting society's norms to suit himself and the limits of his partly imagined and partly real potential, he has made lying, assault, theft, and unprovoked violence—and especially violence—the major activities of his life.

[23]The very fact that it is *senseless* rather than premeditated violence which is more highly prized by the gang, tells us a great deal about the role violence plays for the gang boy. He is looking for a quick, almost magical way of achieving power and prestige, and in a single act of unpremeditated intensity he at once establishes a sense of his own existence and impresses this existence on others. No special ability is required—not even a plan—and the anxiety attendant upon executing a premeditated (or "rational") act of violence is minimized in the ideal of a swift, sudden, and "meaningless" outbreak. (To some extent, the public's reaction to this violence, a reaction, most obviously of horror, also expresses a sort of covert aggrandizement—and this the gang boy instinctively understands.)

[24]Thus the violent gang provides an alternative world for the disturbed young who are ill-equipped for success in a society which in any case blocks their upward mobility. The irony is that this world with its nightmare inversion of the official values of our society is nevertheless constructed out of elements that are implic-

itly (or unconsciously) approved—especially in the mass media — and that its purpose is to help the gang boy achieve the major value of respectable society: success. "I'm not going to let anybody be better than me and steal my 'rep' . . . when I go to a gang fight, I punch, stomp, and stab harder than anyone."

COMMENT

Yablonsky uses division in two ways in the course of the essay. First he divides gangs of the past from gangs of the present; then he defines their purpose and structure. Second, he divides gangs of the present—the violent street gangs—according to their "levels." This division is, in fact, a more detailed analysis of the structure of the gang, for Yablonsky's earlier discussion of that structure is concerned only with its general features. Characterized by constant change or "flux," and existing to express spontaneous violence, the violent gang "lacks all the features of an organized group." The three levels reveal the various motives of the gang members. Reflecting the values of the fifties, the violent gang shows how people are directed by forces beyond their control. Yablonsky's concern over the death of Michael Farmer is in part a concern over wanton acts by boys who did not know their victim or themselves. He returns to this point at the end. His essay shows how an episode (the murder of Michael Farmer) can be used to say much about a society—its values, its structure, the motives of acts that seem "senseless."

QUESTIONS FOR STUDY AND DISCUSSION

1. How does Yablonsky explain the difference between gangs of the past and the violent gang of the fifties?

2. By what other principles might the violent gang be divided? To what use could these divisions be put in another essay?

3. Yablonsky states: "In contemporary American society, youth is constantly bombarded by images—from the media, schools, and parents," and he identifies those images and their effect. Yablonsky was writing in 1960. Do you believe youth in the late seventies is bombarded by the same images? Are the effects of images the same today?

4. What does Yablonsky mean in paragraph 14 by "the inadequate relation between means and ends"? How does the context of the statement help to explain it?

5. Yablonsky cites the Second World War and the atomic bomb as causes of certain attitudes and behavior in youth of the fifties. Do you believe war and fear of destruction are a major cause of juvenile crime today? Do you believe the pressures to conform are as strong today as they were in the fifties?

6. The phrase "society's norms" (paragraph 22) refers to the values or standards by which people live. How does Yablonsky show that not all of these "norms" are admitted or recognized by the people who live by them?

7. What is Yablonsky's thesis and where is it first stated? How does he restate it in the course of the essay?

8. To what extent does Yablonsky depend on formal transitions?

VOCABULARY STUDY

Complete the following sentences, using the italicized word according to one of its dictionary meanings:
   a. It is a *truism* of life that
   b. One *aspect* of the energy crisis is
   c. There was no *consensus*
   d. The *phenomenon* of flying saucer reports
   e. The teacher was *amenable* to
   f. She could distinguish between *fantasy* and
   g. They could not *emulate*
   h. The contract *entails*
   i. There was a *covert* recognition

SUGGESTIONS FOR WRITING

1. Compare Yablonsky and Jim Brown on the causes of juvenile gang life. Discuss whether the experiences Brown describes fit in part or in whole the pattern Yablonsky describes, or do not fit it at all.

2. Analyze the "levels" of a group you belong to, or divide the group by another principle. Use your analysis to develop a thesis or to support or argue against one of Yablonsky's conclusions.

comparison and contrast

Like definition and division, comparison and contrast is an important method of analysis in exposition. *Comparison* deals with similarities, *contrast* with differences. In comparing, we show what two or more people or objects or places have in common; in contrasting, how they are unlike. There are many ways of organizing paragraphs of comparison or contrast. One way is to list the qualities of the first person or place, then to list the qualities of the second—in the same order:

> Chicago, at the southern tip of Lake Michigan, is a port city and an important commercial and industrial center of the Middle West. It is also an important cultural and recreational center, drawing thousands to its concert halls, art museum, and sports arenas. Cleveland, on the south shore of Lake Erie, is similarly a port city and a commercial and industrial center important to its area. Like Chicago, it has a distinguished symphony orchestra, one of the fine art museums of the world, and many recreational centers. The two cities may have developed as they did because of their location, but this similarity is not sufficient to explain their wide cultural diversity. (paragraph of comparison)

A second way is to make the comparison or contrast point by point:

> Chicago is at the southern tip of Lake Michigan; Cleveland, on the south shore of Lake Erie. Both are important commercial and

industrial centers of the Middle West, and both offer a wide range of cultural and recreational activities.

In developing such paragraphs, transitions like *similarly, likewise, by comparison,* and *by contrast* may be needed to clarify the organization. The purpose of comparison and contrast is sometimes to provide a relative estimate: we discover the qualities of the first person or object or place *through* the qualities of the second (or third). If Cleveland and Chicago share these characteristics and have the same history of growth, we are better able to understand the causes that shape cities. A contrast with Atlanta or Omaha— large inland cities—would clarify these causes further through a similar relative estimate.

ON FRIENDSHIP

Margaret Mead and Rhoda Metraux

Margaret Mead, born in 1901, is one of America's most distinguished anthropologists. From 1926 to 1969 she was a curator of ethnology at the Museum of Natural History in New York City, and she has taught at Columbia and other universities. Her many books include *Male and Female* (1949), *And Keep Your Powder Dry* (1942), and *Growing Up in New Guinea* (1930).

Rhoda Metraux is also a distinguished anthropologist. She has done field research in many countries including Haiti, Mexico, Argentina, and New Guinea. She and Mead have worked together for many years, collaborating in the writing of *The Study of Culture at a Distance* (1953) and *Themes in French Culture* (1954).

[1]Few Americans stay put for a lifetime. We move from town to city to suburb, from high school to college in a different state, from a job in one region to a better job elsewhere, from the home where we raise our children to the home where we plan to live in retirement. With each move we are forever making new friends, who become part of our new life at that time.

[2]For many of us the summer is a special time for forming new friendships. Today millions of Americans vacation abroad, and they go not only to see new sights but also—in those places where they do not feel too strange—with the hope of meeting new people. No one really expects a vacation trip to produce a close friend. But surely the beginning of a friendship is possible? Surely in every country people value friendship?

[3]They do. The difficulty when strangers from two countries meet is not a lack of appreciation of friendship, but different expectations about what constitutes friendship and how it comes into being. In those European countries that Americans are most likely to visit, friendship is quite sharply distinguished from other, more casual relations, and is differently related to family life. For a Frenchman, a German or an Englishman friendship is usually more particularized and carries a heavier burden of commitment.

[4]But as we use the word, "friend" can be applied to a wide range of relationships—to someone one has known for a few weeks in a new place, to a close business associate, to a childhood playmate, to a man or woman, to a trusted confidant. There are real differences among these relations for Americans—a friendship may be superficial, casual, situational or deep and enduring. But to a European, who sees only our surface behavior, the differences are not clear.

[5]As they see it, people known and accepted temporarily, casually, flow in and out of Americans' homes with little ceremony and often with little personal commitment. They may be parents of the children's friends, house guests of neighbors, members of a committee, business associates from another town or even another country. Coming as a guest into an American home, the European visitor

From *A Way of Seeing* by Margaret Mead and Rhoda Metraux. Copyright © 1970, 1969, 1968, 1967, 1966, 1965, 1964, 1963, 1962, 1961 by Margaret Mead and Rhoda Metraux. Reprinted by permission of the publishers, Saturday Review Press/E. P. Dutton & Co., Inc.

finds no visible landmarks. The atmosphere is relaxed. Most people, old and young, are called by first names.

⁶Who, then, is a friend?

⁷Even simple translation from one language to another is difficult. "You see," a Frenchman explains, "if I were to say to you in France, 'This is my good friend,' that person would not be as close to me as someone about whom I said only, 'This is my friend.' Anyone about whom I have to say *more* is really less."

⁸In France, as in many European countries, friends generally are of the same sex, and friendship is seen as basically a relationship between men. Frenchwomen laugh at the idea that "women can't be friends," but they also admit sometimes that for women "it's a different thing." And many French people doubt the possibility of a friendship between a man and a woman. There is also the kind of relationship within a group—men and women who have worked together for a long time, who may be very close, sharing great loyalty and warmth of feeling. They may call one another *copains*— a word that in English becomes "friends" but has more the feeling of "pals" or "buddies." In French eyes this is not friendship, although two members of such a group may well be friends.

⁹For the French, friendship is a one-to-one relationship that demands a keen awareness of the other person's intellect, temperament and particular interests. A friend is someone who draws out your own best qualities, with whom you sparkle and become more of whatever the friendship draws upon. Your political philosophy assumes more depth, appreciation of a play becomes sharper, taste in food or wine is accentuated, enjoyment of a sport is intensified.

¹⁰And French friendships are compartmentalized. A man may play chess with a friend for thirty years without knowing his political opinions, or he may talk politics with him for as long a time without knowing about his personal life. Different friends fill different niches in each person's life. These friendships are not made part of family life. A friend is not expected to spend evenings being nice to children or courteous to a deaf grandmother. These duties, also serious and enjoined, are primarily for relatives. Men who are friends may meet in a café. Intellectual friends may meet in larger groups for evenings of conversation. Working people may meet at the little *bistro* where they drink and talk, far from the family. Marriage does not affect such friendships; wives do not have to be taken into account.

[11] In the past in France, friendships of this kind seldom were open to any but intellectual women. Since most women's lives centered on their homes, their warmest relations with other women often went back to their girlhood. The special relationship of friendship is based on what the French value most—on the mind, on compatibility of outlook, on vivid awareness of some chosen area of life.

[12] Friendship heightens the sense of each person's individuality. Other relationships commanding as great loyalty and devotion have a different meaning. In World War II the first resistance groups formed in Paris were built on the foundation of *les copains*. But significantly, as time went on these little groups, whose lives rested in one another's hands, called themselves "families." Where each had a total responsibility for all, it was kinship ties that provided the model. And even today such ties, crossing every line of class and personal interest, remain binding on the survivors of these small, secret bands.

[13] In Germany, in contrast with France, friendship is much more articulately a matter of feeling. Adolescents, boys and girls, form deeply sentimental attachments, walk and talk together—not so much to polish their wits as to share their hopes and fears and dreams, to form a common front against the world of school and family and to join in a kind of mutual discovery of each other's and their own inner life. Within the family, the closest relationship over a lifetime is between brothers and sisters. Outside the family, men and women find in their closest friends of the same sex the devotion of a sister, the loyalty of a brother. Appropriately, in Germany friends usually are brought into the family. Children call their father's and their mother's friends "uncle" and "aunt." Between French friends, who have chosen each other for the congeniality of their point of view, lively disagreement and sharpness of argument are the breath of life. But for Germans, whose friendships are based on mutuality of feeling, deep disagreement on any subject that matters to both is regarded as a tragedy. Like ties of kinship, ties of friendship are meant to be irrevocably binding. Young Germans who come to the United States have great difficulty in establishing such friendships with Americans. We view friendship more tentatively, subject to changes in intensity as people move, change their jobs, marry, or discover new interests.

[14] English friendships follow still a different pattern. Their basis

is shared activity. Activities at different stages of life may be of very different kinds—discovering a common interest in school, serving together in the armed forces, taking part in a foreign mission, staying in the same country house during a crisis. In the midst of the activity, whatever it may be, people fall into step—sometimes two men or two women, sometimes two couples, sometimes three people—and find that they walk or play a game or tell stories or serve on a tiresome and exacting committee with the same easy anticipation of what each will do day by day or in some critical situation. Americans who have made English friends comment that, even years later, "you can take up just where you left off." Meeting after a long interval, friends are like a couple who begin to dance again when the orchestra strikes up after a pause. English friendships are formed outside the family circle, but they are not, as in Germany, contrapuntal to the family nor are they, as in France, separated from the family. And a break in an English friendship comes not necessarily as a result of some irreconcilable difference of viewpoint or feeling but instead as a result of misjudgment, where one friend seriously misjudges how the other will think or feel or act, so that suddenly they are out of step.

[15] What, then, is friendship? Looking at these different styles, including our own, each of which is related to a whole way of life, are there common elements? There is the recognition that friendship, in contrast with kinship, invokes freedom of choice. A friend is someone who chooses and is chosen. Related to this is the sense each friend gives the other of being a special individual, on whatever grounds this recognition is based. And between friends there is inevitably a kind of equality of give-and-take. These similarities make the bridge between societies possible, and the American's characteristic openness to different styles of relationship makes it possible for him to find new friends abroad with whom he feels at home.

COMMENT

The essay is developed mainly through contrast, beginning with the initial one between the American idea of friendship and the European. The European styles of friendship are described one by one: first the French, then the German, finally the English. The authors do, however, return to earlier styles for contrast:

Between French friends, who have chosen each other for the congeniality of their point of view, lively disagreement and sharpness of argument are the breath of life. But for Germans, whose friendships are based on mutuality of feeling, deep disagreement on any subject that matters to both is regarded as a tragedy.

The essay closes with comparison, for the authors state the similarities between Americans and Europeans. This careful ordering of ideas allows the authors to present many different ones without confusing the reader about the central purpose of the analysis. Comparison and contrast are fitted to a thesis—anticipated in the opening paragraphs and stated fully in the concluding one.

QUESTIONS FOR STUDY AND DISCUSSION

1. What is the thesis of the essay? How is it anticipated in the opening paragraphs?

2. What kind of definition do Mead and Metraux use in defining friendship toward the beginning, and later in the essay? What is the purpose of this definition?

3. How is the American style of friendship different from the European? Which of the three European styles does the American most and least resemble? Are these resemblances important to the thesis?

4. Why do the authors begin with the French and end with the English, before proceeding to the final comparison? Could the essay just as well have begun with the English and ended with the French?

5. The authors are describing the world of 1966, when the essay first appeared in print. Do you believe styles of American friendships—as you have experienced them—have changed in the seventies?

VOCABULARY STUDY

1. Examine the dictionary meanings of the following words. Then write a sentence for each, making the content reveal the meaning of the word: *affection, love, acquaintance, pal, buddy, confidante.*

2. Complete each of the following sentences, using the italicized word in its dictionary meaning:
   a. He felt no *commitment*
   b. The *niche* she was searching for
   c. The *bistro* on the corner of the Rue de Rivoli

    d. We get *sentimental* about
    e. The decision to make the change *irrevocable*
    f. We are *tentatively* scheduled

SUGGESTIONS FOR WRITING

1. Illustrate the following statement from your own experience, and use comparison and contrast to develop it: "There are real differences among these relations for Americans—a friendship may be superficial, casual, situational or deep and enduring." Define each of the adjectives in the course of your discussion.

2. Compare or contrast two of your friendships to show how they resemble or differ from one of the styles described in the essay.

3. Discuss the extent to which the gang relationships described by Lewis Yablonsky fit one or more of the styles of friendships described in the essay.

ARE CHILDREN PEOPLE?

Phyllis McGinley

Phyllis McGinley was born in 1905 in Ontario, Oregon, and attended the University of Utah and the University of California. She has written light verse, many articles and children's books, and she has won numerous literary prizes, including the 1961 Pulitzer Prize for poetry.

    [1]The problem of how to live with children isn't as new as you might think. Centuries before the advent of Dr. Spock or the PTA, philosophers debated the juvenile question, not always with compassion. There's a quotation from one of the antique sages floating around in what passes for my mind which, for pure cynicism, could set a Montaigne or a Mort Sahl back on his heels.

[2]"Why," asks a disciple, "are we so devoted to our grandchildren?"

[3]And the graybeard answers, "Because it is easy to love the enemies of one's enemies."

[4]Philosopher he may have been but I doubt his parental certification. Any parent with a spark of natural feeling knows that children aren't our enemies. On the other hand, if we're sensible we are aware that they aren't really our friends, either. How can they be, when they belong to a totally different race?

[5]Children admittedly are human beings, equipped with such human paraphernalia as appetites, whims, intelligence, and even hearts, but any resemblance between them and people is purely coincidental. The two nations, child and grown-up, don't behave alike or think alike or even see with the same eyes.

[6]Take that matter of seeing, for example. An adult looks in the mirror and notices what? A familiar face, a figure currently overweight, maybe, but well-known and resignedly accepted; two arms, two legs, an entity. A child can stare into the looking glass for minutes at a time and see only the bone buttons on a snowsuit or a pair of red shoes.

[7]Shoes, in fact, are the first personal belongings a child really looks at in an objective sense. There they are to adore—visible, shiny, round-toed ornamental extensions of himself. He can observe them in that mirror or he can look down from his small height to admire them. They are real to him, unlike his eyes or his elbows. That is why, for a child, getting a pair of new shoes is like having a birthday. When my daughters were little they invariably took just-acquired slippers to bed with them for a few nights, the way they'd take a cuddle toy or smuggle in a puppy.

[8]Do people sleep with their shoes? Of course not. Nor do they lift them up reverently to be fondled, a gesture children offer even to perfect strangers in department stores. I used to think that a child's life was lived from new shoe to new shoe, as an adult lives for love or payday or a vacation.

[9]Children, though, aren't consistent about their fetish. By the time they have learned to tie their own laces, they have lapsed into an opposite phase. They start to discard shoes entirely. Boys, being natural reactionaries, cling longer than girls to their first loves, but girls begin the discalced stage at twelve or thirteen—and it goes on interminably. Their closets may bulge with footwear, with every-

thing from dubious sneakers to wisps of silver kid, while most of the time the girls themselves go unshod. I am in error, too, when I speak of shoes as reposing in closets. They don't. They lie abandoned under sofas, upside down beside the television set, rain-drenched on verandas. Guests in formal drawing rooms are confronted by them and climbers on stairways imperiled. When the phase ends, I can't tell you, but I think only with premature senescence.

[10] My younger daughter, then a withered crone of almost twenty, once held the odd distinction of being the only girl on record to get her foot stabbed by a rusty nail at a Yale prom. She was, of course, doing the Twist barefoot, but even so the accident seems unlikely. You can't convince me it could happen to an adult.

[11] No, children don't look at things in the same light as people. Nor do they hear with our ears, either. Ask a child a question and he has an invariable answer: "What?" (Though now and then he alters it to "Why?")

[12] Or send one on a household errand and you will know that he—or she—is incapable of taking in a simple adult remark. I once asked an otherwise normal little girl to bring me the scissors from the kitchen drawer, and she returned, after a mysterious absence of fifteen minutes, lugging the extension hose out of the garage. Yet the young can hear brownies baking in the oven two blocks away from home or the faintest whisper of parents attempting to tell each other secrets behind closed doors.

[13] They can also understand the language of babies, the most esoteric on earth. Our younger child babbled steadily from the age of nine months on, although not for a long while in an intelligible tongue. Yet her sister, two years older, could translate for us every time.

[14] "That lady's bracelet—Patsy wishes she could have it," the interpreter would tell me; and I had the wit hastily to lift my visitor's arm out of danger.

[15] Or I would be instructed, "She'd like to pat the kitten now."

[16] We used occasionally to regret their sibling fluency of communication. Once we entertained at Sunday dinner a portrait painter known rather widely for his frequent and publicized love affairs. He quite looked the part, too, being so tall and lean and rakish, with such a predatory moustache and so formidable a smile, that my husband suggested it was a case of art imitating nature.

[17]The two small girls had never met him, and when the baby saw him for the first time she turned tail and fled upstairs.

[18]The older, a gracious four, came back into the living room after a short consultation, to apologize for her sister's behavior. "You see," she told him winningly, "Patsy thinks you're a wolf."

[19]It was impossible to explain that they had somehow confused the moustache and the smile with a description of Little Red Riding Hood's arch foe and were not referring to his private life. We let it pass. I often thought, however, that it was a pity the older girl's pentecostal gifts did not outlast kindergarten. She would have been a great help to the United Nations.

[20]Young mothers have to study such talents and revise their methods of child rearing accordingly. To attempt to treat the young like grown-ups is always a mistake.

[21]Do people, at least those outside of institutions, drop lighted matches into wastebaskets just to see what will happen? Do they tramp through puddles on purpose? Or prefer hot dogs or jelly-and-mashed-banana sandwiches to lobster Thermidor? Or, far from gagging on the abysmal inanities of *Raggedy Ann,* beg to have it read to them every evening for three months?

[22]Indeed, the reading habits alone of the younger generation mark them off from their betters. What does an adult do when he feels like having a go at a detective story or the evening paper? Why, he picks out a convenient chair or props himself up on his pillows, arranges the light correctly for good vision, turns down the radio, and reaches for a cigarette or a piece of chocolate fudge.

[23]Children, however, when the literary urge seizes them, take their comic books to the darkest corner of the room or else put their heads under the bedcovers. Nor do they sit *down* to read. They wander. They lie on the floor with their legs draped over the coffee table, or, alternatively, they sit on the coffee table and put the book on the floor. Or else they lean against the refrigerator, usually with the refrigerator door wide open. Sometimes I have seen them retire to closets.

[24]Children in comfortable positions are uncomfortable—just as they are miserable if they can't also have the phonograph, the radio, the television and sometimes the telephone awake and lively while they pore on *The Monster of Kalliwan* or *The Jungle Book.*

[25]But then, children don't walk like people, either—sensibly,

staidly, in a definite direction. I am not sure they ever acquire our grown-up gaits. They canter, they bounce, they slither, slide, crawl, leap into the air, saunter, stand on their heads, swing from branch to branch, limp like cripples, or trot like ostriches. But I seldom recall seeing a child just plain walk. They can, however, dawdle. The longest period of recorded time is that interval between telling children to undress for bed and the ultimate moment when they have brushed their teeth, said their prayers, eaten a piece of bread and catsup, brushed their teeth all over again, asked four times for another glass of milk, checked the safety of their water pistols or their tropical fish, remembered there was something vital they had to confide to you, which they have forgotten by the time you reach their side, switched from a panda to a giraffe and back to the panda for the night's sleeping companion, begged to have the light left on in the hall, and finally, being satisfied that your screaming voice is in working order, fallen angelically into slumber.

[26] Apprentice parents are warned to disregard at least nine-tenths of all such requests as pure subterfuge but to remember that maybe one of the ten is right and reasonable, like the night-light or the value of a panda when one is in a panda mood.

[27] Not that reason weighs much with children. It is the great mistake we make with a child, to think progeny operate by our logic. The reasoning of children, although it is often subtle, differs from an adult's. At base there is usually a core of sanity, but one must disentangle what the lispers mean from what they say.

[28] "I believe in Santa Claus," a daughter told me years ago, when she was five or six. "And I believe in the Easter Rabbit, too. But I just can't believe in Shirley Temple."

[29] Until I worked out a solution for this enigmatic statement, I feared for the girl's mind. Then I realized that she had been watching the twenty-one-inch screen. After all, if you are six years old and see a grown-up Shirley Temple acting as mistress of ceremonies for a TV special one evening and the next day observe her, dimpled and brief-skirted, in an old movie, you are apt to find the transformation hard to credit.

[30] I managed to unravel that utterance, but I never did pierce through to the heart of a gnomic pronouncement made by a young friend of hers. He meandered into the backyard one summer day when the whole family was preparing for a funeral. Our garden is

thickly clustered with memorials to defunct wildlife, and on this particular afternoon we were intent on burying another robin.

[31]John looked at the hole.

[32]"What are you doing?" he asked, as if it weren't perfectly apparent to the most uninformed.

[33]"Why, John," said my husband, "I'm digging a grave."

[34]John considered the matter a while. Then he inquired again, with all the solemnity of David Susskind querying a senator, "Why don't you make it a double-decker?"

[35]Not even Echo answered that one, but I kept my sense of proportion and went on with the ceremonies. You need a sense of proportion when dealing with children, as you also need a sense of humor. Yet you must never expect the very young to have a sense of humor of their own. Children are acutely risible, stirred to laughter by dozens of human mishaps, preferably fatal. They can understand the points of jokes, too, so long as the joke is not on them. Their egos are too new, they have not existed long enough in the world to have learned to laugh at themselves. What they love most in the way of humor are riddles, elementary puns, nonsense, and catastrophe. An elderly fat lady slipping on the ice in real life or a man in a movie falling from a fifteen-foot ladder equally transports them. They laugh at fistfights, clowns, people kissing each other, and buildings blowing up. They don't, however, enjoy seeing their parents in difficulties. Parents, they feel, were put on earth solely for their protection, and they cannot bear to have the fortress endangered.

[36]Their peace of mind, their safety, rests on grown-up authority; and it is that childish reliance which invalidates the worth of reasoning too much with them. The longer I lived in a house with children, the less importance I put on cooperatively threshing out matters of conduct or explaining to them our theories of discipline. If I had it to do over again I wouldn't reason with them at all until they arrived at an *age* of reason—approximately twenty-one. I would give them rules to follow. I would try to be just, and I would try even harder to be strict. I would do no arguing. Children, in their hearts, like laws. Authority implies an ordered world, which is what they— and, in the long run, most of the human race—yearn to inhabit. In law there is freedom. Be too permissive and they feel lost and alone. Children are forced to live very rapidly in order to live at all. They are given only a few years in which to learn hundreds of thousands

of things about life and the planet and themselves. They haven't time to spend analyzing the logic behind every command or taboo, and they resent being pulled away by it from their proper business of discovery.

[37]When our younger and more conversational daughter turned twelve, we found she was monopolizing the family telephone. She would reach home after school at 3:14 and at 3:15 the instrument would begin to shrill, its peal endless till bedtime. For once we had the good sense neither to scold nor to expostulate. We merely told her she could make and receive calls only between five and six o'clock in the afternoon. For the rest of the day, the telephone was ours. We expected tears. We were braced for hysterics. What we got was a calm acceptance of a Rule. Indeed, we found out later, she boasted about the prohibition—it made her feel both sheltered and popular.

[38]But, then, children are seldom resentful, which is another difference between them and people. They hold grudges no better than a lapdog. They are too inexperienced to expect favors from the world. What happens to them happens to them, like an illness; and if it is not too extravagantly unfair, they forget about it. Parents learn that a child's angry glare or floods of tears after a punishment or a scolding may send the grown-up away feeling like a despotic brute; but that half an hour later, with adult feelings still in tatters, the child is likely as not to come flying into the room, fling both carefree arms about the beastly grown-up's neck, and shout, "I love you," into her ear.

[39]The ability to forget a sorrow is childhood's most enchanting feature. It can also be exasperating to the pitch of frenzy. Little girls return from school with their hearts broken in two by a friend's treachery or a teacher's injustice. They sob through the afternoon, refuse dinner, and go to sleep on tear-soaked pillows. Novice mothers do not sleep at all, only lie awake with the shared burden for a nightlong companion. Experienced ones know better. They realize that if you come down in the morning to renew your solacing, you will meet—what? Refreshed, whole-hearted offspring who can't under*stand* what you're talking about. Beware of making childhood's griefs your own. They are no more lasting than soap bubbles.

[40]I find myself hoaxed to this day by the recuperative powers of the young, even when they top me by an inch and know all about

modern art. More than once I have been called long distance from a college in New England to hear news of impending disaster.

[41]"It's exam time and I'm down with this horrible cold," croaks the sufferer, coughing dramatically. "Can you rush me that prescription of Dr. Murphy's? I don't trust our infirmary."

[42]Envisioning flu, pneumonia, wasting fever, and a lily maid dead before her time, I harry the doctor into scribbling his famous remedy and send it by wire. Then after worrying myself into dyspepsia, I call two days later to find out the worst. An unfogged voice answers me blithely.

[43]"What cold?" it inquires.

[44]Ephemeral tragedies, crises that evaporate overnight are almost certain to coincide with adolescence. Gird yourselves for them. Adolescence is a disease more virulent than measles and difficult to outgrow as an allergy. At its onset parents are bewildered like the victim. They can only stand by with patience, flexibility, and plenty of food in the larder. It's amazing how consoling is a batch of cookies in an emergency. If it doesn't comfort the child, at least it helps the baker. I stopped in at a neighbor's house the other day and found her busily putting the frosting on a coconut cake.

[45]"It's for Steven," she told me. "His pet skunk just died, and I didn't know what else to do for him."

[46]Food helps more than understanding. Adolescence doesn't really want to be understood. It prefers to live privately in some stone tower of its own building, lonely and unassailable. To understand is to violate. This is the age—at least for girls—of hidden diaries, locked drawers, unshared secrets. It's a trying time for all concerned. The only solace is that they do outgrow it. But the flaw there is that eventually they outgrow being children too, becoming expatriates of their own tribe.

[47]For, impossible as it seems when one first contemplates diapers and croup, then tantrums, homework, scouting, dancing class, and finally the terrible dilemmas of the teens, childhood does come inexorably to an end. Children turn into people. They speak rationally if aloofly, lecture you on manners, condescend to teach you about eclectic criticism, and incline to get married. And there you are, left with all that learning you have so painfully accumulated in twenty-odd years and with no more progeny on whom to lavish it.

[48]Small wonder we love our grandchildren. The old sage recog-

nized the effect but not the cause. Enemies of our enemies indeed! They are our immortality. It is they who will inherit our wisdom, our experience, our ingenuity.

[49]Except, of course, that the grandchildren's parents will listen benevolently (are they not courteous adults?) and not profit by a word we tell them. They must learn for themselves how to speak in another language and with an alien race.

COMMENT

"The two nations, child and grown-up, don't behave alike or think alike or even see with the same eyes," Phyllis McGinley says toward the start of the essay. Her statement suggests a relative estimate of the two worlds—much like that of Mead and Metraux in their contrast of American and European friendships. McGinley's contrast of child and grown-up world is, however, mainly for the purpose of illustration. We are asked throughout the essay whether we recognize the behavior of children in our own grown-up behavior. Assuming that the answer is no, McGinley does not develop the differences. At several points in the essay, the contrast is implied: "You need a sense of proportion when dealing with children, as you also need a sense of humor. Yet you must never expect the very young to have a sense of humor of their own." The statement tells us that grown-ups do have a sense of proportion and can laugh at themselves. The strength of McGinley's essay is in its lively examples drawn from her own experience; no idea in the essay is without illustration. She also maintains a clear and consistent focus on those qualities that distinguish children from grown-ups—her central topic.

QUESTIONS FOR STUDY AND DISCUSSION

1. According to McGinley, in what ways are children different from grown-ups? Through what transitions and topic sentences does she remind the reader of these differences?

2. What kind of transitions does she use? How many of them refer to the ideas of the immediately preceding paragraph?

3. In what order are the qualities of children presented?

4. What point is McGinley making about the differences between children and grown-ups? Is this point stated or implied?

5. Look up the word *reactionary*. In what sense are boys "natural

reactionaries" (paragraph 9)? How does the context explain the statement? If boys are reactionaries, what are girls? Do you agree with this
distinction?

6. How many of the qualities of children discussed in the essay illustrate
their "proper business of discovery"?

VOCABULARY STUDY

Use each of the following pairs of words in sentences that reveal their
difference. If you can, use the pair in a sentence that contrasts them:
   a. *premature, early*
   b. *withered, worn out*
   c. *babbled, raved*
   d. *formidable, threatening*
   e. *inanities, absurdities*
   f. *saunter, dawdle*
   g. *exasperating, annoying*
   h. *blithely, happily*

SUGGESTIONS FOR WRITING

1. Develop one of the following statements from your own experience.
   Explain why you agree or disagree with it:
   a. "Boys, being natural reactionaries, cling longer than girls to their
      first loves."
   b. "Children in comfortable positions are uncomfortable."
   c. "Children, in their hearts, like laws."
   d. "Children are forced to live very rapidly in order to live at all."
   e. "Children are seldom resentful."
   f. "The ability to forget sorrow is childhood's most enchanting
      feature."
   g. "Adolescence doesn't really want to be understood."

2. The author distinguishes between boys and girls, childhood and
   adolescence, children and grown-ups. Provide illustrations of your
   own for one of these distinctions. If you wish, distinguish between
   them in your own way.

3. Compare the rules set for you as a child or adolescent with those you
   would set for your own children. Be sure to explain the reasons for the
   differences.

example

In explaining our ideas and making points in arguing, we fit our examples to the knowledge and experience of our readers or listeners. Explaining to a child that pinpoints of light in the night sky are in fact very large distant objects, we might first explain why large objects can appear small. An example suited to the experience of the child might be a ball that seems to get smaller as it flies through the air. Explaining to college physics students why the space of the universe is said to be "curved," we might draw on laboratory experiments for illustrations, but for the person who knows little or nothing about science, we would again have to draw on common experiences.

The word *example* usually carries the meaning of typical; that is, the example represents the many occurrences or forms of the idea or experience we are trying to convey. Examples are essential to exposition, particularly to the explanation of complex ideas. It would be difficult if not impossible, for instance, to explain how children are different from grown-ups emotionally without giving examples of their responses to various situations.

PURGING STAG WORDS

Russell Baker

Russell Baker was born in 1925 in Loudon County, Virginia. He studied at Johns Hopkins University and served in the Second World War. Later he joined the staff of the *Baltimore Sun,* and from 1954 to 1962 he was with the *New York Times'* Washing-

ton Bureau. Since 1962 he has been a columnist for the *Times*.
Baker is a keen and witty observer of American life, and has
written much about popular language. His books include *Our
Next President* (1968), *All Things Considered* (1965), and *Poor
Russell's Almanac* (1972).

[1]Everybody at some time has probably felt blood pressure rise
and pulse when loaded words have been used to diminish him. The
laborer who is called "a hardhat," the poor white who is called "a
redneck," the black man who is called "boy," the intellectual who is
called "an egghead," the liberal who is called "a bleeding heart," the
policeman who is called "a pig"—all these and many others are
painfully aware how brutally the English language can be used to
humiliate them.

[2]In such instances, words become weapons. Their victims see
English as an enemy to be disarmed and, so, when they acquire
political muscle one of their first goals commonly is to purge the
language.

[3]This is what feminists are now struggling to do in their
assault on the heavily masculine freight that has been built into
English from the time of the Angles, the Saxons and the Normans.
When sensible adults are called "the weaker sex," or "the girls,"
they are apt to feel at least mildly ridiculed and possibly assaulted.

[4]Hearing men refer to "the little woman," "the better half,"
"the ball and chain" or "a sweet young thing" may make them
suspect they are being crushed in a velvet vise. Not surprisingly,
then, the feminist movement is heavily engaged in a language
purge.

[5]It is not easy once they get beyond putting the taboo on
"weaker sex," "ball and chain," "sweet young thing" and similar
ancient clichés that were ready for retirement anyhow, for masculine primacy is deeply entrenched in English.

[6]Some of the difficulties are illustrated in McGraw-Hill's
"Guidelines for Equal Treatment of the Sexes in McGraw-Hill Book
Company Publications," an admirable analysis of how firmly modern English confines women to the masculine mentality. The
author, Timothy Yohn, describes the mental trap very persuasively
but is less successful in suggesting how to break out.

⁷The most awkward problem arises with all those words that are compounds of "man." Mr. Yohn tackles "Congressman" and suggests "member of Congress" as a better alternative. His "businessman" becomes "business executive" or "business manager." His "fireman" is a "fire fighter," his "mailman" a "mail carrier," his "salesman" a "sales representative," "salesperson" or "sales clerk," his "insurance man" an "insurance agent," his "statesman" a "leader" or "public servant," his "chairman" a "presiding officer," "the chair," "head," "leader," "coordinator" or "moderator," his "cameraman" a "camera operator" and his "foreman" a "supervisor."

⁸In almost every case the alternative for the "sexist" word to be purged is either a longer word or a combination of words. Instead of "sexism," we have verbosity. It is a dilemma that feminists will have no trouble resolving, but whether it is a good idea to encourage more windiness in an age when most of us already talk like politicians on television is arguable.

⁹One of feminism's goals, presumably, is to establish woman's right, too, to speak in words of one syllable. It will be a pity if everybody has forgotten how by the time equality is finally attained.

¹⁰The trouble with most of Mr. Yohn's "nonsexist" alternatives—although "fire fighter" isn't bad—is that they abolish "man" only to bring on a Latin-root substitute, and Latin-root words tend to be not only pompous but also vague and long-winded.

¹¹Feminists with a classic turn of mind might object that the "or" endings on "operator," "supervisor," "moderator" and "coordinator" smack heavily of the masculine "or" ending common on Latin nouns and are, thus, merely "sexist" words concealed in a toga.

¹²Ideally, someone should invent brand new words that are devoid of gender implication in their job descriptions without weighting the language down like lead settling into swamp water. A scouring of the dictionaries might even turn up some good old words that would serve.

¹³Mr. Yohn suggests one when, in cautioning against "language that assumes all readers are male," he rules out "you and your wife" and suggests, instead, "you and your spouse." The trouble with "spouse" is that nobody but a lawyer can say it with a straight face. It belongs to W. C. Fields and dry wits in sawdust saloons, and in the plural who could resist saying, "you and your spice"?

¹⁴Why not "you and your mate," Mr. Yohn? "Mate" has the strength of one unequivocal syllable. It also has sex in it, without gender, and that's what we are looking for, isn't it?

COMMENT

Baker illustrates the attitudes implied in certain words and expressions and the difficulty of finding substitutes for some of these. Through these examples he makes points about language itself—for example, the effect of Latin-root words on English sentences. Without examples, Baker would be stating generalities—essentially, vague opinions unsupported by evidence. Generalizations by contrast are well supported, and can be tested through the examples and evidence amassed. Baker's examples are strong ones, and his ability to amass so many of them shows the seriousness of the problem he discusses.

QUESTIONS FOR STUDY AND DISCUSSION

1. What examples does Baker give of words that are used as weapons? What examples can you give of words used in this way?

2. Are all the words cited used to ridicule women? Or are other attitudes implied in them?

3. What is "verbose"about some of the words suggested as alternatives for sexist words?

4. What general philosophy of language is implied in Baker's comments, as well as stated directly? In other words, what does Baker believe that words should and should not do?

5. Do you agree that substitutes should be found for words that exhibit "masculine primacy"? Do you find yourself belittled or injured by words used about your sex or racial or cultural background?

6. How prevalent do you find sexist language in newspapers and on television? Have you noticed changes in the use of words that apply to men and women equally?

VOCABULARY STUDY

Analyze a newspaper or magazine article or editorial for words that Baker would consider weighted toward the masculine or "loaded" in some other way. Make a list of these words, and be prepared to explain your choice.

SUGGESTIONS FOR WRITING

1. Discuss your agreement or disagreement with Baker on the issues raised in the article. Base your discussion on your experience with these or similar words and expressions.

2. Trace your attitude toward women or a racial, national, or religious minority through the words you use in talking about them. You might want to discuss how you came to use these words.

3. Discuss a television show or a cartoon strip in which men or women (possibly both) are ridiculed or portrayed falsely. Contrast this treatment with one that you consider fair and true.

ABOUT LANGUAGE: A RICHNESS OF WORDS, A BABEL OF TONGUES

Wallace L. Chafe

Wallace L. Chafe was born in 1927 in Cambridge, Massachusetts. He studied at Yale University, and from 1959 to 1962 worked as a linguist for the Bureau of American Ethnology at the Smithsonian Institution. He has taught at the State University of New York at Buffalo, and since 1962 has taught linguistics at the University of California at Berkeley. His interest in American Indian languages and anthropology is expressed in the essay printed here.

¹Exploring a Canadian headland in 1534, one of Jacques Cartier's longboats encountered a large band of Indians. Outnumbered, the Frenchmen rowed off. Seven canoes paddled after them, the chronicle relates, the Indians "showing many signs of joy and of their desire to be friends, saying to us in their language: *Napou tou daman asurtat,* and other words we did not understand."

²Those were the first Indian words recorded by Europeans north of the Rio Grande, and they evidently were spoken in friendship. But the shape of things to come was foreshadowed in the explorers' reaction: " . . . we shot off two fire-lances which . . . frightened them so much that they began to paddle off in very great haste. . . ."

From *The World of the American Indian,* National Geographic Society, 1974. Reprinted with permission.

[3]No one knows the language recorded; likely it was Micmac, of the Algonquian family and one of 500 to 600 spoken in North America at that time. Scholars have sought to link them with Asian languages; the results remain inconclusive. Thousands of years of separation have obscured any clear linguistic connections between the continents. And there is no special reason to think that all Indian tongues had a common origin; probably separate migrations at different times introduced linguistic variety from the very beginning.

[4]A reasonable consensus today distinguishes 18 language families, each containing from one to more than 20 languages. Those in a family are believed to have a common ancestor. For all we know, the families themselves may be as independent in ancestry as, say, English and Japanese.

[5]Language and culture are sometimes closely related; Eskimos from Alaska to Greenland share an Arctic culture and a single language. On the other hand, tribes in the same language family may be quite distant in culture and geography. The Penobscot of Maine, the Ojibwa of the Great Lakes, and the Blackfoot of the Great Plains all speak Algonquian languages. The 20 members of the Athapaskan language family include the Kutchin of Alaska, the Hupa of northern California, the Navajo and Apache of the southwest. Of the southeastern people who came to be known as the Five Civilized Tribes, the Chickasaw, Choctaw, Creek, and Seminole speak Muskogean languages; the Cherokee speak an Iroquoian language.

[6]Europeans often mistakenly concluded that Indian languages were somehow more "primitive" than those of "civilized" Europe. Indians, it was alleged, could not express general concepts, and therefore used several specific terms where Europeans might employ one generic word.

[7]As an example, one eminent linguist claimed that Cherokee had no single word for "washing," but instead used different words according to what is washed: "*Gadawo'a*—I am washing myself"; "*Gagun'sgwo'a*—I am washing my face."

[8]Actually, the verb stem—(*a*)*wo*—is the same in each instance. The confusion arises from the fact that in Cherokee, as in other Indian languages, a single word may incorporate all the elements of a sentence. And the word can vary to indicate the tense and grammatical mood of the verb, as well as the person, gender, and number of the subject and object nouns. Far from primitive,

such languages show a grammatical complexity which can take a lifetime of scholarship to unravel.

[9]Some Indian languages also express subtleties which English glosses over. When I say "He is chopping wood," the words give no hint about how I came to know this. In the Wintu language of northern California, I would say *"pi k'upabe"* if I had seen the woodsman at work. If I had heard but not seen him, I would say *"pi k'upanthe."* If someone told me about it, the form would be *"pi k'upake*—I understand he is chopping wood." Or if I guess the act is going on because that is what the person usually does at this time, I would make it *"pi k'upa'el*—I assume he is chopping wood." Distinctions like these are hard to reconcile with the notion that Wintu is "primitive."

[10]The richness of vocabulary on a given topic varies, depending upon its importance to the community. Woodland Indians have many more words dealing with wood and trees than do Plains Indians. In the southwest elaborate religious ceremonials gave rise to rich ceremonial vocabularies.

[11]Sometimes such evidence helps us reconstruct prehistory. The Iroquois, for instance, have two kinds of traditional religious practices, one associated with the agricultural cycle and the other with the curing and prevention of disease—with the so-called medicine societies. Linguistic studies show that the vocabulary of the healing rites is much older. Since medicine societies are characteristic of northeastern cultures, the evidence suggests that the Iroquois have lived in the northeast a long time. Apparently they are not, as was once thought, recent immigrants from the south who brought agriculture with them. Thus language can serve the culture historian in the way that rock strata help the geologist read the past.

[12]But unlike solid rock, languages are remarkably adaptable, easily borrowing or coining new words as circumstances change. The horse, unknown when the Spanish landed, soon took on a central role among many tribes, and words for the horse and its many uses were introduced. One device was to borrow some form of the Spanish word *caballo*. Another was to invent a descriptive term. Indians of eastern New York State used a word meaning "one rides its back"; in the western part the word for horse means "it hauls out logs." Presumably these were the first uses of horses seen in the two areas. Among the Kwakiutl of British Columbia a steamboat was "fire on its back moving on the water." To the Tsimshian of the same area the word for rice was "looking like maggots."

[13]Borrowing worked both ways. English acquired Indian words for many plants and animals and for aspects of culture first found in North America—such words as raccoon, skunk, moose, squash, pecan, persimmon, moccasin, tipi, wampum, toboggan, totem, succotash, and hominy.

[14]Translation at times mangled the meaning of Indian words. A chief's title which meant "recklessly brave" was recorded in English as "crazy." "Bear bearing down (an opponent)" was rendered "Stumbling Bear." A Kiowa title lauded its holder as a fighter always on the warpath, too busy to remove his horse's saddle blanket; in English the name became "Stinking Saddle Blanket."

[15]Indian languages show a great variety of sounds, but this is not really surprising. We find such variety even among the related languages of Europe; witness the nasal vowels of French, the trilled *r* of Spanish, the "guttural" *ch* of German. Many Indian languages make use of the so-called glottal stop, or catch in the throat (we do the same thing in the middle of the exclamation "oh oh!"). Indian speech treats the stop as a consonant as common as *p* or *t*. And though tone languages of the Chinese variety are lacking, some Indian languages do have a "pitch accent," whereby different syllables of a word are given either high, low, or falling pitch, or some other distinctive pitch pattern.

[16]Attempts by explorers and settlers to spell Indian words could lead to surprising results. The Caddo term *tayša* (pronounced roughly "tie Shah") meant "friend" or "ally"; it often referred to people of the Caddo Confederacy of what is now Louisiana and Texas. The Spanish at the time spelled the *sh* sound as *x*; adding the plural yielded *Texas*. We have reinterpreted the *x* by English conventions and produced a word that sounds quite remote from its origin. Finally, the Caddo borrowed back the word as a place name; in Caddo the Lone Star State is called *tihsis*.

[17]Though Sequoyah's syllabary was the most famous, several Indian writing systems were devised by missionaries to provide religious materials in native languages. The most workable of these was the Cree syllabary invented by James Evans around 1840. A unique feature of Evans's creation is that the orientation of the character indicates the vowel; thus triangles pointed in different directions, ▲, ▼, ▶, ◀, represent the syllables *hee, hay, ho,* and *hah* respectively. The Cree system has been adapted for the Eskimo language and is still in use for both.

[18]Language provides the most elaborate form of human communication, but Indians, like people everywhere, have developed other forms to serve limited functions. Sign language was one of these. Smoke signaling was another; across the open country of the plains and the southwest, Indians apparently employed combinations of long and short puffs to represent such messages as the presence of buffalo or the approach of enemies.

[19]In view of the treatment accorded Indian speakers by Cartier's men and the Europeans who came after, it is remarkable that more than half of the native languages survived into the late 20th centry. But the number of Indian languages in active use continues to decline. Probably the greatest single factor in their disappearance is the increasing importance of mass media in the lives of all of us, including Indians. Radio, the movies, and television have revolutionized the kind of contact people have with the world beyond their immediate surroundings. And almost all of this contact takes place in the English language.

[20]Most Indian communities are aware of the great loss in the disappearance of their languages, and many have established programs to teach their native tongues to the children. It is too early to tell whether such programs will succeed. It may be that only a few of the most widely spoken languages, such as Cree, Ojibwa, Dakota, Cherokee, Navajo, and Eskimo, will survive indefinitely.

[21]The white man has destroyed many fine and beautiful things on this continent, not the least of them the rich cultures that had evolved here for unknown millenniums. Language is the lifeblood of a culture. When the last speaker of a language dies, a wonderful tradition of thought and expressive power, extending from the infinite depths of man's history, dies too. Sadly, such a passing goes almost totally unnoticed, even now, as if an entire world were lost without anyone caring.

COMMENT

"Language and culture are sometimes closely related," Chafe points out, and he illustrates the statement with the Eskimos of the area from Alaska to Greenland. Each of his ideas is illustrated carefully, for they would have little if any meaning without concrete examples. A reader unfamiliar with linguistic ideas probably would not understand the difference between "general concepts" and "specific terms"; the example from

Cherokee not only clarifies the difference but reveals even more complex features of language, including the subtleties possible in Indian languages. The whole discussion is used to develop a thesis—which Chafe delays stating until he has fully illustrated it.

QUESTIONS FOR STUDY AND DISCUSSION

1. What is Chafe's thesis, and where does he state it? How do the many features of Indian languages illustrate it?

2. How does Chafe make transitions from one feature to another? Do you see an order of ideas in the whole essay?

3. How exactly does English gloss over the subtleties Chafe illustrates in paragraph 8?

4. Are the examples in paragraph 12 the same kind of adaptation, or do these show different adaptations?

5. Chafe states in paragraph 14: "Translation at times mangled the meaning of Indian words." Would this statement be clear without an example? Could it be explained without one?

VOCABULARY STUDY

Use your dictionary to investigate the etymology of the following words. Then write a sentence for each, stating what its etymology contributes to your understanding of one or more of its current meanings:

a. cattle	c. deck	e. reveille	g. kibitzer
b. tulip	d. alcohol	f. slogan	h. hoodlum

SUGGESTIONS FOR WRITING

Chafe writes: "Radio, the movies, and television have revolutionized the kind of contact people have with the world beyond their immediate surroundings. And almost all of this contact takes place in the English language." Illustrate how the language you hear in popular songs or in radio and television advertisements influences how you think and feel about one of the following:

a. falling in love
b. getting along with parents
c. making decisions about a career
d. buying a car
e. making friends

process

When we give a set of directions for changing a tire or baking a cake, we are describing a *process*. The process we describe may be a mechanical or invented one, like those just mentioned; or a natural one, like the circulation of the blood; or a historical one, describing something that happened in the past, like making the decision to attend college. Unlike the others named, the historical process happens once only, and the stages or steps of the process are usually described according to strict chronology. In mechanical or invented processes, however, which can happen over and over, there is sometimes a choice of several procedures or tools, and the writer may choose to describe more than one of these—for example, the several kinds of car jack and their operation. Many processes are complex—that is, they contain several related processes, each of which must be carefully distinguished. In writing about such a process, we may have to explain or illustrate terms and make comparisons, and we may also want to comment on the implications of the process as we analyze it. We should not, however, introduce any distracting details unrelated to the process.

MOVING ROCKS

John W. Brainerd

John Brainerd was born in 1918 in Boston, Massachusetts, and was educated at Harvard, where he received his Ph.D. in plant ecology in 1949. In the same year he began teaching at Springfield College in Massachusetts. He worked for the United States Forest Service and Fish and Wildlife Service, and has been

active in the conservation movement, twice receiving awards of
the Massachusetts Audubon Society and receiving also the John
F. Kennedy Conservation Award. The essay printed here is taken
from a book that teaches people how to live in nature.

[1] Most rocks are dense, so all but the smallest are heavy. (A
very few, like frothy lavas, pumice, and tuff, are lighter than water.)
Moving rocks without machine-power is hard work but lets you feel
nature's laws intimately. Gravity is experienced a little differently
than when you lift yourself out of bed, hoist a fork to your mouth, or
pump blood from your feet to your lungs. You will have to both
counteract gravity and use it thoughtfully.

[2] When possible, quarry rock uphill from where you will use it.
When rock removed is surplus at the site, use it as close to the site as
possible, preferably downhill. But don't be tempted to fill a low spot
which should be kept as a hollow. Even cart it uphill for a worthy
purpose.

[3] When lifting rock, bend your knees, not your back, to let your
legs do the work. Keep your toes out from under; you can never
predict when a rock may slip and drop accidentally. Do not let your
fingers be pinched between your rock and another; one slip can in a
second crush a finger or hand if a rock is heavy.

[4] When a stone is too heavy or awkward to lift by yourself, get a
helper. Roll or slide the stone onto a burlap bag or canvas which can
form a sling between you, to distribute the weight and keep it
farther from your feet in case it falls. Stones can be hoisted a bit at a
time by using a *pry bar* at one corner. Slide small stones or sticks
under the lifted edge to hold it up while you repeat the process at
another corner. More help comes from using a *block-and-tackle*
pulley system hung from a *tripod* for lifting straight up or from a
gin pole for swinging stones sideways.

[5] When possible, roll or slide a large stone rather than lift it.
When rolling a large stone, do not get down-hill from it. Roll stones
at right angles to their short axis, except sometimes when rounding
a corner; then be extra careful. When moving a large stone that does
not roll easily, use a *following stone* to hold it up partially while you
prepare for your next shove. Use a *nudging stick* to poke the
following stone under, thus keeping your fingers out. Use a pry bar
(crowbar, strong pole, or iron pipe) to lift a corner of a heavy stone or

From *Working with Nature: A Practical Guide* by John W. Brainerd. Copyright
© 1973 by Oxford University Press, Inc. Reprinted by permission.

to slide it. Prepare the surface along which a stone is to be rolled or slid. Remove obstacles, grade the way, or provide a plank. Greasing a plank reduces friction for sliding. A rock rolled onto it can often best be moved not by sliding the rock on the plank but by putting rollers such as short logs under it and moving the entire plank with the stone on it. (This is probably the most primitive wagon, forerunner of modern diesel trucks.) The larger the diameter of the rollers, the more easily they traverse the terrain, but the higher the stone must be hoisted to put it on the plank, or the higher the plank must be lifted with the stone to put it on the rollers.

[6]If a stone is too large to lift, roll, or slide by manpower supplemented by simple machines like inclined planes, levers, and pulleys, you can perhaps solve your problem by breaking the stone into movable pieces; or give in and hire a bulldozer and truck. Or maybe you decide the rock belongs where it is "to hold the world together," so you work creatively around it, enjoying it.

COMMENT

Brainerd's purpose is to give instructions on moving rocks—not to describe a landscape or arouse feelings of pleasure or disgust concerning it. But he takes time anyway to comment on the feeling of the experience and its difference from other activities. He wants his reader to remember that rocks may have their own purposes, but he does not insist. His main concern is with several processes—quarrying rock, lifting and rolling and sliding it. Each process is described in the order in which the steps are performed; terms are defined through their use in the process (illustrations that accompany this discussion in Brainerd's book have been omitted here).

QUESTIONS FOR STUDY AND DISCUSSION

1. The opening paragraph states the purpose of the discussion and the chief problem to be solved. What is that problem and what instructions bear on it?

2. The author first describes how to lift rocks, then how to roll or slide them. Given what he tells us about these processes, did he first have to tell us how to lift them? Could these processes have been described in reverse order?

3. In paragraph 5 the author twice pauses to define his terms and to digress briefly. Is his digression needed to understand the process?

4. How does the final sentence reveal the author's attitude toward nature and working outdoors? What impression do you get of him in the whole discussion?

5. If the author wanted to focus on how to "feel nature's laws intimately," how might he have organized the details and presented them?

6. If you were describing how to start a fire in an open field, what steps would have to be presented chronologically? What additional details might be presented without disturbing the focus?

VOCABULARY STUDY

Brainerd defines or illustrates several words in the essay elsewhere in his book. Select several of the words unfamiliar to you and, with the use of your dictionary, write definitions of them in your own words.

SUGGESTIONS FOR WRITING

1. Describe how to change a bicycle or automobile tire or how to thread and operate a sewing machine or how to knit or crochet—or a similar process. Assume that your reader knows nothing about the tools or machinery required. Before writing consider what details must be provided and what terms defined at each stage of the process.

2. Certain jobs can be performed in more than one way—for example, training a dog not to jump on people. Discuss the various ways of doing a similar job. Keep these ways distinct for your reader.

3. Trace a historical process like making the decision to attend college. Comment on the implications of some of the stages of this process as you describe it.

HOW TO EAT AN ICE-CREAM CONE

L. Rust Hills

L. Rust Hills was born in 1924 in Brooklyn, New York, and attended the United States Merchant Marine Academy and Wesleyan University. He was fiction editor of *Esquire* and *The Saturday Evening Post*, has taught writing, and is now a free-lance writer.

[1]Before you even get the cone, you have to do a lot of planning about it. We'll assume that you lost the argument in the car and that the family has decided to break the automobile journey and stop at an ice-cream stand for cones. Get things straight with them right from the start. Tell them that after they have their cones there will be an imaginary circle six feet away from the car and that no one—man, woman, or especially child—will be allowed to cross the line and reënter the car until his ice-cream cone has been entirely consumed and he has cleaned himself up. Emphasize: Automobiles and ice-cream cones don't mix. Explain: Melted ice cream, children, is a fluid that is eternally sticky. One drop of it on a car-door handle spreads to the seat covers, to trousers, to hands, and thence to the steering wheel, the gearshift, the rearview mirror, all the knobs of the dashboard—spreads *everywhere* and lasts *forever,* spreads from a nice old car like this, which might have to be abandoned because of stickiness, right into a nasty new car, in secret ways that even scientists don't understand. If necessary, even make a joke: "The family that eats ice-cream cones together sticks together." Then let their mother explain the joke and tell them you don't mean half of what you say, and no, we won't be getting a new car.

[2]Blessed are the children who always eat the same flavor of ice cream or always know beforehand what kind they will want. Such good children should be quarantined from those who want to "wait and see what flavors there are." It's a sad thing to observe a beautiful young child who has always been perfectly happy with a plain vanilla ice-cream cone being subverted by a young schoolmate who has been invited along for the weekend—a pleasant and polite visitor, perhaps, but spoiled by permissive parents and scarred by an overactive imagination. This schoolmate has a flair for contingency planning: "Well, I'll have banana if they have banana, but if they don't have banana then I'll have peach, if it's fresh peach, and if they don't have banana or fresh peach I'll see what else they have that's like that, like maybe fresh strawberry or something, and if they don't have that or anything like that that's good I'll just have chocolate marshmallow chip or chocolate ripple or something like that." Then—turning to one's own once simple and innocent child, now already corrupt and thinking fast—the schoolmate invites a similar rigmarole. "What kind are *you* going to have?"

From *How to Do Things Right* by L. Rust Hills. First appeared in *The New Yorker,* copyright © 1968 by The New Yorker Magazine, Inc. Reprinted by permission of Doubleday & Company, Inc.

[3]I'm a great believer in contingency planning, but none of this is realistic. Few adults, and even fewer children, are able to make up their minds beforehand what kind of ice-cream cone they'll want. It would be nice if they could all be lined up in front of the man who is making up the cones and just snap smartly when their turn came, "Strawberry, please," "Vanilla, please," "Chocolate, please." But of course it never happens like that. There is always a great discussion, a great jostling and craning of necks and leaning over the counter to see down into the tubs of ice cream, and much interpersonal consultation—"What kind are *you* having?"—back and forth, as if that should make any difference. Until finally the first child's turn comes and he asks the man, "What kinds do you have?"

[4]Now, this is the stupidest question in the world, because there is always a sign posted saying what kinds of ice cream they have. As I tell the children, that's what they put the sign up there for—so you won't have to ask what kinds of ice cream they have. The man gets sick of telling everybody all the different kinds of ice cream they have, so they put a sign up there that *says*. You're supposed to read it, not ask the man.

[5]"All right, but the sign doesn't say strawberry."

[6]"Well, that means they don't have strawberry."

[7]"But there *is* strawberry, right there."

[8]"That must be raspberry or something." (Look again at the sign. Raspberry isn't there, either.)

[9]When the child's turn actually comes, he says, "Do you have strawberry?"

[10]"Sure."

[11]"What other kinds do you have?"

[12]The trouble is, of course, that they put up that sign saying what flavors they have, with little cardboard inserts to put in or take out flavors, way back when they first opened the store. But they never change the sign—or not often enough. They always have flavors that aren't on the list, and often they don't have flavors that *are* on the list. Children know this—whether innately or from earliest experience it would be hard to say. The ice-cream man knows it, too. Even grownups learn it eventually. There will always be chaos and confusion and mind-changing and general uproar when ice-cream cones are being ordered, and there has not been, is not, and will never be any way to avoid it.

[13]Human beings are incorrigibly restless and dissatisfied, always in search of new experiences and sensations, seldom content

with the familiar. It is this, I think, that accounts for people wanting to have a taste of your cone, and wanting you to have a taste of theirs. "*Do* have a taste of this fresh peach—it's delicious," my wife used to say to me, very much (I suppose) the way Eve wanted Adam to taste her delicious apple. An insinuating look of calculating curiosity would film my wife's eyes—the same look those beautiful, scary women in those depraved Italian films give a man they're interested in. "How's *yours?*" she would say. For this reason, I always order chocolate chip now. Down through the years, all those close enough to me to feel entitled to ask for a taste of my cone— namely, my wife and children—have learned what chocolate chip tastes like, so they have no legitimate reason to ask me for a taste. As for testing other people's cones, never do it. The reasoning here is that if it tastes good, you'll wish you'd had it; if it tastes bad, you'll have had a taste of something that tastes bad; if it doesn't taste either good or bad, then you won't have missed anything. Of course no person in his right mind ever *would* want to taste anyone else's cone, but it is useful to have good, logical reasons for hating the thought of it.

[14]Another important thing. Never let the man hand you the ice-cream cones for the whole group. There is no sight more pathetic than some bumbling disorganized papa holding four ice-cream cones in two hands, with his money still in his pocket, when the man says, "Eighty cents." What does he do then? He can't hand the cones back to the man to hold while he fishes in his pocket for the money, for the man has just given them to *him.* He can start passing them out to the kids, but at least one of them will have gone back to the car to see how the dog is doing, or have been sent round in back by his mother to wash his hands or something. And even if papa does get them distributed, he's still going to be left with his own cone in one hand while he tries to get his money with the other. Meanwhile, of course, the man is very impatient, and the next group is asking him, "What flavors do you have?"

[15]No, never let the man hand you the cones of others. Make him hand them out to each kid in turn. That way, too, you won't get those disgusting blobs of butter pecan and black raspberry on your own chocolate chip. And insist that he tell you how much it all costs and settle with him *before* he hands you your own cone. Make sure everyone has got paper napkins and everything *before* he hands you your own cone. Get *everything* straight before he hands you your own cone. Then, as he hands you your own cone, reach out and take

it from him. Strange, magical, dangerous moment! It shares something of the mysterious, sick thrill that soldiers are said to feel on the eve of a great battle.

[16]Now, consider for a moment just exactly what it is that you are about to be handed. It is a huge, irregular mass of ice cream, faintly domed at the top from the metal scoop, which has first produced it and then insecurely balanced it on the uneven top edge of a hollow inverted cone made out of the most brittle and fragile of materials. Clumps of ice cream hang over the side, very loosely attached to the main body. There is always much more ice cream than the cone could hold, even if the ice cream were tamped down into the cone, which of course it isn't. And the essence of ice cream is that it melts. It doesn't just stay there teetering in this irregular, top-heavy mass; it also melts. And it melts *fast.* And it doesn't just melt—it melts into a sticky fluid that *cannot* be wiped off. The only thing one person could hand to another that might possibly be more dangerous is a live hand grenade from which the pin had been pulled five seconds earlier. And of course if anybody offered you that, you could say, "Oh. Uh, well—no thanks."

[17]Ice-cream men handle cones routinely, and are inured. They are like professionals who are used to handling sticks of TNT; their movements are quick and skillful. An ice-cream man will pass a cone to you casually, almost carelessly. Never accept a cone on this basis! Too many brittle sugar cones (the only good kind) are crushed or chipped or their ice-cream tops knocked askew, by this casual sort of transfer from hand to hand. If the ice-cream man is attempting this kind of brusque transfer, keep your hands at your side, no matter what effort it may cost you to overcome the instinct by which everyone's hand goes out, almost automatically, whenever he is proffered something delicious and expected. Keep your hands at your side, and the ice-cream man will look up at you, startled, questioning. Lock his eyes with your own, and *then,* slowly, calmly, and above all deliberately, take the cone from him.

[18]Grasp the cone with the right hand firmly but gently between thumb and at least one but not more than three fingers, two-thirds of the way up the cone. Then dart swiftly away to an open area, away from the jostling crowd at the stand. Now take up the classic ice-cream-cone-eating stance: feet from one to two feet apart, body bent forward from the waist at a twenty-five-degree angle, right elbow well up, right forearm horizontal, at a level with your collarbone and about twelve inches from it. But don't start eating yet!

Check first to see what emergency repairs may be necessary. Sometimes a sugar cone will be so crushed or broken or cracked that all one can do is gulp at the thing like a savage, getting what he can of it and letting the rest drop to the ground, and then evacuating the area of catastrophe as quickly as possible. Checking the cone for possible trouble can be done in a second or two, if one knows where to look and does it systematically. A trouble spot some people overlook is the bottom tip of the cone. This may have been broken off. Or the flap of the cone material at the bottom, usually wrapped over itself in that funny spiral construction, may be folded in a way that is imperfect and leaves an opening. No need to say that through this opening—in a matter of perhaps thirty or, at most, ninety seconds—will begin to pour hundreds of thousands of sticky molecules of melted ice cream. You know in this case that you must instantly get the paper napkin in your left hand under and around the bottom of the cone to stem the forthcoming flow, or else be doomed to eat the cone far too rapidly. It is a grim moment. No one wants to eat a cone under that kind of pressure, but neither does anyone want to end up with the bottom of the cone stuck to a messy napkin. There's one other alternative—one that takes both skill and courage: Forgoing any cradling action, grasp the cone more firmly between thumb and forefinger and extend the other fingers so that they are out of the way of the dripping from the bottom, then increase the waist-bend angle from twenty-five degrees to thirty-five degrees, and then eat the cone, *allowing* it to drip out of the bottom onto the ground in front of you! Experienced and thoughtful cone-eaters enjoy facing up to this kind of sudden challenge.

[19]So far, we have been concentrating on cone problems, but of course there is the ice cream to worry about, too. In this area, immediate action is sometimes needed on three fronts at once. Frequently the ice cream will be mounted on the cone in a way that is perilously lopsided. This requires immediate corrective action to move it back into balance—a slight pressure downward with the teeth and lips to seat the ice cream more firmly in and on the cone, but not so hard, of course, as to break the cone. On other occasions, gobs of ice cream will be hanging loosely from the main body, about to fall to the ground (bad) or onto one's hand (far, far worse). This requires instant action, too; one must snap at the gobs like a frog in a swarm of flies. Sometimes, trickles of ice cream will already (already!) be running down the cone toward one's fingers, and one

must quickly raise the cone, tilting one's face skyward, and lick with an upward motion that pushes the trickles away from the fingers and (as much as possible) into one's mouth. Every ice-cream cone is like every other ice-cream cone in that it potentially can present all of these problems, but each ice-cream cone is paradoxically unique in that it will present the problems in a different order of emergency and degree of severity. It is, thank God, a rare ice-cream cone that will present all three kinds of problems in exactly the same degree of emergency. With each cone, it is necessary to make an instantaneous judgment as to where the greatest danger is, and to *act!* A moment's delay, and the whole thing will be a mess before you've even tasted it *(Fig. 1)*. If it isn't possible to decide between any two of the three basic emergency problems (i.e., lopsided mount, dangling gobs, running trickles), allow yourself to make an arbitrary adjudication; assign a "heads" value to one and a "tails" value to the other, then flip a coin to decide which is to be tended to first. Don't, for heaven's sake, *actually* flip a coin—you'd

Fig. 1

have to dig in your pockets for it, or else have it ready in your hand before you were handed the cone. There isn't remotely enough time for anything like that. Just decide *in your mind* which came up, heads or tails, and then try to remember as fast as you can which of the problems you had assigned to the winning side of the coin. Probably, though, there isn't time for any of this. Just do something, however arbitrary. Act! *Eat!*

[20]In trying to make wise and correct decisions about the ice-cream cone in your hand, you should always keep the objectives in mind. The main objective, of course, is to get the cone under control. Secondarily, one will want to eat the cone calmly and with pleasure. Real pleasure lies not simply in eating the cone but in eating it *right*. Let us assume that you have darted to your open space and made your necessary emergency repairs. The cone is still dangerous—still, so to speak, "live." But you can now proceed with it in an orderly fashion. First, revolve the cone through the full three hundred and sixty degrees, snapping at the loose gobs of ice cream; turn the cone by moving the thumb away from you and the forefinger toward you, so the cone moves counterclockwise. Then, with the cone still "wound," which will require the wrist to be bent at the full right angle toward you, apply pressure with the mouth and tongue to accomplish overall realignment, straightening and settling the

whole mess. Then, unwinding the cone back through the full three hundred and sixty degrees, remove any trickles of ice cream. From here on, some supplementary repairs may be necessary, but the cone is now defused.

[21] At this point, you can risk a glance around you. How badly the others are doing with their cones! Now you can settle down to eating yours. This is done by eating the ice cream off the top. At each bite, you must press down cautiously, so that the ice cream settles farther and farther into the cone. Be very careful not to break the cone. Of course, you never take so much ice cream into your mouth at once that it hurts your teeth; for the same reason, you never let unmelted ice cream into the back of your mouth. If all these procedures are

Fig. 2

followed correctly, you should shortly arrive at the ideal—the way an ice-cream cone is always pictured but never actually is when it is handed to you *(Fig. 2)*. The ice cream should now form a small dome whose circumference exactly coincides with the large circumference of the cone itself—a small skullcap that fits exactly on top of a larger, inverted dunce cap. You have made order out of chaos; you are an artist. You have taken an unnatural, abhorrent, irregular, chaotic form, and from it you have sculpted an

ordered, ideal shape that might be envied by Praxiteles or even Euclid.

[22] Now at last you can begin to take little nibbles of the cone itself, being very careful not to crack it. Revolve the cone so that its rim remains smooth and level as you eat both ice cream and cone in the same ratio. Because of the geometrical nature of things, a constantly reduced inverted cone still remains a perfect inverted cone no matter how small it grows, just as a constantly reduced dome held within a cone retains *its* shape. Because you are constantly reshaping the dome of ice cream with your tongue and nibbling at the cone, it follows in logic—and in actual practice, if you are skillful and careful—that the cone will continue to look exactly the same, except for its size, as you eat it down, so that at the very end you will hold between your thumb and forefinger a tiny, idealized replica of an ice-cream cone, a thing perhaps one inch high. Then, while the others are licking their sticky fingers, preparatory to wiping them on their clothes, or going back to the ice-cream stand for more paper napkins to try to clean themselves up—*then* you can hold the miniature cone up for everyone to see, and pop it gently into your mouth.

COMMENT

Hills is writing about the joys of eating ice-cream cones, and he is writing humorously. The problems he describes are real ones, but these are part of the fun of eating ice-cream cones, and he knows that his readers will share this view. He therefore can describe the process of eating a cone without having to present each step in order. He is instructing his reader in each step, though the reader probably knows all of the details. The purpose of the essay, then, is to give the pleasure of recognition. The many kinds of analysis—from comparison and contrast to process—can be used for many different purposes, as this delightful essay shows.

QUESTIONS FOR STUDY AND DISCUSSION

1. What in the description of the process depends on the reader's recognition of the problems? How does Hills remind the reader of these problems?

2. What explains the order of the steps in the process? Is Hills moving from the easier to the more difficult steps, or has he chosen another principle of order?

3. What is the overall tone of the essay? How do the drawings contribute to it?

4. Are the various statements about human nature to be taken seriously, though they are presented humorously?

5. The most effective humor develops out of genuine problems and observations—not out of invented ones. Is this true of the humor of this essay?

6. What impression do you get of the writer—his personality, his outlook on life perhaps, his sense of humor?

VOCABULARY STUDY

Formal words will often seem humorous in an informal setting: "This schoolmate has a flair for *contingency* planning. . . ." Identify formal words of this sort in the essay, and explain the humor they provide.

SUGGESTIONS FOR WRITING

Write a humorous description of a process similar to eating an ice-cream cone—perhaps wrapping a large gift, or eating an unfamiliar food for the first time. Let your details reveal something unusual and important about human beings.

COVERING A SPOT NEWS STORY

Robert W. Tyrrell

Robert W. Tyrrell was born in Harwich, England, in 1929. He has worked as a newspaper man and for twenty years as a radio and television reporter, writer, director and producer, mainly in Great Britain. Several of his television documentaries have won awards, and he has produced programs for American television. He now makes industrial and information films.

[1] A newsflash comes over the teleprinter—fire at a paint warehouse. Armed only with this and the location of the fire, he sets out with no idea of how the story will turn out. As an old hand, he knows enough to take some protective clothing—an old hat, a waterproof coat, gum boots, a pair of gloves. As an old hand, he also knows that most fires look alike on the screen unless some special feature is clearly picked out in the viewfinder. This one should be fairly spectacular—it's probably a big paint store, being in the docks area, and there must be a lot of other buildings close by. As he nears the scene, he notices the large cloud of black smoke billowing up. Worth a shot? No. It is not spectacular enough yet, and by the time he finds a good vantage point to film it, he may be missing better shots closer to the blaze.

[2] Sooner or later, his car is stopped by police. A quick word, and he is allowed to park out of the way of fire engines. On with the protective clothing, stuff some spare rolls of film in the pockets, sling the camera battery over one shoulder, and go in on foot. As the earliest cameraman on the scene, he must get first the basic shots before trying to build up any special story. He starts to look for scenes that show the blazing building with some action in the foreground to give it scale. Check the exposure value of flames, daylight and shadow, work out a compromise diaphragm setting, focus the lens at fifteen or twenty feet, set the zoom at wide angle. This is no time or place for a tripod: if necessary, the camera can be kept steady by leaning on a wall or resting the elbows on a car roof.

[3] After establishing shots of the blaze itself, he turns to cut-in

shots of the firemen, their faces lit by the orange glow. A low angle
will dramatise them, so he drops on one knee and shoots up, keeping
the hoses and water jets running from corner to corner of the frame.
The sound of a siren alerts him to the arrival of another fire engine,
and he gets a shot of it drawing up and the firemen leaping out. As
soon as their feet touch the ground, he switches off, hurries round to
another angle and films again as they unload their gear. With so
much movement and the change of angle, it will all look like one
continuous action.

⁴With nearly a hundred feet (or about three minutes) shot,
there is enough now to give the basic coverage of the story, and
there is time to find out how the fight against the fire is going.
Keeping an eye on the blaze, he seizes the chance to talk to a fire
officer. The firemen, he learns, have written off the paint warehouse, and are now trying to prevent the flames from spreading to
the buildings nearby. What do they contain? Sugar. The only evidence of this on the outside is the nameplate of a well-known sugar
firm. He finds an angle to film this, and pans from it to the burning
building, then films the firemen spraying the roof with water.
Sparks are falling. Looking around, he sees a pool of water, and
films a close shot of the sparks falling into it. This takes some time.
Such shots always do. The problem is to find an angle where the
sparks can be seen clearly and separately from the general orange
and yellow glow over everything. To integrate the shot more closely
with the rest of the footage, he seizes the chance to ask a passing
fireman to walk through the puddle, and pans with his feet into a
long shot of the sugar warehouse.

⁵It is now 3 pm. The next newscast is at 6 pm. There is just time
to get the film back. He hurries to the car, and calls the office on the
radio. They tell him to stay with the story. A despatch rider is on his
way to collect the film, and is telephoning in to know exactly where
the cameraman is. The news desk has been following the agency
tapes on the fire story, and there is a report that sabotage may be
involved. They have decided to send a sound unit. Does he know that
a fireman is reported seriously injured?

⁶Rapidly, the cameraman scribbles a dope sheet, parcels up the
exposed film with camera tape, and leaves it on the seat of the car.
He reports what he has done and the exact position of the car, to the
office, then heads back to the blaze, taking fresh film with him.

⁷Contact with base is vital for a cameraman. Nothing changes

and develops so fast as news, and what looked like a number one story at nine o'clock can be relegated to the spares category at ten. A reporter or cameraman who does not check with base is a liability to the office and to himself.

COMMENT

Considering one's audience is particularly crucial in process analysis, for the author must decide what special terms need definition. This essay is part of a book that reviews the various skills and assignments of the television journalist. If Tyrrell were instructing a student cinematographer in the operation described, he probably would define *pan* and *compromise diaphragm setting*. Too much definition, however, will distract the reader from the main process. For this reason definitions are sometimes made before the description of the process begins.

QUESTIONS FOR STUDY AND DISCUSSION

1. What special terms are defined by their context—by the use Tyrrell makes of them?

2. At what points does he interrupt the process to discuss problems?

3. Is the analysis presented entirely in chronological order?

4. At what points does Tyrrell use formal transitions, and where does he depend instead on pronoun reference and the repetition of key words?

5. What details of the scene does Tyrrell present, and why does he choose these, given his purpose in writing?

VOCABULARY STUDY

Identify the special terms and see whether your dictionary defines them. Check the reference section of your library for special dictionaries concerned with photography and cinematography.

SUGGESTIONS FOR WRITING

1. Rewrite those sentences in the essay that contain special terms. Briefly define the terms without disturbing the focus on the passage.

2. Describe a process that uses complicated equipment like the camera. Keep a particular audience in mind and define only those terms that would be unfamiliar to them.

cause
and
effect

Cause-and-effect reasoning is often a simple connecting of two events. When I come in soaking wet during a thunderstorm, I know that rain is the cause of my being wet. But usually making connections is not this simple. If I catch cold the same day, I blame it on the rain. The fact is that I might have caught cold even if I had not been outside; and if I had been, the rain by itself probably would not have been the single cause. A number of conditions probably acted together to produce the cold: a run-down state arising from overwork and lack of sleep, bad eating habits, a virus waiting to be "triggered," and exposure to the storm, which may have triggered the virus. If in the past I caught colds under the identical circumstances, I have good reason to believe I have discovered the conditions that produced the cold. The sum of these conditions is in the broadest sense what we mean by "cause." But we may point to one or more of them as the "cause" also. Notice that causal reasoning is always of a probable nature, except where an immediate action (exposure to the storm) produces a direct and certain consequence (getting wet). Having identified the conditions that produced a cold in the past, I cannot be sure that their occurrence in the present *must* produce one again. The identical conditions may be present in the future, without producing a cold.

Informal discussions of cause and effect appeal to common sense as well as probability, and usually indicate in what limited way causes will be identified. Implied in all discussions of cause and effect are assumptions or beliefs about people, society, and behavior: human beings are aggressive by nature; the Irish have hot tempers; adolescents are naturally rebellious; little girls are sugar and spice and everything nice; cats and dogs are natural enemies; opposites attract. Such assumptions are sometimes left unstated because writers accept them as "givens"—that is, they assume that their readers would agree to the statement without question—or because they do not know that they hold the belief. In testing the causal reasoning of an essay, it is sometimes necessary to ask whether the details or evidence are based on and support a hidden assumption.

VIOLENCE: TV'S CROWD-CATCHER

Robert Lewis Shayon

> Robert Lewis Shayon was born in New York City. He has worked as a producer for CBS and NBC, written for television, and written a column on television and other media for *Saturday Review*. He teaches at the Annenberg School of Communications at the University of Pennsylvania.

[1] The President's Commission on the Causes and Prevention of Violence continues to hold hearings and to conduct studies on the subject of violence in TV programs. The commission's activities have energized the press to make surveys of its own. The editors of *McCall's* recently urged its readers to write letters to television executives to protest against the outpouring of TV violence. *The Christian Science Monitor* has reported the results of a six-week survey that show that video violence "still rides high on the air-

waves, in spite of assurances by network chiefs that they are doing all they can to minimize the incidence of shootings, stabbings, killings, and beatings."

[2]Social scientists discuss for the commission members the subtleties of defining violence, calculating its effects in terms of aggression, catharsis, and impact on social norms. Some witnesses have urged regulation and control even though research has as yet established no clear, causal relationship between violence in the media and in real life. Nobody, however, seems willing to talk about the true options that are available to the public, as it tries to decide what ought to be done about the problem of violence on TV. The implicit assumptions are that networks could cut down violence if they really wanted to do it; that corporations and advertising agencies have the power to reform the networks if they wished.

[3]Thus, Dr. Leo Bogart, general manager of the Bureau of Advertising of the American Newspaper Publishers Association, told the Commission on Violence that "it must appeal to top managers of corporations . . . in order to induce change in TV programing, and other advertiser-supported media. There is still among them an overwhelming acceptance of the need to do what is right." Perhaps so, but the question is not one of regulation by the industry, government, or any other constituted authority of "them" (people in TV). The real question is whether we—all of us—wish to regulate the American way of life, which is inextricably interwoven with violence on TV.

[4]To understand what the game is all about, one has to get rid of the notion that television is in the program business; nothing could be further from the truth. Television is in the crowd-catching business. The networks and stations are instant crowd-catchers who deliver their catch to the advertisers who inoculate them with consumer messages. Proof of this is at hand in any broadcasting or advertising trade journal, where broadcasters, addressing their real clients, boast of what great crowd-catchers they are at how cheap a cost.

[5]The catching of instant crowds is necessary for the sale of instant tea, coffee, headache relief, spot remover, and other assorted goods and services—not for profit maximization, as John Kenneth Galbraith has argued, but for the instant managing of demand. Planned growth, in his theory, is the driving rod of our industrial

state; growth depends on assured flow of capital for long-term projections. Corporations cannot depend on the whims of the old "free market"—where the consumer was sovereign—for steady, reliable demand. Therefore, demand has to be "managed." Advertising is the manager, and broadcasting is the crowd-catcher.

[6]Now, the essence of the art of catching crowds is conflict—the most contagious of all human experiences, the universal language. Of conflict there are many varieties, ranging from parliamentary debates and elections to strikes, games, and fights. Television could, and occasionally does, present conflicts of ideas, but you can't run a crowd-catching business at this level. Instant crowds require simple phenomena, quickly grasped. Furthermore, ideas are controversial, dangerous; people have convictions, they take sides, are easily offended. Crowd-catchers want only happy consumers.

[7]The type of conflict that will deliver instant crowds most efficiently is physical violence. Consider what would happen if a crowd had three viewing choices on a street: watching a clown, a nude woman, or a no-holds-barred fight—which do you think would attract the biggest crowd? Physical violence grows in mesmeric power, while sex and humor diminish relatively. Violence, internal and external, is the young generation's hang-up, not sex. This is the way our world is; TV tells us so—TV is the true curriculum of our society. We fear violence and enjoy it with guilt, because it calls to our own deeply latent potential for violence in response to a violent world. With such a sure-fire, instant crowd-catcher providing the essential energy which runs our industries, our networks, our advertising agencies—in short, our style of life—to call for the voluntary or involuntary regulation of violence on TV is to call for instant self-destruction of the system. By "system," I mean TV based on advertiser support. Television can run on a different system, of course; it does so in other countries. Public funds can support TV directly; license-fees on sets, along with marginal income from controlled advertising, can provide another basis. But to choose another system is to opt for another style of life, one where corporate and consumer acquisitions are not the dominant values.

[8]If the American citizen is to be addressed maturely on the subject of violence in TV, he ought, at least, to be accorded the dignity of being told what his real choices are. Anything less—any talk of regulating and minimizing physical violence on TV, while

retaining the present advertiser-supported crowd-catching system—is to contribute to instant self-delusion.

COMMENT

Shayon is concerned with several cause-and-effect relationships in his discussion of television violence. The cause, he tries to show, is "the American way of life"—which he identifies with the "advertiser-supported crowd-catching system." The relationship is not, however, a direct one, nor does Shayon suggest it is. Advertisers support physical violence on television not because they want to promote violence but because it can best "deliver instant crowds." American business executives make certain assumptions about people—and so does Shayon. We know that his argument is merely probable, not certain, for he appeals to experience for support; it is from experience that he has drawn his own assumptions. The strength of his reasoning depends on the strength of his one example—the probable behavior of the street crowd. He does not try to probe deeply into the "hang-up" with violence. He can merely assert that this hang-up exists and ask his reader to consider his "real choices." The discussion is informal; Shayon does not try to deal with the problem as the social scientists mentioned in paragraph 2 probably would.

QUESTIONS FOR STUDY AND DISCUSSION

1. How does Shayon identify the "implicit assumptions" in the public discussion of television violence?

2. What does Shayon assume about the viewing habits and attitudes of his reader toward television violence? Is he addressing himself to readers who share the views of *McCall's* and *The Christian Science Monitor?*

3. In what ways is "the American way of life . . . inextricably interwoven with violence on TV"? Is Shayon saying that Americans are basically prone to violence, and always have been?

4. Is Shayon opposing planned growth in his comments on the "system," or is his analysis a limited one? Is he suggesting that it is possible to change the system, or that it is possible only to change one's thinking about television violence? What exactly is Shayon recommending?

5. How would you answer the question he asks about the street crowd? If you disagree with his comments on Americans today, need you disagree with his analysis of television violence? Do you think he has identified its cause?

VOCABULARY STUDY

Write a paraphrase of paragraphs 2 and 7. Be sure to explain the following in your own words: *catharsis, social norms,* and *true curriculum.*

SUGGESTIONS FOR WRITING

1. Draw on your experience with and attitudes toward physical violence on television and in everyday life to answer Shayon's question and comment on his views.

2. Shayon wrote his essay in 1969. Discuss how much you believe the situation he describes has changed in the late seventies. Comment on the issue of television violence today compared to other issues, such as legalized marijuana.

WHY SMALLER REFRIGERATORS CAN PRESERVE THE HUMAN RACE

Appletree Rodden

Appletree Rodden did research in biochemistry at Stanford University and has been a member of the Staatstheater Ballet Company, in West Germany.

[1] Once, long ago, people had special little boxes called refrigerators in which milk, meat, and eggs could be kept cool. The grandchildren of these simple devices are large enough to store whole cows, and they reach temperatures comparable to those at the South Pole.

Their operating costs increase each year, and they are so complicated that few home handymen attempt to repair them on their own.

[2] Why has this change in size and complexity occurred in America? It has not taken place in many areas of the technologically advanced world (the average West German refrigerator is about a yard high and less than a yard wide, yet refrigeration technology in Germany is quite advanced). Do we really need (or even want) all that space and cold?

[3] The benefits of a large refrigerator are apparent: a saving of time (one grocery-shopping trip a week instead of several), a saving of money (the ability to buy expensive, perishable items in larger, cheaper quantities), a feeling of security (if the car breaks down or if famine strikes, the refrigerator is well stocked). The costs are there, too, but they are not so obvious.

[4] Cost number one is psychological. Ever since the refrigerator began to grow, food has increasingly become something we buy to store rather than to eat. Few families go to market daily for their daily bread. The manna in the wilderness could be gathered for only one day at a time. The ancient distaste for making food a storage item is echoed by many modern psychiatrists who suggest that such psychosomatic disorders as obesity are often due to the patient's inability to come to terms with the basic transitoriness of life. Research into a relationship between excessive corpulence and the size of one's refrigerator has not been extensive, but we might suspect one to be there.

[5] Another cost is aesthetic. In most of Europe, where grocery marketing is still a part of the daily rhythm, one can buy tomatoes, lettuce, and the like picked on the day of purchase. Many European families have modest refrigerators for storing small items (eggs, milk, butter) for a couple of days, but the concept of buying large quantities of food to store in the refrigerator is not widely accepted. Since fresh produce is easily available in Europe, most people buy it daily.

[6] Which brings to mind another price the large refrigerator has cost us: the friendly neighborhood market. In America, time is money. A large refrigerator means fewer time-consuming trips to the grocery store. One member of a deep-freeze-owning family can do the grocery shopping once or twice a month rather than daily. Since shopping trips are infrequent, most people have been willing

to forego the amenities of the little store around the corner in favor of the lower prices found in the supermarket.

[7] If refrigerators weren't so large—that is, if grocery marketing were a daily affair—the "entertainment surcharge" of buying farm-fresh food in a smaller, more intimate setting might carry some weight. But as it is, there is not really that much difference between eggs bought from Farmer Brown's wife and eggs bought from the supermarket which in turn bought them from Eggs Incorporated, a firm operated out of Los Angeles that produces 200,000 eggs a day from chickens that are kept in gigantic warehouses lighted artificially on an eighteen-hour light-and-dark cycle and produce one-and-a-half times as many eggs—a special breed of chickens who die young and insane. Not much difference if you don't mind eating eggs from crazy chickens.

[8] Chalk up Farmer and Mrs. Brown as cost number four of the big refrigerator. The small farmer can't make it in a society dominated by supermarkets and big refrigerators; make way for super-farmers, super yields, and pesticides (cost number five).

[9] Cost number six of the big refrigerator has been the diminution of regional food differences. Of course the homogenization of American fare cannot be blamed solely on the availability of frozen food. Nonetheless, were it not for the trend toward turning regional specialties into frozen dinners, it might still be possible to experience novelty closer to home.

[10] So much for the disadvantages of the big refrigerator. What about the advantages of the small one? First of all, it would help us to "think small," which is what we must learn anyway if the scary predictions of the Club of Rome *(The Limits of Growth)* are true. The advent of smaller refrigerators would set the stage for reversing the "big-thinking" trends brought on with the big refrigerator, and would eventually change our lives.

[11] Ivan Illich makes the point in *Tools for Conviviality* that any tool we use (the automobile, standardized public education, public-health care, the refrigerator) influences the individual, his society, and the relationship between the two. A person's automobile is a part of his identity. The average Volkswagen owner has a variety of characteristics (income, age, occupation) significantly different from those of the average Cadillac owner. American society, with more parking lots than parks, and with gridded streets rather than winding lanes, would be vastly different without the private automobile.

Similar conclusions can be drawn about any of the tools we use. They change us. They change our society. Therefore, it behooves us to think well before we decide which tool to use to accomplish a given task. Do we want tools that usurp power unto themselves, the ones called "non-convivial" by Illich?

[12]The telephone, a "convivial tool," has remained under control; it has not impinged itself on society or on the individual. Each year it has become more efficient, and it has not prevented other forms of communication (letter writing, visits). The world might be poorer without the telephone, but it would not be grossly different. Telephones do not pollute, are not status symbols, and interact only slightly (if at all) with one's self-image.

[13]So what about the refrigerator? Or back to the more basic problem to which the refrigerator was a partial answer: what about our supply of food? When did we decide to convert the emotion-laden threat of starvation from a shared community problem (of societal structure: farm-market-home) to a personal one (of storage)? How did we decide to accept a thawed block taken from a supermarket's freezer as a substitute for the voluptuous shapes, smells, and textures of fresh fruits and vegetables obtained from complex individual sources?

[14]The decision for larger refrigerators has been consistent with a change in food-supply routes from highly diversified "trails" (from small farms to neighborhood markets) to uniform, standardized highways (from large farms to centrally located supermarkets). Desirable meals are quick and easy rather than rich and leisurely. Culinary artistry has given way to efficiency, the efficiency of the big refrigerator.

[15]People have a natural propensity for running good things into the ground. Mass production has been a boon to mankind, but its reliance on homogeneity precludes its being a paradigm for all areas of human life. Our forebears and contemporaries have made it possible to mass-produce almost anything. An equally challenging task now lies with us: to choose which things of this world should be mass-produced, and how the standards of mass production should influence other standards we hold dear.

[16]Should houses be mass-produced? Should education? Should food? Which brings us back to refrigerators. How does one decide how large a refrigerator to buy, considering one's life, one's society, and the world, and not simply the question of food storage?

[17]As similar questions are asked about more and more of the things we mass-produce, mass production will become less of a problem and more of a blessing. As cost begins to be measured not only in dollars spent and minutes saved, but in total richness acquired, perhaps smaller refrigerators will again make good sense. A small step backward along some of the roads of "technological progress" might be a large step forward for mankind, and one our age is uniquely qualified to make.

COMMENT

If the author wished to persuade West German readers to buy large refrigerators, the benefits they provide would be emphasized. Writing to persuade Americans to give up large refrigerators, Rodden focuses on one cause of their preference for them, the attitude that "time is money." If this attitude is one necessary condition of the American preference—that is, a condition that must be present for this preference to exist—attacking the attitude may help to diminish the incentive. Rodden attacks this attitude by showing the disadvantages of thinking about life in this way; these include the sacrifice of fresh food and the fun of buying it, the gradual disappearance of the small farmer, the use of dangerous pesticides—in general, the limits of choice imposed by technology. There may be other necessary conditions, but Rodden need not identify all of them and does not claim to have done so. The "natural propensity for running good things into the ground" is a necessary condition that would be difficult to eliminate. Writers seldom try to identify all the causes of a situation or attitude—not only because it would be difficult to do so, but because they need not do so to make their point.

· QUESTIONS FOR STUDY AND DISCUSSION

1. In what order does Rodden present the costs of large refrigerators?

2. What other causes does Rodden state or imply for the American preference? What is the thesis of the essay, and where is it first stated?

3. Does Rodden explain why Europeans prefer small refrigerators? Is Rodden implying that Americans are more easily captivated by "technological progress"?

4. What in Rodden's comments on storing food and the problem of obesity shows that he is stating some of the reasons, not all of them— that he is concerned with probabilities?

5. Does Rodden assert or imply that the greater efficiency a tool has, the greater control it exerts over people?

6. Do you agree that the telephone is a "convivial tool"? If you agree with Rodden's conclusions about tools, can you provide other examples? If you disagree, can you provide another explanation of why tools shape our lives as they do?

7. How formal are the transitions of the essay? What is the overall tone? Do you find shifts in tone?

VOCABULARY STUDY
Write sentences using each of the following words to show its dictionary meaning: *psychosomatic, transitoriness, corpulence, aesthetic, amenities, homogenization, convivial, usurp, culinary, propensity.*

SUGGESTIONS FOR WRITING
1. Analyze your preference for a certain make or size of automobile, or your opinion about the role of the telephone or a comparable tool. Discuss as many causes of your preference or opinion as you can, and present them in the order of their importance.

2. Discuss your eating habits, or those of your family, with attention to the role of the refrigerator in shaping these habits.

argument

Arguments are generally *inductive* or *deductive*. *Inductive arguments* reason from observations or particulars of experience to general conclusions:

> The Salk vaccine has reduced the incidence of polio in the United States.
>
> Vaccination for smallpox has virtually eradicated the disease.
>
> Vaccination for German measles has reduced the incidence of birth defects resulting from the disease.
>
> *Vaccination is an effective method of fighting contagious diseases.*

The conclusions of inductive arguments are only as strong as the evidence warrants. The evidence above does not, for example, warrant the conclusion that vaccination is the *most* effective method available.

The cause-and-effect reasoning described in the previous section is one form of inductive argument: identifying the "conditions" that produce an event is the same as drawing a conclusion from particulars of experience. Another inductive form is the argument from analogy, a special kind of comparison. Seeking to persuade an audience that a certain man should be elected president, I might show his resemblance to President Truman—a man particularly admired by the audience I am addressing. Through a point-by-point comparison or analogy, I build to a conclusion: since my candidate resembles Truman in all these ways, he probably will make as good a president. The strength of the analogy depends on the points of similarity that strengthen the analogy. It would be immaterial if my candidate is shorter than

Truman; it would be material if he had no important experience in government. Important differences will weaken the analogy.

Notice the qualification that the candidate *probably* would make as good a president as Truman. That qualification applies to all inductive arguments. While inductive arguments can be highly probable, they can never be certain, for we cannot be sure that we have discovered all the facts—that an exception may not exist to the generalization we have drawn. Some contagious diseases may be resistant even to vaccination, and when and if that fact is discovered, our conclusion would have to be severely qualified.

Deductive arguments, by contrast, derive conclusions from statements assumed to be self-evident or well enough established to provide certain and decisive evidence for the conclusion. These statements usually concern classes rather than individuals:

> All human beings are mortal.
>
> Human beings wish to conquer the unknown.
>
> Sharks are voracious eaters.

In a deductive argument, the statements themselves provide evidence for the conclusion:

> Devices that use great amounts of gasoline waste a natural resource.
>
> Eight-cylinder engines are devices that use great amounts of gasoline.
>
> Eight-cylinder engines waste a natural resource.

Usually the argument is worded less formally and more concisely:

> Eight-cylinder engines, like all devices that use great amounts of gasoline, waste an important natural resource—petroleum.

A deductive argument depends on the evident truth of its statements to establish its conclusion; and more than this, deductive evidence is considered to be certain enough to establish the conclusion without qualification. When writing a deductive argument, we may choose to explain or illustrate our statements, perhaps as a way of reminding our readers of what they already know to be true. But that explanation or illustration is not presented as *proof* of our statements, as in inductive arguments.

We must understand that not everyone will agree with our premises and that we may have to defend them in the course of a deductive argument. However we defend them, the argument is a deductive one as long as the premises themselves provide the decisive evidence for the conclusion. In some arguments, statements may be implied rather than made explicitly, as was mentioned in the previous discussion. Appletree Rodden *implies* that people are reasonable and capable of changing their habits when given good reasons for doing so. Rodden implies also that people need not be victims of technology: they need not own large refrigerators just because they exist. These assumptions are basic to the argument—particularly to the response Rodden wants—and yet they are unstated in the essay. When we disagree with an argument yet cannot say why we do, we may be in disagreement with such implied assumptions. Identifying hidden assumptions—for example, prejudices that may color an argument in subtle ways—is of course a more difficult job.

Deductive arguments in particular must be developed and written with care. For if the premises are not well-established truths, but rather "glittering generalities"—statements that cannot be easily supported and do not cover all instances they presume to—the argument will be hollow. In inductive arguments, the major problem is not to claim more in the conclusion than the evidence presented warrants.

STRIKE OUT LITTLE LEAGUE

Robin Roberts

Robin Roberts was born in Springfield, Illinois, in 1926. After his graduation from high school in 1944, he joined the Air Force Student Training Reserve Unit at Michigan State University, where he played basketball and baseball while he earned his

Bachelor of Science degree. In 1946 he was named Michigan's Outstanding Basketball Player. Two years later he joined the Philadelphia Phillies and played with that baseball team until 1962. In 1976, he was made a member of the National Baseball Hall of Fame.

[1]In 1939, Little League baseball was organized by Bert and George Bebble and Carl Stotz of Williamsport, Pa. What they had in mind in organizing this kids' baseball program, I'll never know. But I'm sure they never visualized the monster it would grow into.

[2]At least 25,000 teams, in about 5,000 leagues, compete for a chance to go to the Little League World Series in Williamsport each summer. These leagues are in more than fifteen countries, although recently the Little League organization has voted to restrict the competition to teams in the United States. If you judge the success of a program by the number of participants, it would appear that Little League has been a tremendous success. More than 600,000 boys from 8 to 12 are involved. But I say Little League is wrong—and I'll try to explain why.

[3]If I told you and your family that I want you to help me with a project from the middle of May until the end of July, one that would totally disrupt your dinner schedule and pay nothing, you would probably tell me to get lost. That's what Little League does. Mothers or fathers or both spend four or five nights a week taking children to Little League, watching the game, coming home around 8 or 8:30 and sitting down to a late dinner.

[4]These games are played at this hour because the adults are running the programs and this is the only time they have available. These same adults are in most cases unqualified as instructors and do not have the emotional stability to work with children of this age. The dedication and sincerity of these instructors cannot be questioned, but the purpose of this dedication should be. Youngsters eligible for Little League are of the age when their concentration lasts, at most, for five seconds—and without sustained concentration organized athletic programs are a farce.

[5]Most instructors will never understand this. As a result there is a lot of pressure on these young people to do something that is unnatural for their age—so there will always be hollering and tremendous disappointment for most of these players. For acting

their age, they are made to feel incompetent. This is a basic fault of Little League.

⁶If you watch a Little League game, in most cases the pitchers are the most mature. They throw harder, and if they throw strikes very few batters can hit the ball. Consequently, it makes good baseball sense for most hitters to take the pitch. Don't swing. Hope for a walk. That could be a player's instruction for four years. The fun is in hitting the ball; the coach says don't swing. That may be sound baseball, but it does nothing to help a young player develop his hitting. What would seem like a basic training ground for baseball often turns out to be a program of negative thoughts that only retards a young player.

⁷I believe more good young athletes are turned off by the pressure of organized Little League than are helped. Little Leagues have no value as a training ground for baseball fundamentals. The instruction at that age, under the pressure of an organized league program, creates more doubt and eliminates the naturalness that is most important.

⁸If I'm going to criticize such a popular program as Little League, I'd better have some thoughts on what changes I would like to see.

⁹First of all, I wouldn't start any programs until the school year is over. Any young student has enough of a schedule during the school year to keep busy.

¹⁰These programs should be played in the afternoon—with a softball. Kids have a natural fear of a baseball; it hurts when it hits you. A softball is bigger, easier to see and easier to hit. You get to run the bases more and there isn't as much danger of injury if one gets hit with the ball. Boys and girls could play together. Different teams would be chosen every day. The instructors would be young adults home from college, or high-school graduates. The instructor could be the pitcher and the umpire at the same time. These programs could be run on public playgrounds or in schoolyards.

¹¹I guarantee that their dinner would be at the same time every night. The fathers could come home after work and relax; most of all, the kids would have a good time playing ball in a program in which hitting the ball and running the bases are the big things.

¹²When you start talking about young people playing baseball at 13 to 15, you may have something. Organize them a little, but be

careful; they are still young. But from 16 and on, work them really hard. Discipline them, organize the leagues, strive to win championships, travel all over. Give this age all the time and attention you can.

[13]I believe Little League has done just the opposite. We've worked hard with the 8- to 12-year-olds. We overorganize them, put them under pressure they can't handle and make playing baseball seem important. When our young people reach 16 they would appreciate the attention and help from the parents, and that's when our present programs almost stop.

[14]The whole idea of Little League baseball is wrong. There are alternatives available for more sensible programs. With the same dedication that has made the Little League such a major part of many of our lives, I'm sure we'll find the answer.

[15]I still don't know what those three gentlemen in Williamsport had in mind when they organized Little League baseball. I'm sure they didn't want parents arguing with their children about kids' games. I'm sure they didn't want to have family meals disrupted for three months every year. I'm sure they didn't want young athletes hurting their arms pitching under pressure at such a young age. I'm sure they didn't want young boys who don't have much athletic ability made to feel that something is wrong with them because they can't play baseball. I'm sure they didn't want a group of coaches drafting the players each year for different teams. I'm sure they didn't want unqualified men working with the young players. I'm sure they didn't realize how normal it is for an 8-year-old boy to be scared of a thrown or batted baseball.

[16]For the life of me, I can't figure out what they had in mind.

COMMENT

Roberts does not begin with general truths about boys and girls. He begins with and presents his specific experience and observations and draws limited conclusions from them. How much evidence he presents for these depends on how he views his reader. He clearly expects the reader to know from experience that eight-year-old boys are scared of hard balls, and that most adults who instruct the boys are unqualified; on other points he presents more evidence. In an inductive argument of this sort, depending on particulars of experience, the strength of the argument depends on the amount and variety. It depends, too, on the reputation of the author. Roberts has a claim to authority in writing about Little League baseball; an author with less impressive credentials may need to cite more particulars and verify them.

QUESTIONS FOR STUDY AND DISCUSSION

1. What audience does Roberts have in mind? Is his purpose to inform them of the situation, or to inform and persuade them to take action?

2. How does Roberts establish his authority on the subject? Does he make direct reference to his experience in baseball? Does he ask his audience to accept his views on the basis of his authority alone?

3. Roberts anticipates an objection sometimes called a *dilemma:* either we have Little League baseball, or we have no organized baseball for boys and girls. How does he "go between the horns" of this dilemma by suggesting a third possibility?

4. How might Roberts answer those who object that only parents with children playing Little League baseball currently have a right to judge the sport?

VOCABULARY STUDY

Identify those words in the essay that you consider negative in connotation. State whether Roberts could have substituted neutral words for them, and should have done so.

SUGGESTIONS FOR WRITING

1. Discuss your experience with and attitude toward an organized sport like Little League baseball. Use this discussion to state your agreement or disagreement with Roberts on planned sports for children.

2. Discuss how the supporters of Little League baseball might answer the charges Roberts makes. Then state how Roberts might answer these people.

3. Write your own essay using the title "Strike Out _____." Try to persuade your readers of the disadvantages of an organization or activity. Remember that you will not convince readers without strong evidence based on your observations and experience.

. . . MEANWHILE, HUMANS EAT PET FOOD

Edward H. Peeples Jr.

Edward H. Peeples Jr. was born in 1935 in Richmond, Virginia. He attended the Richmond Professional Institute, the University of Pennsylvania, and the University of Kentucky, where he received his Ph.D. in 1972. He is associate professor of preventive medicine at Virginia Commonwealth University. In the sixties he gained knowledge of urban poverty as a social worker in Richmond and South Philadelphia. He has been a leader of the Richmond Human Rights Coalition and Council on Human Relations and is deeply concerned with the nutritional problems and medical care of poor people.

[1]The first time I witnessed people eating pet foods was among neighbors and acquaintances during my youth in the South. At that time it was not uncommon or startling to me to see dog-food patties sizzling in a pan on the top of a stove or kerosene space heater in a dilapidated house with no running water, no refrigerator, no heat, no toilet and the unrelenting stench of decaying insects. I simply thought of it as the unfortunate but unavoidable consequence of being poor in the South.

[2]The second time occurred in Cleveland in the summer of 1953. Like many other Southerners, I came to seek my fortune in one of those pot-at-the-end-of-the-rainbow factories along Euclid Avenue. Turned away from one prospective job after another ("We don't hire hillbillies," employers said), I saw my nest egg of $30 dwindle to nothing. As my funds diminished and my hunger grew, I turned to pilfering food and small amounts of cash. With the money, I surreptitiously purchased, fried and ate canned dog and cat food as my principal ration for several weeks.

[3]I was, of course, humiliated to be eating something that, in my experience, only "trash" consumed. A merciless pride in self-sufficiency kept me from seeking out public welfare or asking my friends

or family for help. In fact, I carefully guarded the secret from everyone, because I feared being judged a failure.

[4]Except for the humiliation I experienced, eating canned pet food did not at the time seem to be particularly unpleasant. The dog food tasted pretty much like mealy hamburger, while the cat food was similar to canned fish that I was able to improve with mayonnaise, mustard or catsup.

[5]The next time I ate dog food was in 1956 while struggling through a summer session in college without income for food. Again, I was ashamed to admit it, fearing that people would feel sorry for me or that others who had even less than I would feel compelled to sacrifice for my comfort. I never again had to eat pet food.

[6]Later, while working as a hospital corpsman at the Great Lakes Illinois Naval Training Center in the late 1950's I had the opportunity to ask new recruits about their home life and nutrition practices. While I was not yet a disciplined scientist, I was able to estimate that about 5 to 8 percent of the thousands of young men who came to Great Lakes annually consumed pet foods and other materials not commonly thought to be safe or desirable for humans. Among these substances were baking soda, baking powder, laundry starch, tobacco, snuff, clay, dirt, sand and various wild plants.

[7]My later experience as a public assistance caseworker in Richmond, a street-based community worker in South Philadelphia, and my subsequent travels and studies as a medical sociologist throughout the South, turned up instances of people eating pet food because they saw it as cheaper than other protein products. Through the years, similar cases found in the Ozarks, on Indian reservations and in various cities across the nation have also been brought to my attention.

[8]While there do exist scattered scientific reports and commentary on the hazards and problems associated with eating such things as laundry starch and clay, there is little solid epidemiological evidence that shows a specific percentage of American households consume pet food. My experience and research, however, suggest that human consumption of pet food is widespread in the United States. My estimate, one I believe to be conservative, is that pet foods constitute a significant part of the diet of at least 225,000 American households, affecting some one million persons. Who knows how many more millions supplement their diet with pet-food products? One thing that we can assume is that current economic

conditions are increasing the practice and that it most seriously affects the unemployed, poor people, and our older citizens.

[9]There are those who argue that we do not have enough hard data on the human consumption of pet foods. Must we wait for incontrovertible data before we seriously seek to solve the problems of hunger and malnutrition in America? I submit that we have data enough. Isn't it sufficient to know that one American child or a single elderly person in this bountiful land is reduced to eating the forage of animals or exposed to unknown toxic levels of mercury, lead or salmonella to know that something very extraordinary must be done?

COMMENT

An important decision for writers of inductive argument is how much evidence is sufficient to draw conclusions from—to make the "inductive leap." This phrase sometimes means that writers have drawn their conclusions too soon, on the basis of incomplete evidence. Probably few writers are satisfied that they have all the evidence needed to make the argument decisive and fully convincing. Like Peeples, writers may feel it necessary to draw conclusions from limited evidence because a current situation is growing critical and must be exposed immediately. Peeples bases his conclusion on one person's experience. Though he is an expert on the subject, he admits the limitation his personal experience imposes on his conclusions. He is careful to state this limitation, and also the basis of his estimate—a conservative estimate, he notes—that about a million people in the United States eat pet food in significant amounts. If writers have wide experience in their subject, as Peeples has, their experience alone may be sufficient to give weight to the conclusion. As in inductive arguments generally, Peeples' conclusion is probable only, not certain.

QUESTIONS FOR STUDY AND DISCUSSION

1. For what reason does Peeples suggest that people eat pet food?

2. What is his purpose in writing and where does he state it?

3. To what audience is he writing, and how do you know?

4. How does Peeples qualify his conclusions—that is, state the degree of their probability? How does he relate this qualification to his purpose in writing?

VOCABULARY STUDY

Complete the following sentences to show the meaning of the italicized words:

a. His *disciplined* way of living was shown by

b. A *conservative* action is one that

c. An *incontrovertible* proof can never

d. The *bountiful* harvest

SUGGESTIONS FOR WRITING

1. Write an essay that builds to a thesis through a series of observations and experiences. Qualify your thesis by indicating the limitations of your experience and knowledge of the subject.

2. Compare Peeples' attitude toward poor people with Dwayne Walls' attitude toward the North Carolina tobacco farmers. Comment on the ways they reveal their attitudes.

THE TRUTH ABOUT THE BLACK MIDDLE CLASS

Vernon E. Jordan Jr.

Vernon E. Jordan Jr. was born in Atlanta, Georgia, in 1935. He studied at De Pauw University and at the Howard University law school. Later he worked for the National Association for the Advancement of Colored People and the United Negro College Fund and served as advisor to the U.S. government on selective service and civil rights. In 1972 he succeeded Whitney M. Young Jr. as executive director of the National Urban League.

[1]Recent reports of the existence of a vast black middle class remind me of daring explorers emerging from the hidden depths of a strange, newly discovered world bearing tales of an exotic new phenomenon. The media seem to have discovered, finally, black families that are intact, black men who are working, black house-

wives tending backyard gardens and black youngsters who aren't sniffing coke or mugging old ladies.

[2]And out of this "discovery" a new black stereotype is beginning to emerge. Immaculately dressed, cocktail in hand, the new black stereotype comes off as a sleek, sophisticated professional light-years away from the ghetto experience. As I turn the pages of glossy photos of these idealized, fortunate few, I get the feeling that this new black image is all too comforting to Americans weary of the struggle against poverty and racism.

[3]But this stereotype is no more real than was the old image of the angry, fire-breathing militant. And it may be just as damaging to black people, for whom equal opportunity is still a theory and for whom a national effort to bring about a more equitable distribution of the fruits of an affluent society is still a necessity. After all, who can argue the need for welfare reform, for guaranteed jobs, for integrated schools and better housing, when the supposed beneficiaries are looking out at us from the pages of national magazines, smiling at the camera between sips from their Martinis?

[4]The "new" black middle class has been seen recently in prime time on a CBS News documentary; it has adorned the cover of The New York Times Magazine, and it has been the subject of a Time cover story. But its much ballyhooed emergence is more representative of wishful thinking than of reality. And important as it is for the dedication and hard work of countless black families finally to receive recognition, the image being pushed so hard may be counterproductive in the long run.

[5]The fact is that the black middle class of 1974, like that of earlier years, is a minority within the black community. In 1974, as in 1964, 1954 and in the decades stretching into the distant past, the social and economic reality of the majority of black people has been poverty and marginal status in the wings of our society.

[6]The black middle class traditionally included a handful of professionals and a far larger number of working people who, had they been white, would be solidly "working class." The inclusion of Pullman porters, post-office clerks and other typical members of the old black middle class was due less to their incomes—which were well below those of whites—than to their relative immunity from the hazards of marginal employment that dogged most blacks. They were "middle class" relative to other black people, not to the society at large.

[7]Despite all the publicity, despite all the photos of yacht-club cocktail parties, that is where the so-called black middle class stands today. The CBS broadcast included a handyman and a postal worker. Had they been white they would be considered working class, but since they were black and defied media-fostered stereotypes, they were given the middle-class label.

[8]Well, is it true that the black community is edging into the middle class? Let's look at income, the handiest guide and certainly the most generally agreed-upon measurement. What income level amounts to middle-class status? Median family income is often used, since that places a family at the exact midpoint in our society. In 1972 the median family income of whites amounted to $11,549, but black median family income was a mere $6,864.

[9]That won't work. Let's use another guide. The Bureau of Labor Statistics says it takes an urban family of four $12,600 to maintain an "intermediate" living standard. Using that measure, the average black family not only is *not* middle class, but it earns far less than the "lower, non-poverty" level of $8,200. Four out of five black families earn less than the "intermediate" standard.

[10]What about collar color? Occupational status is often considered a guide to middle-class status, and this is an area in which blacks have made tremendous gains, breaking into occupations unheard of for non-whites only a decade ago. When you look at the official occupation charts, there is a double space to separate higher-status from lower-status jobs such as laborer, operative and service worker. That gap is more than a typographical device. It is an indicator of racial separation as well, for the majority of working whites hold jobs above that line, while the majority of blacks are still confined to the low-pay, low-status jobs below it. At the top of the job pinnacle, in the elite categories of the professions and business, the disparity is most glaring, with one out of four whites in such middle-class jobs in contrast to every tenth black worker.

[11]Yes, there are black doctors, dentists and lawyers, but let no one be fooled into thinking they are typical—these professions include only 2 per cent blacks. Yes, there are black families that are stable, who work, often at more than one job, and who own cars and homes. And yes, they are representative of the masses of black people who work the longest hours at the hardest jobs for the least pay in order to put some meat on the table and clothes on their backs. This should be emphasized in every way possible in order to remind this forgetting nation that there is a dimension of black

reality that has never been given its due.

[12]But this should not blind us to the realization that even with such superhuman efforts, the vast majority of blacks are still far from middle-class status. Let us not forget that the gains won are tenuous ones, easily shaken from our grasp by an energy crisis, a recession, rampant inflation or nonenforcement of hard-won civil-rights laws.

[13]And never let us fall victim to the illusion that the limited gains so bitterly wrenched from an unwilling nation have materially changed the conditions of life for the overwhelming majority of black people—conditions still typified by discrimination, economic insecurity and general living conditions inferior to those enjoyed by the majority of our white fellow citizens.

COMMENT

Jordan attacks the mistaken confidence of those who write about the black middle class; he then draws conclusions from his own observations. His main point is that "the black middle class of 1974, like that of earlier years, is a minority within the black community." To establish this point, he must show that, in the past at least, the black middle class was *defined* differently from the white middle class; he is, in fact, exposing the fallacy of "hasty generalization"—generalizing from exceptional rather than typical instances. Jordan's evidence of this difference is the inclusion of the handyman and postal worker in the CBS broadcast: "Had they been white they would be considered working class, but since they were black and defied media-fostered stereotypes they were given the middle-class label." He then measures black people by the standards of white middle-class status—median family income, "intermediate" living standard, "collar color." Not only do fewer black families meet these standards, but the few that do are untypical of American blacks. Jordan uses this inductive argument to drive home his point: "There is a dimension of black reality that has never been given its due." The concern with the definition of the black middle class is inductive also because Jordan is concerned with an implied analogy between the white and black middle class that he shows to be false.

QUESTIONS FOR STUDY AND DISCUSSION

1. What is the implied analogy that the media make between the white and black middle class? How does Jordan show the analogy to be false?

2. How does Jordan show that the media have generalized about the black middle class from exceptional instances?

3. Does Jordan attribute a motive to those who generalize hastily or use a false analogy? Or is he blaming the stereotype on widespread ignorance about black people?

4. How does Jordan show that it is important to define the black middle class properly?

VOCABULARY STUDY
The following words and phrases have exact denotative meanings and strong connotative ones. Show how both types of meaning are used in the essay: *immaculately dressed, stereotype, affluent, militant, dogged, elite, tenuous, recession.*

SUGGESTIONS FOR WRITING
1. Explore the effects of a stereotype—possibly of black teenagers, or high school students, or motorcyclists—for those being stereotyped. You might discuss the view they hold of themselves, or their relations to other people, as these are affected by the stereotype.

2. Discuss an "illusion" people hold about a group you belong to, and state the real facts as Jordan does. You might discuss the consequence of this illusion for you personally.

3. Trace the growth of your feelings toward a particular minority. Discuss the various influences that shaped your feelings, including perhaps television and movies.

AGGRESSION IN ANIMALS

Robin Clarke

Robin Clarke was born in Bedford, England, in 1937. He has edited the British scientific magazines *Discovery* and *Science Journal* and has also appeared on the British Broadcasting Company science program *Scientific Discovery*. He is the author of *The Secret Weapons* (1968) and *The Science of War and Peace*

(1972), from which the essay printed here is taken. In his introduction to the chapter in which the essay appears, Clarke says this about the psychology of war and peace:

Because the field is young and poorly funded, the evidence that can be drawn on is limited. Most of it has been produced by scientists whose first interest is in other fields. Most of it has relevance to war and peace by implication only. In quality, it compares unfavorably with the mass of painfully acquired literature available on, say, the theoretical accuracy of low-level bombing. In short, we know far more about how to kill than about why we kill.

[1] There are two popular views of animal aggression. One is that animals in the wild spend all their time fighting. The other is that if wild animals are not interfered with they will never fight. Both ideas have been perpetuated by Walt Disney's films, and they are as wrong as they are different. They do grave injustice to the richness of animal behavior patterns and serve only to confuse those who turn to animals to seek knowledge of human aggression. So before starting we must dispose of some hoary old myths.

[2] The first is that animal species habitually fight other species. On the contrary, snakes do not fight lions and kangaroos do not attack cows. And when we are shown gory pictures of one animal tearing another limb from limb, we would do well to forget about aggression. Almost certainly the animal is stocking its larder. If this process has any message for humanity, it is not one for generals or politicians but one for the managers of abattoirs. Nature is no redder in tooth and claw than is a slaughterhouse. And that is not the place to start any inquiry about the origin of war.

[3] The second myth is that because some species seem to spend most of their time fighting other members of the same species, they are engaged in killing one another. Catfights and dogfights have now entered the human language as a means of describing any vicious and bloody duel. The analogy is precisely wrong. Such fights rarely end in death and only occasionally do they draw blood. Here a better understanding of the significance of these displays of animal aggression is more rewarding.

[4] Conventional wisdom has it that the brilliant colors of many tropical and subtropical fish are the means by which different sexes

attract their mates. In fact, they are the signals used to warn other members of the species that they are on foreign ground. Fish that live singly or in pairs mark out their own territory by parading their colors around the edges of it. Birds do the same thing with their characteristic songs, which warn not only that a territory is occupied but tell a potential intruder something of the age and ferocity of the defender. Cats and many other animals stake out their hunting grounds with their characteristic smells.

[5] All these signs signify that "trespassers will be prosecuted." But it is what happens during the process of prosecution that may have relevance for man. To an inexperienced eye, the sight of deer with their antlers interlocked, swaying to and fro in apparently mortal combat, looks like the prelude to a bloody death. What is actually happening is more nearly the culmination of the conflict. Sometime before, the two deer will have paced one another, side by side. Then, instead of swinging their antlers viciously into the haunches of their opponent, they stop, lower their heads, engage antlers, and wrestle. The winner is the one who stays the course the longer. And if one should start the fight before the other, rarely if ever will it drive its antlers into its opponent's body. Instead it stops short, as if brought up by some unseen command.

[6] Much the same process marks the combats of other species. Fish will bite ineffectively at one another's mouths, but, as the famous ethologist Konrad Lorenz has written, "never, never does a fish bite into an opponent's unprotected flank." In fact, most animal combatants never touch one another. Instead they engage in an elaborate but entirely psychological trial of strength. Fish will turn sideways on to one another, extending their fins to show their opponent just how large they are. Cats arch their backs and apes stand their hair on end for the same reason. These are the symbols of aggression, the deterrent threats of the animal world. They are designed to bring the opponent's escape mechanism into play, and they are markedly successful.

[7] They are also functional. In territorial animals, these encounters occur mainly when one animal is venturing onto the territory of another. And it seems that the amount of aggression an animal will display is related to its distance from home. Near its lair, it has no alternative but to show that its deterrent is real and will be used if necessary. Further from home the animal becomes less aggressive and quickly yields to the threat display of an animal on its own

territory. All this is also regulated by the size of the animal. Larger animals need larger territories on which to forage for food, and, appropriately, larger animals are able to make more convincing threats.

[8]Animals that live in flocks use similar techniques to establish a hierarchy of rank or "pecking order"—so named because the phenomenon was first observed in chickens. The pecking order, too, has social functions. Once established by trial fights or psychological showmanship, it eliminates unnecessary competition. Only those close to one another will jockey for position, and senior and junior animals rarely fight. In jackdaws the order is so well-established that senior members will interfere in fights breaking out among junior members, thus controlling their squabbling. And it is usually the more experienced members that become the leaders, taking on themselves the task of warning their fellows against dangers which their greater experience enables them to judge more effectively. From them the junior members of the group learn the tricks of survival.

[9]With so many vital aspects of wild life depending on aggressive encounters, it is surprising that all forms of higher life have not long ago fought themselves off the face of the earth. But the fact that so few fights end in death means that some very powerful rules of animal warfare have evolved to protect the species.

[10]These rules are the basis of the ritual that underlies each animal combat. Weapons evolved by animal life have two functions: to protect the species from attack by predators and to catch prey, and to provoke fright in other members of the same species for the territorial or other reasons which I have mentioned. Significantly, an animal species does not always use the same weapon for the same job. Many of what appear to us as the most ferocious bits of animal armory are for threat only—but like all realistic threats can be put to effective use if need be. Thus the deer's antlers have been evolved for the exclusive function of ritualized fighting within the species. If a deer is attacked by another animal for prey, it defends itself not with its antlers but with its forelimbs (the reindeer also uses its antlers as a snow scoop, but that is another matter). So the first rule of animal warfare is that the ritual weapons, and not the real ones, are used in interspecies combat.

[11]The second rule is that even the ritualized weapons are used as rarely as possible. The first "control system" is for the losing

animal to turn off its threatening signals. The cock turns its bright red comb away and the cat's arched back resumes its normal shape. These are signs of impending defeat, but they are often insufficiently strong to deter the victor quickly. And here a second mechanism comes into play.

[12]The defeated animal then offers up to the victor the most vulnerable parts of its body. This may be part of the same movement in which the aggressive signals are turned off, or it may occur as an almost separate signal. The wolf, in this situation, turns his head away from his opponent, offering his jugular vein to the teeth of the winner. The jackdaw holds the unprotected base of its skull under the beak of its rival. And the dog, as everyone has seen, rolls onto his back, offering his throat and belly to the victor.

[13]All these actions evoke a reaction as positive as did the original signs of aggression. They are aggression inhibitors and they have saved countless millions of animals from death by their own species. The attacking animal, perhaps with a final gesture of triumph such as a quick worry at a dog's throat or a slap on a monkey's behind, calls the contest off. The defeated then has the chance to flee back to his own territory or knows that he has fallen by one in the pecking order of his species. Either result is beneficial for both the species and the individuals.

[14]To zoologists I must now apologize for the inadequacy of this description of animal behavior. What I have said does grave injustice to the richness and variability of the rituals that compose animal aggression. But it should be sufficient to provide the background against which we might view human aggression. Our need is not to examine the intricate social life of the tropical fish but to see if the principles on which it rests carry any message for humanity.

COMMENT

As Roberts warns against the false analogy arising in statements about the black middle class, so Clarke deals with the popular analogy that justifies war and social warfare by pointing to "nature red in tooth and claw"—in short, the assumption that aggression is widespread in nature. Clarke attacks the popular myths of animal aggression through particulars of experience. He does not dismiss the view completely, but instead qualifies it by explaining the ways and reasons animals do attack, but avoid inflicting gratuitous harm. As in all presentations of this sort, the quality of the evidence rather than its quantity is decisive, though its amount and variety lend considerable weight to the conclusion. As he writes in the final paragraph, Clarke is defining animal aggression as a preliminary to a statement about human aggression. Though he does not draw direct conclusions about human aggression in this discussion, he implies certain lessons, for example, that "control systems" are needed for the preservation of the species.

QUESTIONS FOR STUDY AND DISCUSSION

1. Clarke uses his analysis to limit the inquiries to be made through a comparison of humans and animals. What are these inquiries?

2. What lessons can be drawn from animal aggression without necessarily drawing analogies with humans?

3. How does Clarke show that animals do not kill for the sake of killing?

4. Clarke is concerned with assumptions people make about animals and human beings. How does he identify these assumptions in the course of the discussion, directly and indirectly?

VOCABULARY STUDY

Suffixes express different meanings. The suffix -*hood*, for example, expresses the state of a noun, as in *motherhood* and *brotherhood; -ing*, the substance which constitutes the noun, as in *stuffing*; or the state produced by the action of a verb, as in *running*. Your dictionary lists suffixes (and prefixes, too.) Determine what meanings the suffixes express in each of the following groups of words:

   a. actress, laundress, tigress
   b. kinship, friendship, hardship
   c. theocracy, democracy, plutocracy
   d. Siamese, Burmese, Cantonese
   e. pluralism, Zen Buddhism, fascism
   f. enlargement, arrangement, government
   g. amplify, certify, modify
   h. modernize, cauterize, organize
   i. restless, helpless, wordless

Identify groups of words in the essay having the same suffixes and expressing similar meanings.

SUGGESTIONS FOR WRITING
Analyze the influence of children's books, films, and possibly cartoons on your ideas about animals. You might analyze how closely these ideas resemble those discussed by Clarke or how closely they are supported by your experience with animals.

DIALOG: DOES STANDARD GRADING ENCOURAGE EXCESSIVE COMPETITIVENESS?

David Swanger teaches at the University of California at Santa Cruz. He is the author of *The Poem as Process* (1974) and the editor of *Quarry West* and his poems and articles on education have appeared in numerous journals.

Phyllis Zatlin Boring holds a Ph.D. from the University of Florida and is associate professor of Spanish and associate dean at Rutgers University. She is the coauthor of a Spanish textbook, *Lengua y lectura* (1970), and has written numerous articles on Hispanic literature, women's rights, and education.

Roy E. Terry is a student at Boise State University in Idaho. He left the university for a time to work as an electronics technician.

Jack Nusan Porter is a sociologist, writer, and critic, living in Boston. He has taught at Northwestern University, Boston College and Boston University's Free University. He is the co-author of *Jewish Radicalism* (1973) and a contributing editor of the *Encyclopedia of Sociology*.

Asheley DiMarco studied at Long Island University and the University of Massachusetts at Amherst, where she is completing her doctoral dissertation. At Long Island University, she received the Creative Writing Award and the Humanities Medal for the Study of Literature.

David Swanger

[1] For those of us who believe that learning can, will, and should take place in a noncompetitive situation, any competitiveness is excessive. The distinction between standard and nonstandard grading is phony. The only real alternative to grading is not to grade, to refuse to turn the classroom into an arena where students are pitted against each other. This is done in several colleges and universities by offering individualized, nongraded evaluations of each student for each course at the end of the term. Ideally, such evaluations describe at length the nature and quality of a student's work but do not rank him or her in competition with others.

[2] Landing jobs and getting into professional graduate schools is becoming more competitive; as a result, colleges and universities are asked *by the students* to grade as if life itself depended on it. At the University of California at Santa Cruz, for example, all analyses of declining admission applications identify ungraded courses at Santa Cruz as a reason many students apply more readily to other University of California campuses. And the *San Francisco Chronicle* ("Inside Colleges Today," February 4, 1975) reports that at places like Berkeley, Yale, and Stanford, students are so preoccupied with grades that their undergraduate lives are clearly desperate. Campus psychologists are kept busy assuaging student anguish over grades, and a popular elective among premeds at one university is "The Fear of Failure Workshop."

[3] The outside political and economic world establishes the priorities of the university. Economic blunders of successive administrations in Washington have set the stage for a massive conservative movement in this country. All of higher education is vulnerable, but the first casualties will be liberalizing educational experiments like those that attempt to replace grading with more humane and pedagogically sound methods of evaluating student work. It is hardly the students, faced with an economy not of their making, who are to blame.

[4] Nor can universities fighting for sheer survival be faulted for responding to the economic needs of their students. But the universities must not give in wholly to that which is obviously antieduca-

From *Change* Magazine, vol. 7, no. 7, September 1975. Reprinted by permission of *Change* and the authors.

tional; they must not be devoted to grade grubbing. The Santa Cruzes and Evergreens and Hampshires must be encouraged by legislators and alumni, by professional associations, by the future employers of their graduates, above all by other colleges and universities, in their efforts to provide alternatives to an otherwise monolithic grading system.

Phyllis Zatlin Boring

[5]In the late 1960s higher education embarked upon a cycle of idealism in grading. By eliminating standard grading, we would eliminate excessive competitiveness. By instituting pass-fail options, we would allow students to learn for learning's sake. Where pass-fail options did not exist, we inflated grades, giving the average students B's instead of C's and the good students A's instead of B's. It was a theory that would have pleased Don Quixote, but it is now time that we listen to the practical wisdom of Sancho Panza: We did not attack the giant Competition; we merely broke our lances on the windmills.

[6]Competition is alive and well and probably always will be. We cannot afford to give legal or medical training to all who seek it. No employer can hire all applicants. If the selection process cannot be based partially on standard grading, then it will be based totally on other criteria: letters of recommendation, which are subjective at best; standardized tests, which will not reflect total ability but will reward those who test well; personal interviews, which will penalize the introverted. Even if we moved to a mastery concept in higher education, we would evaluate people on how fast they moved through the system. Standard grading at least provides the applicant with a composite evaluation of achievement in perhaps 40 courses over a four-year period. The bad exam, the personality conflict with a professor, the discipline the student simply could not grasp average out in the total picture.

[7]At Rutgers College we are finding that the students today are rejecting the pass-fail option an earlier generation of students fought so hard to institute. While freshmen may elect to have their first semester recorded on a pass-fail basis, few of them do. In the real world, those P's hurt far more than they help. All too often pass-

fail merely provides an easy way out for a teacher who does not want to face up to the difficult responsibility of evaluating progress.

[8] We can discourage excessive competitiveness by giving students adequate opportunity to show what they have learned and where they need improvement, and by grading as fairly as is humanly possible. Testing and grading have an educational value, but not if the final grade is based solely on a final exam.

[9] My undergraduate institution, Rollins College, had a grading system which included plus and minus. To improve standard grading, I would move in that direction. When an extra point means the difference between an A and a B, it becomes of much greater significance than the difference between an A− and a B+. But no grading system can eliminate competition. It is our attitudes as teachers that can minimize it.

Roy E. Terry

[10] Grades are the play money in a university Monopoly game. As long as the tokens are offered, the temptation will be largely irresistible to play for them. Students are so busy taking notes, doing tests, and getting tokens that they have forgotten to ask: Of what worth is all this? Or perhaps they ask and the grade is their answer.

[11] One certainly learns something in the passive lecture-note-read-note-test process: how to do it all more efficiently next time (in the hope of eventually owning Boardwalk and Park Place). As Marshall McLuhan has said, we learn what we do. In this process most students come to view learning as studying and remembering what other people have learned. They assume that knowledge is logically and for practical reasons divided up into discrete pieces called "disciplines," and that the highest knowledge is achieved by specializing in a discipline. By getting good grades in a lot of disciplines they conclude they have learned a lot. They have indeed, and it is too bad.

[12] Such harsh judgment seems unjustified to many professors. From their viewpoint a great deal of thinking goes on; they generate most of it themselves and then hear their own echo, often disguised, on tests and papers.

[13] A fair number of students are sensitive enough to distinguish

between grading and learning. They may even have some special interests and an independent perspective. What happens to them? If they see through the token system and decide to pursue their own interests (which seldom fit into a discipline), they immediately discover that tokens control scholarships, special privileges, honors programs, and graduate school entrance. If they opt, on the other hand, to work for a grade (to compete), they deny themselves any true intellectual growth—the growth that comes of deciding for oneself the worth of a paper, a course, a major. Of making one's own major, defining it in one's own terms, and having an emotional stake in its pursuit.

Jack Nusan Porter

[14]Competition need not be destructive; it can be healthy if one's purpose is the pure enjoyment of the chase or the game. Even taking tests can be fun: a prod to do better, a method by which one can sharpen one's mind. However, grades are not used for that purpose but to pigeonhole people in order to fill society's slots. They are a quick way to dispense honors and titles and to divide people into categories. In short, to judge them. Not that I am against tests or judgments per se. But the questions are: What kinds of tests? What kinds of judgments? And to what purpose? Since there will always be some form of competition, let it be a positive one.

[15]In China the emphasis is on mutual aid and cooperative projects in which the group makes collective decisions. Such healthy attitudes would be difficult to inculcate in America. The "new Puritanism" of this society, based on the philosophies of Jefferson, Jackson, Thoreau, Emerson, the Roosevelts, and the Kennedys, is the rationale of rugged individualism, not group cooperation. This "John Wayne complex" is responsible for many of the tensions in America today. What changes can be instituted in education while we wait and hope for a basic shift in our society to take place?

[16]Tests and grades must be deemphasized and more stress put on the joys (and agonies) of acquiring knowledge. When we do test, emphasis should be on the group or individual research project, term paper, essay, essaylike question, open-book exam, and creative gaming, as opposed to the multiple-choice and true-false question,

the highly esoteric test, and the poorly composed and tabulated questionnaire.

[17]Whenever possible, tests should be analogs to the problems that the student will face in the world outside of academe. The sociologist does field work and writes research papers; he does not answer multiple-choice questions. A doctor consults a manual and solves a difficult problem in consultation with others; he does not have to memorize the composition of every drug or even every part of the body.

[18]Let the teacher be honest about his reasons for grading and testing. Group projects or innovative gaming take creative planning. Standard tests take less time to administer and less trouble to evaluate, and therefore most teachers choose them.

[19]Each teacher must examine the purpose of his or her teaching. The vast majority of undergraduates are not going to major in that teacher's specialty. They want insight into the field that will contribute in some way to their philosophy of life. Too often they are bored by lectures and frightened to death by exams. They have become perfect victims of the educational system.

Asheley DiMarco

[20]What standard grading? At my institution, both undergraduate and graduate students generally get high grades. Graduate students expect A's and B's. When we get B's, we feel that we have failed.

[21]What excessive competitiveness? When virtually everyone gets high grades, the only classroom rivalries are for praise or for anonymity. While F's are still given, they represent failure to do work, not work of failing caliber.

[22]If standard grading means not just a range of grades from A to F, but also a typical distribution concentrated around the grade of C, then it no longer exists as a norm. For grading has become an economic act and is likely to remain so for a long time.

[23]There is, moreover, no way to revert to standard grading without jeopardizing teachers, programs, and institutions. What we have lost is not simple classroom competition, but all ability to evaluate student performance except through interviews and stan-

dardized examinations such as SATs and the GREs. Where standardized test scores used to be correlated with grades and letters of recommendation in establishing profiles of student performance, most students now get good recommendations (because of open files) and high grades as a matter of course. This precludes differentiation between excellent students and good ones, between good students and mediocre ones.

[24]Standard grading, like letters of recommendation, relied heavily on subjective judgments. Injustices existed, but these methods of evaluation were better than grades and recommendations so uniform as to be meaningless. As a teaching assistant, I know that easy grading is a matter of economic survival. As a student, I know that easy grading is a system that deludes poor students and penalizes excellent ones. In selection processes based on academic training, I can only hope that admissions officials and employers will rely on standardized test scores and interviews, for they cannot rely on grades and recommendations. As for excessive competition, it's the name of the game. But we are competing for jobs and funding, not grades.

[25]When my peers and I were undergraduates in the late sixties and early seventies, we demanded pass-fail courses, sympathetic teachers, relevant subjects, and other alternatives to traditional classroom fare. Now the alternatives have become more rigid and stifling than the traditions they replaced. We have cut our own throats and those of our teachers. Fiscal pressures may have trapped us in an unhappy quagmire without solid measures of achievement, but we students and you teachers jointly created the mire in the first place.

[26]Standard grading and rigorous standards were effectively dismissed because we demanded adolescent varieties of humanism and relevance in their stead. We were wrong to demand total overhaul with such naiveté and righteous conviction; you were wrong to capitulate so quickly, insecurely, and completely.

COMMENT

These five statements appeared as a dialog in a magazine read by students, teachers, and other people interested in education. The five writers could therefore assume that readers of the magazine were acquainted with both current and recent issues in education. The decision to develop an argument deductively or inductively sometimes depends on what writers assume their readers know or believe, and so does the decision on how much supporting evidence or illustration to provide.

David Swanger's statement is mainly deductive. He states the point-at-issue for him in his first paragraph: "The only real alternative to grading is not to grade, to refuse to turn the classroom into an arena where students are pitted against each other." This point-at-issue is based on a "given" or assumption stated in the first sentence: learning can take place in a noncompetitive atmosphere. And Swanger *implies* more than this: education need not be highly competitive, nor must life be. These assumptions are taken to provide certain and decisive evidence for the conclusions he reaches: this is why the argument is mainly deductive. For example, his stated assumption that "any competitiveness is excessive" provides the certain and decisive evidence for his statement that "individualized, nongraded evaluations" are the only way to keep the classroom from becoming an arena. The details Swanger provides about enrollment at the University of California campuses and other universities show what happens when students compete for grades: these details are not used to prove the assumptions of the argument. Though much of the argument is concerned with the current situation in education, Swanger's analysis of the situation is based on the opening deductive first paragraph.

Roy Terry's statement is mainly inductive: he draws conclusions from his experiences in the classroom. One conclusion is that professors do most of the thinking in the classroom and assume mistakenly that they are testing their students' thinking. From observations such as this, Terry draws a general conclusion: there is more grading than learning going on in schools today. The inductive nature of his argument lies in his drawing probable conclusions from particulars of experiences. But underlying his discussion is a "given"—an ideal of education: students should think for themselves, choose and define their major as they wish, and be emotionally as well as intellectually involved in their education. Though this ideal of education shapes the argument, the question of whether standard grading encourages excessive competitiveness is answered through particulars of experience, and the statement is therefore inductive.

QUESTIONS FOR STUDY AND DISCUSSION
1. In stating that standard and nonstandard grading turn the classroom into an arena, Swanger assumes that grading requires *comparison*

between students. What other statements support this assumption? Do you believe that all grading must involve such comparison, or can you think of a grading system that does not?

2. Do Boring and DiMarco make this same assumption—that grading requires comparison between students? Do you find a stated or implied definition of grading in Terry and Porter?

3. Swanger states as a given, "The outside political and economic world establishes the priorities of the university." What conclusions does he draw from this assumption? What other givens do you find in his statement, and how are they used in the argument?

4. Is Boring's statement mainly deductive or inductive? If deductive, what givens or assumptions provide certain and decisive evidence for the conclusions she reaches? If inductive, what particulars of experience lead to probable conclusions? If deductive, what is the purpose of her information about changes in grading procedures in the sixties? If inductive, what is the purpose of her statements about competition?

5. How does Terry explain his ideal of education? In the course of his statement Terry introduces an objection to his thesis and answers it. What is that objection or alternate opinion, and how does he answer it?

6. Is Porter in more agreement with Swanger's or with Boring's assumptions about competition? Does Porter present his ideas about competition as givens and deduce conclusions from them, or does he instead present probable ideas derived from particulars of experience?

7. Does Porter disagree or agree with Terry's ideal of education? Does he state his ideal or merely imply it?

8. Does Porter define the "new Puritanism" and the "John Wayne complex," or does he assume that his readers will understand these phrases? What do they mean?

9. Why does DiMarco reject alternatives to standard grading? How does she defend standard grading?

10. Do you find any points of agreement among the five writers? Do they make similar or the same assumptions about the knowledge and beliefs of their audience?

11. Do you find yourself in *complete* agreement or disagreement with one or more of the writers? Is your agreement or disagreement with assumptions, with conclusions, or with particulars of experience?

12. To what extent does each writer define terms formally? Does any writer stipulate a definition of an important term?

VOCABULARY STUDY

1. The words *competition, competitive,* and *compete* have special meanings for each of the five writers. Be ready to discuss how each writer establishes the meaning of these words in the course of his or her statement.

2. Identify those words in the five statements chosen for their connotative rather than denotative meaning. Be ready to discuss the appropriateness of these words to the context and general argument.

SUGGESTIONS FOR WRITING

1. Write a statement of your own in answer to the question of the dialog. In the course of your statement, discuss with which of the five writers you are in most and in least agreement. If you base your conclusions on certain givens, identify them as such, and explain or illustrate them. If you develop an inductive argument from particulars of experience, state how probable you consider your conclusions to be.

2. Analyze the reasoning of one of the five statements. Distinguish the deductive or inductive arguments used and analyze the uses the writer makes of particulars of experience (if any). Clarify the difference between deductive and inductive reasoning in the course of your analysis.

3. Develop an argument of your own on a current issue in education— perhaps the pass-fail or credit-noncredit options in courses.

persuasion

An argument need not be organized with a particular audience in mind. But most writers do write for a particular audience and shape their argument in light of that audience's knowledge and beliefs. For example, if the argument is deductive, they may reverse the expected order of statements and state the conclusion first as a way of focusing attention on the point of most concern. Or they may begin the essay with the least controversial statement, proceed to the more controversial, and end with the most controversial. Basic to many arguments on gun control may be the premise that human beings love to kill. Though this premise would be stated first in the formal syllogism or arrangement of proofs, the writer may save it for last in addressing an audience of hunters since it is the idea they may find least acceptable. In short, the premises and conclusions of a deductive argument need not be presented in the order required in the formal logical argument.

The persuasiveness of the inductive argument depends, as we have seen, on the strength of the evidence presented for the conclusion. Precise definition of terms and a clear statement of the thesis in a position of prominence—at the end of the first paragraph, for example—will heighten the force of the argument. Though the inductive argument usually builds through details to the conclusion, the writer may anticipate it through a partial statement of it early in the essay.

Opposed to the logical order of deductive or inductive ideas, then, there is also a rhetorical order of ideas—an order determined by the audience being addressed. Having thought out their ideas logically, writers may arrange them in the most effective order, given a particular audience. Over many years a basic form of argument has emerged, deriving from the legal orations of the ancient Greeks. Here is a brief outline of it:

Introduction or exhortation—an urging or plea to the audience to listen to the evidence and judge it fairly

Narrative—a statement of the facts of the case or appropriate background

Division of proofs—a summary of the main arguments or evidence to be presented

Thesis—the central proposition

Confirmation—arguments presented in support of the thesis

Refutation—arguments and evidence against opponents, or answers to opposing arguments

Recapitulation—a summary of the main arguments and evidence

Final appeal to the audience for their fair consideration of the argument

An argument may include all of these, or it may omit some of them. The order of parts shown may of course be altered to fit a particular audience; the refutation may, for example, precede the confirmation or be combined with it.

LIMITING HANDGUNS

Robert di Grazia

Robert J. di Grazia was born in 1928, in San Francisco, and studied at the University of San Francisco, Michigan State University, and Sonoma State College in California. He served in various law enforcement posts, including sheriff of Marin County, California, 1959–60; chief of police in St. Louis, Missouri, 1963–69; and, later, superintendent of police in the same city. Until late 1976, he was police commissioner of Boston, Massachusetts, and is now police chief of Montgomery County, Maryland.

[1] We buried Donald Brown in May. He was murdered by three men who wanted to rob the supermarket manager he was protecting. Patrolman Brown was 61 years old, six months from retirement. He and his wife intended to retire to Florida at the end of the year. Now there will be no retirement in the sun, and she is alone.

[2] Donald Brown was the second police officer to die since I became commissioner here on Nov. 15, 1972.

[3] The first was John Schroeder, a detective shot in a pawnshop robbery last November. John Schroeder was the brother of Walter Schroeder, who was killed in a bank robbery in 1970. Their names are together on the honor roll in the lobby of Police Headquarters.

[4] John Murphy didn't die. He was shot in the head last February as he chased a robbery suspect into the Washington Street subway station. He lived, but he will be brain-damaged for the rest of his life, unable to walk or talk.

[5] At least two of these police officers were shot by a handgun, the kind one can buy nearly everywhere for a few dollars. Those who don't want to buy one can steal one, and half a million are stolen each year. There are forty million handguns circulating in this country; two and half million are sold each year.

[6] Anybody can get a gun. Ownership of handguns has become so widespread that the gun is no longer merely the instrument of crime; it is now a cause of violent crime. Of the eleven Boston police officers killed since 1962, seven were killed with handguns; of the seventeen wounded by guns since 1962, sixteen were shot with handguns.

[7] Police officers, of course, are not the only people who die. Ten thousand other Americans are dead at the price of our promiscuous right to bear arms. Gun advocates are fond of saying that guns don't kill, people do. But guns do kill.

[8] Half of the people who commit suicide do so with handguns. Fifty-four percent of the murders committed in 1972 were commit-

ted with handguns. Killing with handguns simply is a good deal easier than killing with other weapons.

[9]Rifles and shotguns are difficult to conceal. People can run away from knife-wielding assailants. People do die each year by drownings, bludgeonings and strangulation. But assaults with handguns are five times more likely to kill.

[10]No one can convince me, after returning from Patrolman Brown's funeral, after standing in the rain with hundreds of others from this department and others, that we should allow people to own handguns.

[11]I know that many people feel deeply and honestly about their right to own and enjoy guns. I realize that gun ownership and self-protection are deeply held American values. I am asking that people give them up.

[12]I am committed to doing what I can to take guns away from the people. In my view, private ownership of handguns must be banished from this country. I am not asking for registration or licensing or outlawing cheap guns. I am saying that no private citizen, whatever his claim, should possess a handgun. Only police officers should.

COMMENT

Robert di Grazia recognizes that gun ownership and self-protection are "givens" for people who oppose confiscation: "I realize that gun ownership and self-protection are deeply held American values." He might have focused on these givens, showing them to be unsound, but he chooses not to do so; for he wishes to make the point-at-issue the question of whether gun ownership can be tolerated in face of the hazards named and illustrated in the essay. Some of di Grazia's opponents would make these values the point-at-issue, specifically the claim of individual rights versus the claim of society and its appointed representatives, police officers. In ordinary arguments, the main dispute is often over the point-at-issue. In the courtroom, rulings on the admission of evidence are in effect determinations of the point-at-issue in the case; in his instructions to the jury following the presentation of evidence, the judge defines it in stating the basis on which the defendant is to be judged innocent or guilty. Though di Grazia stakes out his argument by focusing on the hazards of gun ownership, he is fair to his opponents and his readers in saying he has done so, and mentioning the reasons for gun ownership. He does not attack the character or motives of his opponents, nor does he appeal to prejudice or to "force," that is, through the argument that guns will be confiscated with or without the consent of their owners. His essay is a model of fair reasoning.

QUESTIONS FOR STUDY AND DISCUSSION

1. Di Grazia builds his case against gun ownership through particulars of experience. What are these particulars?

2. Is he arguing against gun ownership on the ground that people intend to wound or kill with guns? What is his answer to the slogan in favor of gun ownership, "Guns don't kill, people do"?

3. Why does he oppose registration, licensing, and outlawing cheap guns, and why does he limit his recommendation to handguns?

4. What parts of the essay constitute the narrative, the confirmation, and the refutation? Where is the thesis first stated? Where is it restated?

VOCABULARY STUDY

Look up the following words and determine their exact meaning in the essay: *instrument, promiscuous, advocates, assailants, banished.*

SUGGESTIONS FOR WRITING

1. State your agreement or disagreement with di Grazia—specifically, whether you agree or disagree with his assumptions, the point at issue in the essay, his recommendations. Defend your own assumptions and attitudes in the course of your discussion.

2. Organize a persuasive essay in defense of or in opposition to a current controversy. Include in your essay an introduction, a narrative or statement of the backgrounds, a division of arguments, a statement of your proposition or thesis, your confirming argument, a refutation of your opponents, possibly a summary of your main points, and finally a conclusion. These need not be presented in this order. Write to a specific audience and keep in mind the knowledge and beliefs of that audience.

A LETTER ON STRIP MINING

Harvey and Nancy Kincaid

Harvey and Nancy Kincaid live with their seven children in Fayetteville, West Virginia, near Buffalo Creek. On February 26, 1972, a dam consisting of slag from the mines and owned by a local coal company burst. The ensuing flood killed 125 people and injured many thousands, most of the victims working and disabled coal miners and members of their families. In 1971 Mrs. Kincaid spoke about strip mining to the Congress Against Strip Mining, in Washington, D.C. Her letter was read before the West Virginia State Legislature and it helped to pass the Anti–Strip-Mining Bill. Mrs. Kincaid told an interviewer:

It used to be that the kids could keep fish, catfish, and minnows in the creeks. Now you can see the rocks in the creek where the acid has run off the mountains, off the limestone rocks. The rocks in the creek are reddish-looking, like they're rusted. There's nothing living in the creek now.

Gentlemen:

[1] I don't believe there could be anyone that would like to see the strip mines stopped any more than my husband and myself. It just seems impossible that something like this could happen to us twice in the past three and one half years of time. We have been married for thirteen years and worked real hard at having a nice home that was ours and paid for, with a nice size lot of one acre. Over the thirteen years, we remodeled this house a little at a time and paid for it as we worked and did the work mostly ourselves. The house was located about a quarter of a mile off the road up Glenco Hollow at Kincaid, Fayette County, West Virginia, where it used to be a nice, clean neighborbhood.

[2] Then the strippers came four years ago with their big machinery and TNT. I know that these men need jobs and need to make a living like everyone else, but I believe there could be a better way of getting the coal out of these mountains. Have you ever

From *Hillbilly Women,* copyright © 1973 by Kathy Kahn. Reprinted by permission of Doubleday & Co., Inc.

been on a mountaintop and looked down and seen about five different strips on one mountain in one hollow?

[3]My husband owns a Scout Jeep and he can get to the top of the strip mines with the Scout. I would like to invite you to come and visit us sometime and go for a ride with us. It would make you sick to see the way the mountains are destroyed.

[4]First they send in the loggers to strip all the good timber out and then they come with their bulldozers. If their engineers make a mistake in locating the coal they just keep cutting away until they locate the seam of coal. When the rains come and there isn't anything to stop the drainage, the mountains slide, and the spoil banks fall down to the next spoil bank and so on until the whole mountain slides. There is a small creek in the hollow and when the spring rains come, its banks won't hold the water.

[5]So where does it go?—into people's yards, into their wells, under and into their houses. You have rocks, coal, and a little bit of everything in your yards. When the strippers came they started behind our house in the fall sometime before November. There was a hollow behind our house and we asked them not to bank the spoil the way they did, because we knew what would happen when the spring rains came. My father-in-law lived beside us and the property all ran together in a nice green lawn—four acres.

[6]But the rains came in the spring and the spoil bank broke and the water and debris came into our property every time it rained. It would only take a few minutes of rain and this is what we had for three years.

[7]Then the damage comes to your house because of so much dampness. The doors won't close, the foundation sinks and cracks the walls in the house, your tile comes up off your floors, your walls mold, even your clothes in your closets. Then your children stay sick with bronchial trouble, then our daughter takes pneumonia—X-rays are taken, primary T.B. shows up on the X-ray. This is in July of two years ago. About for a year this child laid sick at home. In the meantime we have already filed suit with a lawyer in Oak Hill when the water started coming in on us, but nothing happens. For three years we fight them for our property—$10,000. The lawyer settles out of court for $4,500. By the time his fee comes out and everything else we have to pay, we have under $3,000 to start over with.

[8]So what do we have to do? Doctor's orders, move out for child's

sake and health. We sell for a little of nothing—not for cash, but for rent payments, take the $3,000 and buy a lot on the main highway four miles up the road toward Oak Hill.

[9]The $3,000 goes for the lot, digging of a well and a down payment on a new house. Here we are in debt for thirty years on a new home built and complete by the first of September. We moved the first part of September and was in this house *one month* and what happens? The same strip company comes up the road and puts a blast off and damages the new house—$1,400 worth. When they put one blast off that will crack the walls in your house, the foundation cracked the carport floor straight across in two places, pull a cement stoop away from the house and pull the grout out of the ceramic tile in the bathroom. This is what they can get by with.

[10]How do they live in their $100,000 homes and have a clear mind, I'll never know. To think of the poor people who have worked hard all their lives and can't start over like we did. They have to stay in these hollows and be scared to death every time it rains. I know by experience the many nights I have stayed up and listened to the water pouring off the mountains and the rocks tumbling off the hills.

[11]I remember one time when the strippers put a blast off up the hollow a couple years ago and broke into one of the old mines that had been sealed off for 30 years. They put their blast off and left for the evening. Around seven o'clock that evening it started. We happened to look up the hollow, and thick mud—as thick as pudding—was coming down the main road in the hollow and made itself to the creek and stopped the creek up until the creek couldn't even flow.

[12]The water was turned up into the fields where my husband keeps horses and cattle. I called the boss and told him what was happening and the danger we were in and what did he say? "There isn't anything I can do tonight. I'll be down tomorrow." I called the agriculture and they told us, whatever we did, not to go to bed that night because of the water backed up in those mines for miles.

[13]This is just some of the things that happen around a strip mine neighborhood. But they can get by with it, unless they are stopped. Even if they are stopped it will take years for the trees and grass—what little bit they put on them—to grow enough to keep the water back and stop the slides.

Mr. and Mrs. Harvey Kincaid

COMMENT

A French writer, Amiel, wrote in his journal: "Truth is the secret of eloquence and of virtue, the basis of moral authority." The Kincaids' great letter is an example of eloquence achieved through simple words that state facts plainly and exactly. Instead of reviewing the rights and wrongs of strip mining, Mr. and Mrs. Kincaid describe what happened to them and the land—in enough detail for the reader to imagine the life of people in the hollow. At the end of the letter they state the issue simply and without elaboration: "But they can get by with it, unless they are stopped."

QUESTIONS FOR STUDY AND DISCUSSION

1. The Kincaids state how their life was changed by strip mining. How do they show that their experiences were typical of people in the area?

2. Is the damage caused by strip mining the result of neglect or carelessness, or is it inherent in the process itself—given the details of the letter? Are the Kincaids mainly concerned with this question?

3. What is the point-at-issue for them? Are they arguing against strip mining on moral grounds? Or are they concerned only with the practical consequences? What assumptions about the rights of individuals underlie their argument?

4. Are the Kincaids addressing a general or a special audience? How do you know?

5. What is the tone of the letter, and what in the letter creates it? What do the various questions asked in the letter contribute?

VOCABULARY STUDY

Consult a dictionary of American English or Americanisms on the exact meaning of the following words and phrases and explain their use in the letter: *hollow, strips, spoil banks, grout, pudding.*

SUGGESTIONS FOR WRITING

1. Write a letter protesting an activity that has changed your life in some way. Let the details of the change carry the weight of your protest.

2. Look through magazines and newspapers for a defense of strip mining. You will find authors and titles in the *Reader's Guide to Periodical*

Literature. Analyze the assumptions and reasoning of the writer. (For a general review of the debate, pro and con, see *Business Week,* November 4, 1972.)

THE UNWILLED

Marya Mannes

Marya Mannes was born in New York City in 1904. She has been a feature editor of *Vogue* and *Glamour,* an intelligence analyst for the U.S. government, and from 1952 to 1963 a staff reporter for *The Reporter* magazine. She has written numerous books, including *Who Owns the Air?* (1960) and *Last Rights* (1974), and has received several awards for her journalism.

[1] Those who so passionately uphold the "sanctity of life" do not ask "what life?" nor see themselves as retarded and crippled in an institution for the rest of that life. Nor do they choose to see, or think of, the tens of thousands of lives born crippled and retarded, who, without will or choice, were allowed to be born as, presumably, the "right" of the damaged fetus *to* life.

[2] Rather than seeing the many tangible horrors of that life, the sanctity people choose to emphasize the maternal love and care transcending the agony of a malformed or mindless presence, day after day and year after year. Or they point to those few institutions where a dedicated staff and the latest therapies bring these children or adults to a minimal level of competence: dressing themselves, cleaning themselves, learning small tasks. Since these "inmates" sometimes play and sometimes smile, they are, of course, "happy." They know no other existence, they act on reflexes, not will.

[3] Certainly, love is the prime need of these incomplete beings, whether born that way or the victims of violent and crippling

accident. Two middle-aged couples I know who cannot give such grown sons or daughters the special help they need, visit them where they live every week, stay with them for hours. "Ben is such a beautiful young man," said one father. "It's still hard to believe that his fine face and body can exist without thought processes or directions. The circuits in his brain just don't connect."

[4]Certainly, there are parents who love their mongoloid and retarded children, accept them with their siblings as part of the family. But the "sanctity of life" people forget what an enormous toll it takes of the mother especially, who bore this child before the relatively new science of fetology could have given her the alternative choice: not to bear a permanently deformed or retarded being. For it has now become possible, with extremely delicate instruments and techniques, to establish deformation and brain damage, among other serious handicaps, in the unborn fetus when suspicions of malfunctioning exist.

[5]Yet to the antiabortionists, any birth is presumably better than no birth. They seem to forget that millions of unwanted children all over this world are not only destined for an uncherished and mean existence, but swell a population already threatening the resources of this planet, let alone its bare amenities.

[6]They also choose to ignore the kind of "homes" in every large community where the pitiful accidents of biology sit half-naked on floors strewn with feces, autistic and motionless, or banging their swollen heads against peeling walls.

[7]If the concept of "sanctity" does not include "quality," then the word has no meaning and less humanity. The rights of birth and death, of life itself, require both.

[8]Above all, how can the sanctity-of-life argument prevail in a society that condones death in war of young men who want to live, but will not permit the old and hopelessly ill, craving release, to die?

COMMENT

Mannes attacks the argument against abortion on its own grounds: she asks whether it is consistent to uphold the "sanctity of life" in circumstances where the right to life cannot be enjoyed. She wishes to show that the sanctity-of-life argument ignores fundamental questions, indeed simplifies a complex issue by treating it as a single one and suggesting a single answer. In logic, this simplification is referred to as "the fallacy of the complex question." The essay, indeed, is organized to expose this fallacy: each of the eight paragraphs focuses on a question or problem that must be considered if abortion is to be rejected on the ground that life has sanctity.

QUESTIONS FOR STUDY AND DISCUSSION

1. How does Mannes show the complexities of the abortion controversy?

2. What are Mannes's explicit assumptions about living and dying, and where are they stated? Does her discussion reveal unstated assumptions important to the debate?

3. Is the author saying or implying that abortion should be the decision of the parents alone? Do you believe that it should be?

4. Is Mannes arguing that the capacity to receive and enjoy love is the decisive consideration? Or is she merely stating that incomplete human beings have little if any chance of being loved?

5. Do you agree with the argument against abortion in the essay? Or are you in favor of abortion for different reasons? If you are opposed to abortion, why are you, and how do you answer the argument of the essay?

VOCABULARY STUDY

1. Write a paraphrase of the second paragraph that preserves the tone of the original. Look up the word *sanctity* before you write.

2. Identify those words in the essay that you consider highly connotative or emotional. Use your dictionary to find out whether there are neutral synonyms for these words.

SUGGESTIONS FOR WRITING

1. Write an essay of your own, stating your agreement or disagreement with Mannes's ideas, or some of them, and discussing the origin of your beliefs concerning abortion.

2. Trace the influence of your parents and schooling on one or two ideas you hold relating to the right to live or to die. Use this account to state a thesis. You may wish to build your discussion to the full statement of this thesis.

THE ABORTION CULTURE

Nick Thimmesch

Nick Thimmesch was born in Dubuque, Iowa, in 1927, and graduated from Iowa State University, where he later taught for two years. He served in the U.S. Merchant Marine, and began his journalism career in Iowa with the *Davenport Times* and *Des Moines Register*. From 1955 to 1967 he was a correspondent for *Time*; in 1967 he became Washington Bureau Chief for *Newsday*, and started a syndicated column two years later. He has written for numerous periodicals and has served as reporter and commentator on several television programs.

[1] A journalist often gets caught up in events flaring into instant print and broadcast—a Watergate, feverish inflation, a fretful fuel crisis. We grab at these, try to make some sense out of it all and soon turn to what's next. Occasionally we come on to something that strikes the core and won't go away. For me, it has been the question of the value of human life—a question embracing abortion, letting the newborn die, euthanasia and the creeping utilitarian ethic in medicine that impinges on human dignity. It's all reminiscent of the "what is useful is good" philosophy of German medicine in the '30s—a utilitarianism that sent 275,000 "unworthy" Germans to death and helped bring on the Hitler slaughter of millions of human beings a few years later.

[2] Now super-abortionists and others who relish monkeying around with human life cry that this is scare stuff inspired by hysterical Catholics waving picket signs. Not so. There is growing concern among Protestant and Jewish thinkers about "right to life" and the abortion-binge mentality.

[3] Fetal life has become cheap. There were an estimated 1,340,-000 legal and illegal abortions in the U.S last year. There were a whopping 540,245 abortions in New York City in a 30-month period under the liberalized state abortion law. The abortion culture is upon us. In one operating room, surgeons labor to save a 21-week-old baby; in the next, surgeons destroy, by abortion, another child, who can also be reckoned to be 21 weeks old. Where is the healing?

[4]Look beyond the political arguments and see the fetus and what doctors do to it. An unborn baby's heartbeat begins between the 18th and 25th day; brain waves can be detected at seven weeks; at nine to ten weeks, the unborn squint, swallow and make a fist. Look at the marvelous photographs and see human life. Should these little human beings be killed unless it is to save the mother's life?

[5]Other photos show this human life aborted, dropped onto surgical gauze or into plastic-bagged garbage pails. Take that human life by suction abortion and the body is torn apart, becoming a jumble of tiny arms and legs. In a D and C abortion, an instrument slices the body to pieces. Salt poisoning at nineteen weeks? The saline solution burns away the outer layer of the baby's skin. The ultimate is the hysterotomy (Caesarean section) abortion. As an operation, it can save mother and child; as an abortion it kills the child. Often, this baby fights for its life, breathes, moves and even cries. To see this, or the pictures of a plastic-bagged garbage can full of dead babies, well, it makes believers in right-to-life.

[6]It's unfair to write this way, cry the super-abortionists, or to show the horrible photos. But Buchenwald and Dachau looked terrible, too. Abortions are always grisly tragedies. This truth must be restated at a time when medical administrators chatter about "cost-benefit analysis" factors in deciding who lives and who dies.

[7]The utilitarian ethic is also common in the arguments of euthanasia advocates at work in six state legislatures. Their euphemisms drip like honey (should I say, cyanide?) just as they did in Germany—"death with dignity," the "good death." Their legal arguments fog the mind. Their mentality shakes me. One doctor, discussing the suicide-prone, wrote: "In such instances, positive euthanasia—a nice, smooth anesthetic to terminate life—appears preferable to suicide." Dr. Russell Sackett, author of the "Death With Dignity" bill in Florida, said: "Florida has 1,500 mentally retarded and mentally ill patients, 90 percent of whom should be allowed to die." The German utilitarians had concluded the same when they led the first group of mental patients to the gas chamber at the Sonnestein Psychiatric Hospital in 1939. It bothers me that eugenicists in Germany organized the mass destruction of mental patients, and in the United States pro-abortionists now also serve in pro-euthanasia organizations. Sorry, but I see a pattern.

[8]Utilitarianism isn't all abortion or euthanasia. Utilitarians

ran the experiment in which syphilitic black men died through lack of penicillin. There are also experiments on free-clinic patients, students, the institutionalized. Senate hearings revealed that two experimental birth-control drugs were used on the "vulnerable" for purposes other than those approved by the Food and Drug Administration.

[9]This monkeying around with people is relentless. Some medics would like to sterilize institutionalized people from here to breakfast. Psychosurgery is performed on hundreds of Americans annually, not to correct organic brain damage, but to alter their behavior. This chancy procedure, a first cousin of the now discredited prefrontal lobotomy that turned 50,000 Americans into human vegetables, is performed on unruly children and violence-prone prisoners.

[10]Experimenters produce life outside the womb—combining sperm and ovum—and dispose of the human zygotes by pouring the solution down the sink drain. Recently scientists debated guidelines for experimenting with the live human fetus. To those considering the fetus as an organ, like, say, a kidney, Dr. Andre Hellegers of Georgetown University pointed out that fetuses have their own organs and cannot be considered organs themselves. How does one get consent from a live fetus? he asked. Or even from its donors— the parents who authorized the abortion?

[11]Once fetal experimentation is sanctioned, are children to be next? Farfetched? No. In the New England Journal of Medicine, Dr. Franz Ingelfinger recently advocated removing the World Medical Association's absolute ban on experimenting with children and mental incompetents.

[12]We can brake the tendencies of technocratic-minded doctors and administrators coldly concerned with "cost-benefit analysis." There was no such brake in Germany. After the first killings at Sonnestein, respected German doctors, not Nazi officials, killed 275,000 patients in the name of euthanasia. Many were curable. Eventually the doomed "undesirables" included epileptics, mental defectives, World War I amputees, children with "badly modeled ears" and "bed wetters."

[13]The worst barbarisms often have small beginnings. The logical extension of this utilitarian ethic was the mass exterminations in slave-labor camps. In "A Sign for Cain," Dr. Frederic Wertham tells how death-dealing technicians from German state hospitals

(and their equipment) were moved to the camps in 1942 to begin the big job.

[14]Could the "what is useful is good" mentality lead to such horror in the U.S.? Not so long as I am allowed to write like this—which German journalists couldn't. Not so long as right-to-life Americans can dispute—which Germans couldn't. The extremes of the utilitarian mentality rampaging today through medicine, the drug industry and government will be checked by our press, law-makers and doctors, lawyers and clergymen holding to the traditional ethic. The Germans weren't blessed that way.

COMMENT

Thimmesch knows he is appealing to the emotions of his reader in describing various methods of abortion: "It's unfair to write this way, cry the super-abortionists, or to show the horrible photos. But Buchenwald and Dachau looked terrible, too." The appeal to emotion takes many forms, and in logic may be considered fallacious under some circumstances. One common form, the *argumentum ad hominem* (argument to the man) attacks the motives of the opponent rather than his or her ideas; the *argumentum ad populum* (argument to the people) appeals to the prejudices or feelings of the reader for or against the issue, preventing objective, rational discussion, and judgment.

Thimmesch defends the emotional appeal he is making: the question of abortion cannot be resolved through reason alone, for given the contradictory uses of reason in our time (reason has been used to defend euthanasia and other practices), there must be appeal also to feelings that do not "fog the mind." Though certain "givens" underlie Thimmesch's statement, his argument is mainly inductive: he argues from particulars of experience to probable conclusions about our society today. He also argues from analogy (another form of inductive argument) in identifying the pro-abortionists with the eugenics movement and their counterparts in Nazi Germany. Again, his appeal is to emotion: "Sorry, but I see a pattern." It is the lack of humane feeling, of identification with human emotions, that Thimmesch is chiefly concerned with. We can, he believes, "brake the tendencies of technocratic-minded doctors and administrators coldly concerned with 'cost-benefit analysis.'" The problem is larger than the decision to permit abortion: it is the utilitarian ethic in medicine—the idea that "what is useful is good"—that Thimmesch attacks. He can do so, not by presenting contrary evidence that preserving life is useful (another utilitarian argument), but in stating a contrary given—and appealing to the emotions of his readers in asking for recognition of its truth. The persuasiveness of the argument depends on this simple and direct emotional appeal.

QUESTIONS FOR STUDY AND DISCUSSION

1. Thimmesch traces the consequences of the utilitarian ethic in Nazi Germany. At what points in the essay does he mention these consequences, and why does he? What does he assume about the attitudes and feelings of his audience in mentioning these consequences?

2. Does he state the pro-abortion argument fully and objectively? Does he believe the argument can be stated fully and objectively?

3. What is the point at issue for Thimmesch? Are the rights of women a consideration?

4. Does Thimmesch consider the motives of the pro-abortionists to be at issue? Does he attack their motives?

5. What stated or implied "givens" underlie the argument?

6. Do you agree with Thimmesch's conclusions, and do you share his assumptions? If you disagree, why do you?

VOCABULARY STUDY

Complete the following sentences, using the italicized words according to one of their dictionary meanings:
a. The *utilitarian* argument for attending college is
b. They *liberalized* the rules governing the use of the car by
c. The science of *eugenics* is concerned with
d. *Extermination* has the purpose of
e. The *rampaging* horses
f. Behavior that Americans would consider *barbaric*

SUGGESTIONS FOR WRITING

Write a persuasive argument on one of the following topics. Keeping in mind the outline on page 235, choose a specific audience and fit your arguments and evidence to it.
a. no-fault automobile insurance
b. mercy killing

c. legalized marijuana
d. student participation in course planning
e. compulsory high school education

STARVING THE FUTURE'S CHILDREN

Seward Hiltner

> Seward Hiltner was born in Tyrone, Pennsylvania, in 1909, and attended Lafayette College and the University of Chicago, where he received his Ph.D. in 1952. He taught pastoral theology at Chicago from 1950 to 1961, and has taught at Princeton Theological Seminary since 1961. He has been a minister, a consultant to the Menninger Foundation, and the author of many books on Christian ideas and American life.

[1] While riding my bicycle the other day, keeping severely to the right to avoid being hit by passing cars that were exceeding the speed limit, I had a daydream. The scene was an island of proverbial lushness; its inhabitants were a young man and a young woman, both the picture of health, legally married before being marooned. They had plenty of gear to make shelter and other conveniences. There were, however, three drawbacks. First, there were no possible materials with which to make an escape boat. Second, there were no fish in the sea around the island. Third, the island food supply, though providing all necessary nutrients, grew so slowly that it would be used up in 50 years, while the first fruits of another crop would not be ready for 50.

[2] The crucial connubial dialogue took place on the day the young wife realized that she was irremediably pregnant. The present 2,500-calorie-a-day diet, she noted, would feed the two of them comfortably for their lifetime; but, with junior soon to be added,

such a regimen would sustain the three for only about 35 years. Nonsense, said the husband, arguing that, with his scientific gear, he would figure out in a few years how to turn the abundant seaweed into food.

[3]But suppose he did not succeed, the wife persisted. Could they, on moral grounds, proceed with the abundant diet, knowing of the strong possibility that their child would starve to death in his 30s? The husband discounted such reasoning, and pointed out that in older years they would naturally eat less. The wife proposed that they cut their daily intake to 1,200 calories each, arguing from her knowledge of nutrition that they might thereby be healthier and would, in that way, be sure not to starve their child to death in later years. My daydream stopped before a decision was reached, when a particularly determined car forced me onto the sidewalk.

[4]Instead of exegeting the daydream in terms of the entire energy question, my reflections focused on automobiles as a part of it. Is anyone at all taking a position about them similar to that of the wife on the island? Or are all voices echoing the husband's arguments?

[5] We hardly expect car manufacturers to plump for anything less than a 2,500-calorie automobile diet; or, if they do get down to 2,300, we expect them to sell more cars. It is equally improbable to expect labor unions to suggest that we need fewer cars. In addition, every worker drives his or her own car to work. What of scientists and technologists not in the automobile industry? With few exceptions, their hopes seem to be pinned on finding a way to process the seaweed; and besides, they all drive to work alone.

[6]We look in vain to commuters who, even if they ride a train or bus, complain about the paucity of parking space. The "nonworking" members of households could not get to volunteer activities, to church study groups, or to the grocery store without their individual cars. Students could not get to classes. How could physicians get to their hospitals? Or ministers make pastoral calls?

[7]The concluding message from the recent World Council of Churches meeting in Nairobi advocated the "transformation of civilization," but it seems unlikely that many delegates, upon arrival at their hometown airports, proceeded to their residences by bus, on bicycle, or on foot.

[8]Even the ecologists, while trying to make automobiles either safer or less polluting, have not advocated a 1,200-calorie car diet.

Even if they walk to work and forego a suburban home, they want cars for business trips and family vacations.

[9]Is there the remotest possibility that this nation's people would voluntarily submit to limitations on the ownership and use of cars? Perhaps my crystal ball is clouded, but I cannot put my finger on any group prepared to advocate such a policy, much less to attempt converting others to it. Without exception, we seem addicted to the automobile in such fashion that even the smallest reduction in its use would give us withdrawal pains of unimaginable severity; and by common silent-majority (99 per cent plus) consent, we ignore our collective condition. The thought that our children and grandchildren may starve is successfully repressed. There is nothing like unanimity to make repression work. If almost everybody does it, how can it be immoral?

[10]I do not know what proportion of our current energy usage is drained by the manufacture and use of automobiles, and I cannot think of any source for such data, even the federal government, that would be above suspicion. In view of huge energy expenditures elsewhere, perhaps the proportion for automobiles does not bulk large in the total. But if we do not start somewhere in cutting down on the use of fossil fuels, are we not denying by repression the guilt that we ought to feel?

[11]There ought to be a Christian eschatology for this situation, with some strong guidelines for present practice. I wonder what Nathan would say.

COMMENT

Hiltner is concerned with a very large issue, the "transformation of civilization." Instead of trying to persuade his audience of the need of this transformation through a broad discussion of abstract issues, he focuses on a single transformation that must take place if civilization is to survive at all. This limited focus is one important persuasive device he uses. Another is the use of illustrative analogy to bring his audience to a recognition of the main problem—their own present actions and attitudes. At the end of the essay he suggests that a Christian answer to the repression of guilt and the early end of civilization is needed, and wonders what the biblical Nathan would say about the present situation. These appeals and the biblical allusion are directed to a specific audience—the readers of a magazine devoted to issues of Christianity today.

But Hiltner has the general reader in mind, also. The single transformation he discusses has general importance for readers of many backgrounds and persuasions.

QUESTIONS FOR STUDY AND DISCUSSION

1. What illustrative analogy does Hiltner use to make his audience aware of the single transformation that must take place? How does he encourage his audience to examine their actions and attitudes through this analogy?

2. What in the essay shows that Hiltner is addressing readers of a Christian magazine? Besides the automobile example, what else shows that he is also addressing the general reader?

3. Are you persuaded by Hiltner's reasoning in the essay? Would another example have been more persuasive to you? What other examples would you use to persuade people of the need for transformation?

VOCABULARY STUDY

Write sentences of your own, using equivalent words and phrases for each of the following: *proverbial lushness, connubial dialogue, plump for, unimaginable severity, collective condition, repressed, unanimity.*

SUGGESTIONS FOR WRITING

1. Discuss whether or not you would willingly "submit to limitations on the ownership and use of cars." In the course of your discussion, explain your feelings about cars and describe your driving habits.

2. Choose another transformation that you think must occur if civilization is to survive, and persuade a specific audience to change their thinking and habits so that this transformation can come about.

sentence variety

A string of short sentences, written without connectives, will lose the attention of the reader quickly, owing to their monotony:

> You are watching coal miners at work. You realize momentarily what different universes people inhabit. It is a sort of world apart down there. One can quite easily go through life without ever hearing about that world. Probably a majority of people would even prefer not to hear about it.

Adding connectives and subordinating some of these ideas are ways of removing the monotony and focusing attention on the important ideas:

> Watching coal miners at work, you realize momentarily what different universes different people inhabit. *Down there* where coal is dug it is a sort of world apart *which* one can quite easily go through life without ever hearing about. Probably a majority of people would even prefer not to hear about it.—George Orwell, *The Road to Wigan Pier*

Two of the important connectives in Orwell's original passage have been italicized. Notice that the second sentence of the simplified reduction began with the subject and predicate; Orwell by contrast begins with the modifier *down there* to connect the first two sentences, and he subordinates the third sentence to the second through the word *which.* The more varied sentences are in length and construction, the less monotonous they will seem, though as we shall see parallel ideas need parallel construction to highlight their similarities. Too much variation can be as distracting as too little.

A simple rule to keep in mind when building and revising sentences is that English sentences tend to reserve the end of the sentence for the most important idea. This end focus is seen in the stress we give final words as in this spoken sentence:

My wife's parents live in NEWark.

Even if we have to stress another word in the sentence, we still give a degree of stress to the final word:

My WIFE's parents live in NEWark. (my wife's parents, not my own)

This rule has important consequences for the way we build and vary sentences. It means, simply, that we can "load" the end of the sentence, as we cannot the beginning. We speak or write the following sentence, for example, without thinking twice about its structure:

(1) I know that they won't come because they're out of town.

We would not say or write:

(2) That they won't come because they're out of town I know.

But we can and do on occasion open the sentence with a shorter complement:

(3) That he is coming I have no doubt.

Notice that the complement *that they won't come* in (1) is itself modified by a subordinate clause and therefore cannot appear at the beginning of the sentence, whereas the unmodified complement in (3)—*That he is coming*—can so appear. This is one limitation we face in beginning a sentence, as every speaker and writer knows without being told. By contrast, we can add complex modifiers to the end of the sentence without difficulty, owing to the capacity of the English sentence to carry weight at the end. Notice in the following sentence the relatively short and simple opening modifying phrase and the relatively long concluding subordinate clause:

Despite the Gestapo terror led by Himmler and Heydrich after the Anschluss *Germans flocked by the hundreds of thousands to Aus-*

tria, where they could pay with their marks for sumptuous meals not available in Germany for years and for bargain-priced vacations amid Austria's matchless mountains and lakes.—William L. Shirer, *The Rise and Fall of the Third Reich* (main clause italicized)

If end-of-sentence emphasis is to register as we want it to, we must occasionally introduce a short sentence for contrast, or coordinate main clauses (connecting them by *and, but, for, yet, or, nor*), at the same time keeping our eye on the meaning of the passage.

Compound sentences can run on indefinitely:

John loves Mary, and Mary loves Bill, but Bill loves Sally, and Sally loves Harry . . .

A simple sentence can be modified endlessly:

The dog that is lying on the rug in the living room will be taken for a walk around the block after we have finished supper and then . . .

There is no logical reason why these sentences must end, and many English sentences do continue for considerable length. The old definition of a sentence as a complete thought is of no use in deciding when to end sentences of this kind, for the completeness of the thought lies in the mind of the speaker or writer, who alone knows when everything necessary has been said. Sentence length is thus often determined by how much can be included without losing the reader. Sentences in insurance policies are much longer than those in magazine advertisements. In general, a sentence should be ended when no idea is left hanging, and when the beginning of it seems remote or is hard to remember. The sentence should not seem to run on or drift along monotonously.

Making the sentence express our meaning exactly is our chief concern, and there may be one way only to construct the sentence. Usually, however, we can choose one of several ways to build a sentence, and we do so with a specific audience in mind. Sentence variety is governed as much by considerations of audience as by the requirements of clear, precise meaning.

FIVE-YEAR-OLDS

Harry Reasoner

Harry Reasoner was born in 1923 in Dakota City, Iowa. He studied at Stanford University and the University of Minnesota, was a White House correspondent and commentator for the Columbia Broadcasting System, and is now with ABC News. He is the author of *Tell Me About Women* (1946) and *The Reasoner Report* (1966).

[1]There has been a good deal of talk in recent years to the effect that—except for a formality or two at the beginning—fathers are no longer necessary. There isn't anything for them to do, the articles in the magazines say, and what they do do, they don't do very well. They aren't masculine enough, they don't project the male image to their children, their wives dominate them and it would really be better all the way around if they just stayed in town and mailed the money. Now some of us do not allow our wives and children to read articles by psychologists so we've been spared this attitude, but in behalf of other fellows in the father business, I'd like to note that there is one family role in which the father is indispensable and unique. Somebody has to like five-year-old-girls and only a father seems able to.

[2]It's pretty well known that nobody likes little boys after the age of six months, but little girls are fairly popular—except during that period that begins about age three and reaches a peak at age five and begins to decline at around age seven when little girls begin to see the advantages of being square. Five-year-olds don't care about advantages or popular approval. Their attitude is chiefly negative. They don't like anything to eat except potato chips and ice cream. They lie a good deal and with a splendid disregard for evidence: they will maintain to the point of tears, for instance, that they have eaten most of their dinner even though the untouched plate is sitting there and several brothers and sisters are eager to explain that they are lying.

[3]Five-year-old girls don't like to play outdoors unless it is

slushy and they can go out in party shoes and a clean dress. They don't like to play indoors unless they can wear a snowsuit and sit dangerously near the fire. They don't like kindergarten unless weather or illness or a holiday keeps them home.

[4]Five-year-old girls have some positive talents. Impartial studies indicate that in the case of the average girl her voice reaches a peak of shrillness and carrying power at age five which it never attains again. Five-year-old girls are experts at dealing with both older and younger siblings: a capable five-year-old can reduce a two-and-a-half-year-old sister to helpless tears in four-and-a-half minutes with some simple but expert trick such as showing her a toy, describing its advantages, and then refusing to let her play with it. A talented five-year-old can make a fourteen-year-old boy scream by arguing that sand is put on the roads to make it slippery, that snow is warm, that nobody swims in the summer.

[5]After a series of days in which a five-year-old is acting five years old, sisters and brothers are ready to quit. Even a patient mother who has been through it before finds it hard to remember that the five-year-old will grow into the eight-year-old. Only fathers like five-year-olds, and to some extent vice versa. Maybe these two groups know they need each other.

COMMENT

Reasoner's essay, originally delivered on the air, illustrates the sentence structure and punctuation of informal speech and writing. Reasoner's sentences are mainly compound—that is, they consist of main clauses joined by a coordinating conjunction such as *and* or *but*. In the whole essay only one sentence begins with a subordinate clause. The following sentence is typical of the essay:

> There isn't anything for them to do, the articles in the magazine say, and what they do do, they don't do very well.

The sentence immediately following is built on the same compound pattern:

> They aren't masculine enough, they don't project the male image to their children, their wives dominate them and it would really be better all the way around if they just stayed in town and mailed the money.

Punctuation throughout the essay, as in some informal writing, substitutes for the inflections of voice. Compare the following:

> They lie a good deal and with a splendid disregard for evidence: they will maintain to the point of tears, for instance, that they have eaten most of their dinner . . .

> They lie a good deal and with a splendid disregard for evidence. They will maintain to the point of tears, for instance, that they have eaten most of their dinner . . .

In the first sentence we do not drop the voice at the word *evidence:* we begin *they* at the same pitch. The colon prevents our lowering the pitch to mark a complete stop. In the second sentence we do lower the pitch to show we have completed the sentence.

Because we cannot depend on inflections in voice in written communication, punctuation is used mainly to show the connection of ideas—to make their relation clear at first reading. Consider the following sentence:

> She searched the street for the dog, in her pajamas.

Whether or not we would pause in speaking this sentence, we add the comma in writing to avoid confusion. Sometimes the comma of a written sentence coincides with a pause in speech, sometimes it does not. The comma in the following sentence is optional:

> Despite the heavy rain (,) we packed the car and left for Canada.

It is not optional in the following:

> Knowing that it was going to rain heavily, we decided not to pack the car and leave for Canada.

Written sentences, even informal ones, must be tighter than spoken ones, owing to the loss of vocal inflection and the need to connect ideas precisely and clearly for the reader, who cannot ask us to repeat or rephrase our statements. Punctuation is an important means of showing these relationships.

QUESTIONS FOR STUDY AND DISCUSSION

1. The first sentence of the essay contains an idea set off by dashes. What inflection of voice do these suggest? How would the sentence be read orally if the idea were enclosed in parentheses?

2. What sentence of the essay opens with a subordinate clause?

3. What sentences could Reasoner have varied for emphasis? Would these variations have increased the formality of the essay?

4. What do short sentences in the essay contribute to emphasis?

5. In what paragraph are the sentences the least varied? What ideas are emphasized through the similar structure of the sentences?

6. Reasoner has exaggerated in some of his statements for the sake of humor. Do you agree with the distinction he makes, or do you think he has not exaggerated the truth?

SENTENCE STUDY

The following simple sentences are adapted from the originals in George Orwell's *The Road to Wigan Pier*. Combine them into a single sentence, subordinating where possible, and using semicolons or colons only when necessary:

a. Miners are changed from one shift to another. Their families have to make adjustments to these changes. These adjustments are tiresome in the extreme.

b. If he is on the night shift he gets home in time for breakfast. He gets home in the middle of the afternoon on the morning shift. On the afternoon shift he gets home in the middle of the night. In each case, of course, he wants his principal meal of the day as soon as he returns.

c. The rate of accidents among miners is high. It is high compared with that in other trades. Accidents are so high that they are taken for granted almost as they would be in a minor war.

d. The most obviously understandable cause of accidents is explosions of gas. This cause is always more or less present in the atmosphere of the pit.

e. The gas may be touched off by a spark during blasting operations. It may be touched off by a pick striking a spark from a stone. It may be touched off by a defective lamp. And it may be touched off by "gob fires." These are spontaneously generated fires which smolder in the coal dust and are very hard to put out.

SUGGESTIONS FOR WRITING

Discuss the differences you notice between teenage boys and girls or between the relationships of teenage boys and girls with their fathers or mothers. Use your discussion to develop a thesis about adolescence.

WAITING AND WAITING, BUT NOT FOR NAUGHT

Dorothy Rodgers

Dorothy Rodgers was born in 1909 in New York City, and was educated at Wellesley College. She is a sculptor and the author of several books and a monthly *McCall's* column, *Of Two Minds,* written with her daughter Mary Rodgers. Her husband is the composer Richard Rodgers.

[1]Knowing that I would have to apply for Medicare three months before I reached the marvelous date of becoming 65 years old, I telephoned the Social Security office for information.

[2]I learned that I would have to produce myself in person together with some documents: a photostat of my birth certificate, a W-2 tax form showing Social Security payments made by me and my employer, and an application form which they agreed to mail.

[3]Since I'm self-employed (no one pays any Social Security for me), I didn't have a W-2 form, but I did have two 1099 miscellaneous forms sent me by McCall's and The Ideal Toy Company showing the amount of income I had earned in 1973. I hoped that would do, especially as I wasn't applying for Social Security for the excellent reason that I don't qualify for it.

[4]Armed with these official documents and a book to help pass the time, I set off on a terribly cold morning for the midtown branch of our Department of Health, Education and Welfare where applications for welfare, Social Security and Medicare are processed.

[5]The office is at 1657 Broadway, a building that looks as if it shouldn't be allowed out in daylight.

[6]Next to the entrance was an empty store with double gates stretched across its front, padlocked to protect God knows what inside.

[7]The sidewalk was littered with the remnants of stuff people use when they wait a lot: cigarette butts, chewing-gum and candy

wrappers and crushed paper cups. People were milling around the entrance and I soon found out why. Three polite but firm cops just inside the doors wouldn't let anyone upstairs.

[8] "Social Security?" one of them asked me.

[9] "No," I said, "Medicare."

[10] "Same thing," he said. "Get on the bus."

[11] "What bus? I'm not going anywhere!"

[12] "Lady," he said, "go sit in the bus. It's a waiting room. You'll get a number."

[13] I turned and looked where he was pointing and there were three buses lined up against the curb right in front of the building, so I climbed aboard the first one, which was almost empty.

[14] I took the aisle seat in the second row and watched the bus fill up rapidly with all kinds of people: young, old, mothers with cranky children, children with cranky mothers, people who were obviously ill, blacks, whites, one stoned and at least a few eccentrics.

[15] The bus was soon totally filled and people were being directed to the other buses. Everyone waited unquestioningly and with complete resignation. At last, one of the policemen approached the bus. He gave us all slips of paper with numbers on them and told us to wait.

[16] "Wait" was clearly the name of the game. However, after only a few minutes, the cop came back and told ten people in the front of the bus to get off and go to the second floor.

[17] The second floor was enormous. A whole open space was covered by desks at which applicants were being interviewed. Fluorescent lights in the ceiling provided the only relief from the vast gray area. Immediately in front of the elevators there were two waiting rooms. A girl sat at a desk between them. We were told to find seats in the left section and wait for the guard to call our numbers. Mine was 297 and number 258 had just been called.

[18] Although I came expecting to wait, an hour and a half had already passed and I realized I was going to be late for my next appointment. I certainly didn't want to leave and have to go through the whole performance all over again another day, so I decided to make a phone call and explain why I'd be late. I got up, tripped over a chair and landed flat on the floor.

[19] People were extraordinarily concerned. "Did you hurt yourself?" came at me from applicants and officials in varying accents. Fortunately, I hadn't and, gathering my book, bag, gloves, coat and

dignity, I went up to a woman who seemed to be in charge and asked her where the phone booth was. "Downstairs," she answered.

[20] "But if I go downstairs, I might lose my place."

[21] "I'm so glad you didn't hurt yourself! Use my phone." It was kind and unbureaucratic, and I was grateful. Having completed the phone call, I returned to my old seat and moved my legs to make way for a small black woman of indeterminate age who sank into the chair next to mine and gave a great sigh.

[22] I looked at her face; it wasn't black, it was green. She said: "I like to drop dead out there in the cold—buses all filled up. The policeman said for me to come up and sit where it's warm. I got asthma and I got sugar, I can't work and I'm sick. I can't work—I'm 93—oh, I mean 63."

[23] She talked on unintelligibly for a while. All I could do was to make sympathetic sounds. I felt desperately sorry for her, but there was no way I could help solve her overwhelming problems.

[24] Just then the cop called out 279 and I jumped up, dropping my gloves on the floor. Somebody cried: "Lady, wyn'cha put 'em in your pocket so you don't lose 'em?"

[25] I felt like six going on 65—especially as my number was 297, not 279.

[26] I went back to my chair and the woman resumed her talk until at last my number was called. I wished her luck and told her that I hoped things would work out for her.

[27] The next step took me to the girl at the desk. She asked my name, why I was there, and waved me in the direction of the other waiting room where I was to wait until my name was called. After a relatively short time, someone called my name and I was led to a Mr. Wolfe's desk.

[28] He was young and, like everyone else, pleasant and courteous. He went over my papers, took them to be photostated and returned— all in a matter of about five minutes. That was it. I could leave.

[29] I looked around at everyone—the people being quietly interviewed at the desks, the applicants sitting and waiting, waiting with infinite patience.

[30] Undemanding and submissive, confused and afraid to ask questions, sick or destitute—or merely over 65—they wait, in the cold or on the bus or in the dreary waiting rooms. Wait for Lady Bountiful to hand out our Thanksgiving turkey. Only it isn't Lady

Bountiful. It's our own friendly Uncle Sam and it's not a handout. It's a right paid for by the same people, over many years.

[31]No one had been pushed around; no one had been rude or unkind. I went over to the woman who had allowed me to use her phone to tell her how remarkable I thought it was. She said, "We try."

COMMENT

Mrs. Rodgers' sentences are varied enough so that the short sentences are emphatic. Notice the effect of the one that follows the description of her falling: "People were extraordinarily concerned." And her first sight of the room has the same impact: "The second floor was enormous." If all the sentences in the essay were as short as these, none would convey such impact. The sentence structure expresses feeling in other ways: the statement of the old woman sitting next to the author is punctuated to express her confusion and exhaustion (paragraph 22). Mrs. Rodgers succeeds in doing more than just stating the facts of the episode: she allows us to feel the experience as she felt it.

QUESTIONS FOR STUDY AND DISCUSSION

1. Where else in the essay are short sentences used for emphasis?

2. How does Mrs. Rodgers vary her sentences in paragraphs 14–19 so that not all of them begin with "I"?

3. She might have combined some of her short paragraphs. Which of them could be combined? What is gained by not combining them?

4. Mrs. Rodgers depends on surprise to develop her thesis. How does she build to these surprises? What point is she making?

VOCABULARY STUDY

Explain what the connotations of the following words contribute to the experience: *littered, cranky, eccentrics, sympathetic, submissive, destitute.*

SUGGESTIONS FOR WRITING

Describe a similar experience in which your expectations about what would happen were not realized. Make the details of the experience convey your feelings.

PARENTS MUST MAKE UP
THEIR MINDS

Sydney J. Harris

Sydney J. Harris was born in London, England, in 1917. He attended the University of Chicago and Central College in Chicago, and was employed in public relations for the legal division of the City of Chicago. He has been a journalist most of his life, writing a column for the *Chicago Daily News* since 1941. His columns have been collected into numerous books, including *Majority of One* (1957), *Last Things First* (1961), and *On the Contrary* (1964).

[1]Parents want two opposite things at once: they want their children to excel, and they want their children to be docile. But the two don't go together, and never have.

[2]Every study made of "achievers" in a genuinely creative sense—that is, people who were truly innovative, whose existence made some positive difference for the human race—has shown that as children these people were anything but docile and conformist.

[3]Almost all were independent, in mind and spirit, if not in body. They began thinking for themselves at an early age, and either rejected or modified their parents' code of conduct and scale of values. Many were not popular with their peers, and most of them were found either "stupid" or "difficult" by their teachers.

[4]Actually, when parents say they want a child to "excel," what they customarily mean is that they want him to be successful and to be popular. But genuine achievers are often those who fail for a long time, and who rarely attain popularity outside a small circle. And they have often had severe educational problems, from St. Thomas Aquinas, who was called a "dumb ox" at school, to Thomas Edison, who received depressingly poor grades and left school before the age of twelve.

[5]A creative and imaginative child is a great burden to the ordinary parent, and this is why a repressive society produces so few

of them; the weaker spirits are crushed, and the hardier ones often overreact in a way that turns them into delinquents, or actual criminals if they happen to live in a squalid environment.

⁶As adults, most of us do not care to tolerate the kinetic qualities of children. We want them to stop wriggling or jumping or sloshing through puddles or dangling from fence posts; and in the same way, we resent agile minds and mercurial temperaments. We don't like to answer silly questions, to respond to anxieties that take fantasy form, or to acknowledge the deeper life of the child's spirit.

⁷He is to be quiet, tractable, unquestioning, unthinking, and invisible if possible. Even the so-called permissive parent is doing the same thing in a different way—giving the child too much money or too much false freedom in order to get him out of the way, to leave time and energy for adult pursuits. The TV set is now what the Bible lesson used to be, only more seductive and more effective.

⁸Nothing in the world is harder than rearing a child who will make a difference to his society. But nothing in the world is more worthwhile, if we are breeding for improvement and not just for dumb survival.

COMMENT

English sentences are built by addition: that is the advantage of the coordinating conjunctions *and, but, for, yet, or, nor*. They join closely related ideas that can stand together:

> Many were not popular with their peers, *and* most of them were found either "stupid" or "difficult" by their teachers.

The semicolon in the single sentence of paragraph 5 also joins closely related ideas. Though the discussion and sentence structure of the essay are formal (the subject is abstract, not concrete, like the experience Dorothy Rodgers describes), the sentences are simple or compound, the kind found most in informal writing. Like Reasoner, Harris prefers to break sentences for emphasis rather than connect very long main clauses. If the two sentences of the final paragraph had been combined into one sentence, the final subordinate clause might have been set off in this way:

> Nothing in the world is harder than rearing a child who will make a difference to his society, *but* nothing in the world is more worthwhile—if we are breeding for improvement and not just for dumb survival.

QUESTIONS FOR STUDY AND DISCUSSION

1. What use does Harris make of dashes?

2. How many of his sentences begin with subordinate clauses?

3. Is Harris saying that all delinquent children are creative and imaginative, or that children have trouble in school only for the reasons he gives?

4. Why is the TV set "more seductive and more effective" than the Bible lesson today? Does Harris state or imply the reason?

5. What assumptions about human nature underlie the argument? Are any of these assumptions stated in the essay?

6. What is the thesis of the essay, and where is it first stated? How does Harris restate it in the course of the essay?

VOCABULARY STUDY

1. Explain the special meanings of *creative* and *imaginative* in the essay.

2. Write a paraphrase of paragraphs 4–6 in language that would be clear to high school students. Add examples to your paraphrase if you wish.

SUGGESTIONS FOR WRITING

Develop one of the following statements from your own experience, agreeing or disagreeing with the statement:

   a. "Parents want two opposite things at once: they want their children to excel, and they want their children to be docile."
   b. "A creative and imaginative child is a great burden to the ordinary parent."
   c. "As adults, most of us do not care to tolerate the kinetic qualities of children."
   d. "The TV set is now what the Bible lesson used to be, only more seductive and more effective."

parallelism

When words, phrases, and clauses are worded similarly and used in the same way in a sentence, they are said to be parallel:

> He *jumped off* the porch, *ran through* the woods, and *fell into* the pond.

Sentence parallelism may not be as exact as this. The three subordinate clauses in the following sentence of Reasoner are parallel to the extent that they begin with the same connective, *that:*

> A talented five-year-old can make a fourteen-year-old boy scream by arguing *that* sand is put on the roads to make them slippery,
> > *that* snow is warm,
> > *that* nobody swims in the summer.

The parallelism would be faulty if the clause *and nobody swims . . .* were substituted for the final clause above.

In the same way, sentences in a paragraph may be parallel in structure:

> Five-year-old girls *don't like* to play outdoors *unless* it is slushy and they can go out in party shoes and a clean dress.
>
> They *don't like* to play indoors *unless* they can wear a snowsuit and sit dangerously near the fire.
>
> They *don't like* kindergarten *unless* weather or illness or a holiday keeps them home.

The parallel structure makes the reader aware of the parallelism in ideas. If the ideas were not parallel, the parallel structure might seem awkward. Older writers often aimed for strict parallelism in sentences and paragraphs, whereas modern writers favor the looser parallelism of Reasoner's first sentence above. They may even break the pattern, as Reasoner does in the following sentence (with the words *their wives dominate*) to avoid a formal effect:

> *They aren't* masculine enough, *they don't* project the male image to their children, *their wives dominate* them and it would really be better all the way around if they just stayed in town and mailed the money.

THINGS:
THE THROW-AWAY SOCIETY

Alvin Toffler

Alvin Toffler was born in 1928 in New York City and attended New York University. He has written for many newspapers and magazines, has taught at the New School in New York and at Cornell, and has been an associate editor of *Fortune*. His books are *The Culture Consumers* (1964) and *Future Shock* (1970).

[1]"Barbie," a twelve-inch plastic teen-ager, is the best-known and best-selling doll in history. Since its introduction in 1959, the Barbie doll population of the world has grown to 12,000,000—more than the human population of Los Angeles or London or Paris. Little girls adore Barbie because she is highly realistic and eminently dress-upable. Mattel, Inc., makers of Barbie, also sells a complete wardrobe for her, including clothes for ordinary daytime wear, clothes for formal party wear, clothes for swimming and skiing.

[2]Recently Mattel announced a new improved Barbie doll. The new version has a slimmer figure, "real" eyelashes, and a twist-and-turn waist that makes her more humanoid than ever. Moreover, Mattel announced that, for the first time, any young lady wishing to purchase a new Barbie would receive a trade-in allowance for her old one.

[3]What Mattel did not announce was that by trading in her old doll for a technologically improved model, the little girl of today, citizen of tomorrow's super-industrial world, would learn a fundamental lesson about the new society: that man's relationships with *things* are increasingly temporary.

[4]The ocean of man-made physical objects that surrounds us is set within a larger ocean of natural objects. But increasingly, it is the technologically produced environment that matters for the individual. The texture of plastic or concrete, the irridescent glisten of an automobile under a streetlight, the staggering vision of a cityscape seen from the window of a jet—these are the intimate realities of his existence. Man-made things enter into and color his consciousness. Their number is expanding with explosive force, both absolutely and relative to the natural environment. This will be even more true in super-industrial society than it is today.

[5]Anti-materialists tend to deride the importance of "things." Yet things are highly significant, not merely because of their functional utility, but also because of their psychological impact. We develop relationships with things. Things affect our sense of continuity or discontinuity. They play a role in the structure of situations and the foreshortening of our relationships with things accelerates the pace of life.

[6]Moreover, our attitudes toward things reflect basic value judgments. Nothing could be more dramatic than the difference between the new breed of little girls who cheerfully turn in their Barbies for the new improved model and those who, like their mothers and grandmothers before them, clutch lingeringly and lovingly to the same doll until it disintegrates from sheer age. In this difference lies the contrast between past and future, between societies based on permanence, and the new, fast-forming society based on transience.

[7]That man-thing relationships are growing more and more temporary may be illustrated by examining the culture surrounding the little girl who trades in her doll. This child soon learns that Barbie dolls are by no means the only physical objects that pass into and out of her young life at a rapid clip. Diapers, bibs, paper napkins, Kleenex, towels, non-returnable soda bottles—all are used up quickly in her home and ruthlessly eliminated. Corn muffins come in baking tins that are thrown away after one use. Spinach is

encased in plastic sacks that can be dropped into a pan of boiling water for heating, and then thrown away. TV dinners are cooked and often served on throw-away trays. Her home is a large processing machine through which objects flow, entering and leaving, at a faster and faster rate of speed. From birth on, she is inextricably embedded in a throw-away culture.

[8]The idea of using a product once or for a brief period and then replacing it, runs counter to the grain of societies or individuals steeped in a heritage of poverty. Not long ago Uriel Rone, a market researcher for the French advertising agency Publicis, told me: "The French housewife is not used to disposable products. She likes to keep things, even old things, rather than throw them away. We represented one company that wanted to introduce a kind of plastic throw-away curtain. We did a marketing study for them and found the resistance too strong." This resistance, however, is dying all over the developed world.

[9]Thus a writer, Edward Maze, has pointed out that many Americans visiting Sweden in the early 1950's were astounded by its cleanliness. "We were almost awed by the fact that there were no beer and soft drink bottles by the roadsides, as, much to our shame, there were in America. But by the 1960's, lo and behold, bottles were suddenly blooming along Swedish highways ... What happened? Sweden had become a buy, use and throw-away society, following the American pattern." In Japan today throw-away tissues are so universal that cloth handkerchiefs are regarded as old fashioned, not to say unsanitary. In England for sixpence one may buy a "Dentamatic throw-away toothbrush" which comes already coated with toothpaste for its one-time use. And even in France, disposable cigarette lighters are commonplace. From cardboard milk containers to the rockets that power space vehicles, products created for short-term or one-time use are becoming more numerous and crucial to our way of life.

[10]The recent introduction of paper and quasi-paper clothing carried the trend toward disposability a step further. Fashionable boutiques and working-class clothing stores have sprouted whole departments devoted to gaily colored and imaginatively designed paper apparel. Fashion magazines display breathtakingly sumptuous gowns, coats, pajamas, even wedding dresses made of paper. The bride pictured in one of these wears a long white train of

lacelike paper that, the caption writer notes, will make "great kitchen curtains" after the ceremony.

[11] Paper clothes are particularly suitable for children. Writes one fashion expert: "Little girls will soon be able to spill ice cream, draw pictures and make cutouts on their clothes while their mothers smile benignly at their creativity." And for adults who want to express their own creativity, there is even a "paint-yourself-dress" complete with brushes. Price: $2.00.

[12] Price, of course, is a critical factor behind the paper explosion. Thus a department store features simple A-line dresses made of what it calls "devil-may-care cellulose fiber and nylon." At $1.29 each, it is almost cheaper for the consumer to buy and discard a new one than to send an ordinary dress to the cleaners. Soon it will be. But more than economics is involved, for the extension of the throw-away culture has important psychological consequences.

[13] We develop a throw-away mentality to match our throw-away products. This mentality produces, among other things, a set of radically altered values with respect to property. But the spread of disposability through the society also implies decreased durations in man-thing relationships. Instead of being linked with a single object over a relatively long span of time, we are linked for brief periods with the succession of objects that supplant it.

COMMENT

Parallelism is an important means to emphasis and clarity in Toffler's sentences. The first paragraph contains two important uses of parallel phrases:

> Little girls adore Barbie because she is *highly realistic* and *eminently dress-upable.*

> Mattel, Inc., makers of Barbie, also sells a complete wardrobe for her, including *clothes for ordinary daytime wear, clothes for formal party wear, clothes for swimming and skiing.*

Later in the essay a series of sentences illustrating a topic idea are closely parallel in structure:

> *Corn muffins come* in baking tins that are thrown away after one use. *Spinach is encased* in plastic sacks that can be dropped into a

pan of boiling water for heating, and then thrown away. *TV dinners are cooked* and often served on throw-away trays.

Parallelism is important in comparing and contrasting ideas, as Toffler is doing throughout his discussion.

QUESTIONS FOR STUDY AND DISCUSSION

1. In what other sentences are words and phrases parallel? How does this parallelism promote emphasis and clarity?

2. In what sentences are clauses loosely parallel?

3. How does Toffler move from a single example to a trait of American life? How does he show this example to be typical rather than exceptional?

4. Is Toffler entirely critical of the importance given to "things" in America? Does he state his attitude directly or implicitly?

5. What is the purpose of the comparison with Sweden and Japan? Is Toffler merely illustrating the influence of American consumption?

6. What use does he make of paper and quasi-paper clothing in the discussion? Would this example have been as effective as the Barbie doll in introducing the discussion?

7. What effects does Toffler trace to what causes?

8. To what extent does he depend on formal transitions? Could any of these transitions be omitted without loss of clarity?

VOCABULARY STUDY

1. Use the following words in sentences of your own: *humanoid, benignly, sumptuous, disposable.*

2. Write a paraphrase of paragraph 5, giving particular attention to these phrases: *anti-materialists, functional utility, psychological impact, sense of continuity or discontinuity, structure of situations, foreshortening of our relationships with things.*

SUGGESTIONS FOR WRITING

1. Develop one of the following statements from your own experience. Define your terms, trace cause and effects, and use your discussion to develop a specific thesis:

a. "Yet things are highly significant, not merely because of their functional utility, but also because of their psychological impact."

b. "Our attitudes toward things reflect basic value judgments."

2. Choose a toy like the Barbie doll, and analyze the values that it promotes or represents. Use your analysis to state your agreement or disagreement with Toffler.

concrēteness

To make an idea *concrete* is to make it exist for the reader through the senses. The statement "That car's a beauty!" expresses a general attitude and feeling but nothing more. If we want people to know why it is beautiful or to experience the beauty, we must give particulars or details—those physical qualities that make the car beautiful.

Not all abstract ideas can be expressed through physical details. We can, however, show their application to experience or suggest how we came to the idea; or we can give the details that explain it. In a discussion of the emotional makeup of human beings, Desmond Morris says that people enjoy exploring their emotions. Man, he says, "is constantly pushing things to their limit, trying to startle himself, to shock himself without getting hurt, and then signaling his relief with peals of infectious laughter." The abstract idea is here made specific; for we are told what people *do*. But Morris makes the idea even more concrete through the behavior of teenagers when their idols perform on the stage. "As an audience, they enjoy themselves, not by screaming with laughter, but screaming with screams. They not only scream, they also grip their own and one another's bodies, they writhe, they moan, they cover their faces and they pull at their hair." From these details he draws a conclusion:

> These are all the classic signs of intense pain or fear, but they have become deliberately stylized. . . . They are no longer cries for help, but signals to one another in the audience that they are capable of feeling an emotional response to the sexual idols which is so powerful that, like all stimuli of unbearably high intensity, they pass into the realm of pain.—*The Naked Ape*

The idea has been made concrete. At the same time, we must be careful not to give more details than we need to make the idea clear. Writing can be so colorful—so crowded with details and descriptive words—that the reader is distracted from the main idea.

CHRISTMAS COMES FIRST ON THE BANKS

William G. Wing

William G. Wing was a veteran correspondent of the *New York Herald Tribune.* He is a specialist on natural resources and conservation, writing for *Audubon Magazine,* the *New York Times,* and other periodicals.

[1] The Christmas sun rises first, in America, on trawlermen fishing the undersea meadows of Georges Bank.

[2] At the moment before sunrise a hundred miles east of Cape Cod, the scene aboard a trawler is so unchanging it can be imagined. The net has been hauled and streamed again. The skipper is alone in the pilot house, surrounded by the radiotelephone's racket and the green and amber eyes of electronic instruments, instruments that are supposed to tell him not only where he is but where the fish are, too.

[3] But this is only hope, not science. Despite the instruments, despite the boat's resemblance to a plow horse, methodically criss-crossing the meadow, her men are not engineers or farmers, but hunters who seek their prey in the wilderness of the sea. The trawlermen are, in fact, the last tribe of nomadic huntsmen left in the East.

[4] The skipper is alone, then, with a huntsman's anxieties: the whereabouts of the prey, the uncertainties of the weather, the chances of hitting a good market.

⁵On deck before him the men are processing the catch just brought aboard. They sit in a circle of brilliance, the deck lights reflecting from their yellow and Daybrite-orange oilskins and from the brown curve of the riding sail above.

⁶They sit on the edges of the pens, holding the big white and silver fish between their knees, ripping with knives and tearing with hands, heaving the disemboweled bodies into a central basket. Nothing is visible beyond the cone of light but the occasional flash of a whitecap or comber.

⁷There is much noise, though—wind and water and seabirds that have gathered in mobs for the feast of haulback.

⁸There is an appropriateness to Christmas in this scene, east of the sleeping mainland, so marked that it seems quaint. The names of the trawlers themselves—*Holy Family, Immaculate Conception, St. Mary, St. Joseph*—give the flavor. On the engine room bulkhead of the trawler *Holy Cross,* beyond the ugga-chugging Atlas diesel, is a painting of Christ at Gethsemane.

⁹There is an appropriateness, too, among the men. They share alike—equal shares of profit, equal shares of danger. To work together in such small quarters and stern conditions requires a graciousness of spirit that is the essence of Christmas.

¹⁰The sun is up and the pens are empty. As the deck is hosed down and the trash fish pitchforked overboard, the noise from the birds rises hysterically—barnyard sounds, shrieks, whistles, klaxon horns.

¹¹Now the birds can be seen flying in a circle around the boat. Each can hold position for only a few moments beside the point where the remains of fish are washing over. Then it falls astern and has to come up to windward on the other side of the boat, cross ahead and fall backward to the critical point. The birds pumping up the windward side look like six-day bicycle riders, earnest and slightly ridiculous, but when they reach the critical point there is a miraculous moment of aerobatics as the birds brake, wheel and drop in the broken air.

¹²Gulls snatch, gannets plunge, but the little kittiwakes balance delicately, their tails spread like carved ivory fans. There is a column of descending, shrieking birds, a scintillating feathered mass. The birds revolving about the boat have made themselves not only guests at the feast but have formed the wreath as well.

[13]Christmas Day has begun, but for the men it is time to sleep. They hose each other off and then disappear through the whaleback for a mug-up below.

[14]Boots and oilskins off, they will have a minute or two for a James Bond novel or a crossword puzzle in the bunks, braced against the elevator motions of the hull, not hearing the sounds of Niagara outside. Then the instant unconsciousness that seamen and children know. The skipper alone remains awake, watching Christmas come.

[15]Christmas came first to men on lonely meadows. It will come first again to the men on the lonely meadows offshore, fishing the Bank in boats wreathed by seabirds.

COMMENT

The author tells us that he will seek to make the moment before the sun rises concrete: he will find images that convey the mood and experience of the moment. He does so in the details of the boat, the trawlermen, their relations—"equal shares of profits, equal shares of danger." The seabirds have an unexpected appropriateness, for they wreathe the boats in their circlings. Through careful selection of details, the author succeeds in his purpose; through his description, he is able to make a point without stating it directly.

QUESTIONS FOR STUDY AND DISCUSSION

1. What point is the author making through his description? Is it important to him where the Christmas sun first rises in America?

2. Is the order of details governed by space (moving from one part of the scene to another) or by time, or possibly both?

3. What details or qualities of the scene—stated and implied—suggest Christmas in some way?

4. Is the author saying that the life aboard the trawler and the relations between the men are different during the Christmas season or on Christmas day?

5. How does the author make transitions throughout the essay?

6. What is the point of the concluding comparison?

VOCABULARY STUDY

Look up the following words and then write a sentence for each, explaining what details of the definition contribute to the concreteness of the essay: *klaxon horns, gannets, kittiwakes.*

SUGGESTIONS FOR WRITING

1. Describe a scene at a particular moment on a particular day—perhaps Thanksgiving or July Fourth. Select details that contribute to a central impression. Do not state the impression directly.

2. Describe a day of work, showing how the particular day or the week or season affects you and the people working with you. Use your description to develop a specific thesis.

HOME FOR CHRISTMAS

Carson McCullers

Carson McCullers (1917–1967) was born in Columbus, Georgia. She attended Columbia University and New York University. Her many books include *The Heart Is a Lonely Hunter* (1940), *Reflections in a Golden Eye* (1941), *The Member of the Wedding* (1946), *The Ballad of the Sad Cafe* (1951), and *Clock Without Hands* (1961). She received the National Institute of Arts and Letters Award in 1943, and the New York Drama Critics Circle Award in 1950 for her play *The Member of the Wedding.*

[1] Sometimes in August, weary of the vacant, broiling afternoon, my younger brother and sister and I would gather in the dense shade under the oak tree in the back yard and talk of Christmas and sing carols. Once after such a conclave, when the tunes of the carols

From *The Mortgaged Heart* by Carson McCullers. Reprinted by permission of Floria V. Lasky.

still lingered in the heat-shimmered air, I remember climbing up into the tree-house and sitting there alone for a long time.

2 Brother called up: "What are you doing?"

3 "Thinking," I answered.

4 "What are you thinking about?"

5 "I don't know."

6 "Well, how can you be thinking when you don't know what you are thinking about?"

7 I did not want to talk with my brother. I was experiencing the first wonder about the mystery of Time. Here I was, on this August afternoon, in the tree-house, in the burnt, jaded yard, sick and tired of all our summer ways. (I had read *Little Women* for the second time, *Hans Brinker and the Silver Skates*, *Little Men*, and *Twenty Thousand Leagues under the Sea*. I had read movie magazines and even tried to read love stories in the *Woman's Home Companion*—I was so sick of everything.) How could it be that I was I and now was now when in four months it would be Christmas, wintertime, cold weather, twilight and the glory of the Christmas tree? I puzzled about the *now* and *later* and rubbed the inside of my elbow until there was a little roll of dirt between my forefinger and thumb. Would the *now* I of the tree-house and the August afternoon be the same *I* of winter, firelight and the Christmas tree? I wondered.

8 My brother repeated: "You say you are thinking but you don't know what you are thinking about. What are you really doing up there? Have you got some secret candy?"

9 September came, and my mother opened the cedar chest and we tried on winter coats and last year's sweaters to see if they would do again. She took the three of us downtown and bought us new shoes and school clothes.

10 Christmas was nearer on the September Sunday that Daddy rounded us up in the car and drove us out on dusty country roads to pick elderberry blooms. Daddy made wine from elderberry blossoms—it was a yellow-white wine, the color of weak winter sun. The wine was dry to the wry side—indeed, some years it turned to vinegar. The wine was served at Christmastime with slices of fruitcake when company came. On November Sundays we went to the woods with a big basket of fried chicken dinner, thermos jug and coffee-pot. We hunted partridge berries in the pine woods near our town. These scarlet berries grew hidden underneath the glossy brown pine needles that lay in a slick carpet beneath the tall wind-

singing trees. The bright berries were a Christmas decoration, lasting in water through the whole season.

[11] In December the windows downtown were filled with toys, and my brother and sister and I were given two dollars apiece to buy our Christmas presents. We patronized the ten-cent stores, choosing between jackstones, pencil boxes, water colors and satin handkerchief holders. We would each buy a nickel's worth of lump milk chocolate at the candy counter to mouth as we trudged from counter to counter, choice to choice. It was exacting and final—taking several afternoons—for the dime stores would not take back or exchange.

[12] Mother made fruitcakes, and for weeks ahead the family picked out the nut meats of pecans and walnuts, careful of the bitter layer of the pecans that lined your mouth with nasty fur. At the last I was allowed to blanch the almonds, pinching the scalded nuts so that they sometimes hit the ceiling or bounced across the room. Mother cut slices of citron and crystallized pineapple, figs and dates, and candied cherries were added whole. We cut rounds of brown paper to line the pans. Usually the cakes were mixed and put into the oven when we were in school. Late in the afternoon the cakes would be finished, wrapped in white napkins on the breakfast-room table. Later they would be soaked in brandy. These fruitcakes were famous in our town, and Mother gave them often as Christmas gifts. When company came thin slices of fruitcake, wine and coffee were always served. When you held a slice of fruitcake to the window or the firelight the slice was translucent, pale citron green and yellow and red, with the glow and richness of our church windows.

[13] Daddy was a jeweler, and his store was kept open until midnight all Christmas week. I, as the eldest child, was allowed to stay up late with Mother until Daddy came home. Mother was always nervous without a "man in the house." (On those rare occasions when Daddy had to stay overnight on business in Atlanta, the children were armed with a hammer, saw and a monkey wrench. When pressed about her anxieties Mother claimed she was afraid of "escaped convicts or crazy people." I never saw an escaped convict, but once a "crazy" person did come to see us. She was an old, old lady dressed in elegant black taffeta, my mother's second cousin once removed, and came on a tranquil Sunday morning and announced that she had always liked our house and she intended to stay with us until she died. Her sons and daughters and grandchil-

dren gathered around to plead with her as she sat rocking in our front porch rocking chair and she left not unwillingly when they promised a car ride and ice cream.) Nothing ever happened on those evenings in Christmas week, but I felt grown, aged suddenly by trust and dignity. Mother confided in secrecy what the younger children were getting from Santa Claus. I knew where the Santa Claus things were hidden, and was appointed to see that my brother and sister did not go into the back-room closet or the wardrobe in our parents' room.

[14] Christmas Eve was the longest day, but it was lined with the glory of tomorrow. The sitting-room smelled of floor wax and the clean, cold odor of the spruce tree. The Christmas tree stood in a corner of the front room, tall as the ceiling, majestic, undecorated. It was our family custom that the tree was not decorated until after we children were in bed on Christmas Eve night. We went to bed very early, as soon as it was winter dark. I lay in the bed beside my sister and tried to keep her awake.

[15] "You want to guess again about your Santa Claus?"

[16] "We've already done that so much," she said.

[17] My sister slept. And there again was another puzzle. How could it be that when she opened her eyes it would be Christmas while I lay awake in the dark for hours and hours? The time was the same for both of us, and yet not at all the same. What was it? How? I thought of Bethlehem and cherry candy, Jesus and skyrockets. It was dark when I awoke. We were allowed to get up on Christmas at five o'clock. Later I found out that Daddy juggled the clock Christmas Eve so that five o'clock was actually six. Anyway it was always still dark when we rushed in to dress by the kitchen stove. The rule was that we dress and eat breakfast before we could go in to the Christmas tree. On Christmas morning we always had fish roe, bacon and grits for breakfast. I grudged every mouthful—for who wanted to fill up on breakfast when there in the sitting-room was candy, at least three whole boxes? After breakfast we lined up, and carols were started. Our voices rose naked and mysterious as we filed through the door to the sitting-room. The carol, unfinished, ended in raw yells of joy.

[18] The Christmas tree glittered in the glorious, candlelit room. There were bicycles and bundles wrapped in tissue paper. Our stockings hanging from the mantlepiece bulged with oranges, nuts and smaller presents. The next hours were paradise. The blue dawn

at the window brightened, and the candles were blown out. By nine o'clock we had ridden the wheel presents and dressed in the clothes gifts. We visited the neighborhood children and were visited in turn. Our cousins came and grown relatives from distant neighborhoods. All through the morning we ate chocolates. At two or three o'clock the Christmas dinner was served. The dining-room table had been let out with extra leaves and the very best linen was laid—satin damask with a rose design. Daddy asked the blessing, then stood up to carve the turkey. Dressing, rice and giblet gravy were served. There were cut-glass dishes of sparkling jellies and stateliness of festal wine. For dessert there was always sillabub or charlotte and fruitcake. The afternoon was almost over when dinner was done.

[19]At twilight I sat on the front steps, jaded by too much pleasure, sick at the stomach and worn out. The boy next door skated down the street in his new Indian suit. A girl spun around on a crackling son-of-a-gun. My brother waved sparklers. Christmas was over. I thought of the monotony of Time ahead, unsolaced by the distant glow of paler festivals, the year that stretched before another Christmas—eternity.

COMMENT

Time organizes the author's memory of a childhood Christmas: the sense of Christmas approaching, in the early fall; the rising excitement of the days before Christmas; the long waiting for five o'clock of Christmas morning; the "thought of the monotony of Time ahead" and "the year that stretched before another Christmas." The details and impressions the author records are therefore not presented at random: she connects them to give us the concrete world of a Georgia childhood. This one corner of her life tells us much about her, without our needing other details. Just as one well-chosen example may explain an idea fully and memorably, a few well-chosen details about the experience of Christmas allows the reader to know the world of the author in more than bare outline.

QUESTIONS FOR STUDY AND DISCUSSION

1. In how many ways is the reader reminded of time and its importance to the experience of Christmas?

2. How does the final word of the essay—"eternity"—imply meanings that the whole essay explores?

3. The author gives details of some aspects of Christmas but not of others. Why does she tell us what she thought about in bed? Why does she tell us what she ate for breakfast, instead of describing all the gifts she received? Why does she describe the experiences of September?

4. What other aspects might she have described in more detail? What would have been gained or lost if she had provided these details?

5. What do you discover about the author through this one experience?

6. How is the essay different in tone and purpose from William Wing's description of Christmas on the Banks?

VOCABULARY STUDY

Explain how the connotations of the following phrases contribute to the concreteness of the essay: *heat-shimmered, jaded yard, slick carpet, nasty fur, raw yells of joy, satin damask, stateliness of festal wine.*

SUGGESTIONS FOR WRITING

1. Describe a Christmas morning or another holiday morning and select your details to convey what was special about this day. Let your details reveal what was special. Don't tell your reader directly.

2. Compare the ways William Wing and Carson McCullers make their feelings about Christmas concrete.

JURY DUTY

William Zinsser

William K. Zinsser was born in 1922 in New York City, and studied at Princeton University. He was a feature writer, film critic, and drama editor for the *New York Herald Tribune* and later a columnist for *Look* and *Life,* and has also written numerous books. He has been teaching at Yale University since 1971.

¹Jury duty again. I'm sitting in the "central jurors' room" of a courthouse in lower Manhattan, as I do every two years, waiting to be called for a jury, which I almost never am. It's an experience that all of us have known, in one form or another, as long as we can remember: organized solitude.

²The chair that I sit in is a little island of apartness. I sit there alone, day after day, and I go out to lunch alone, a stranger in my own city. Strictly, of course, I'm not by myself. Several hundred other men and women sit on every side, as closely as in a movie theater, also waiting to be called for a jury, which they almost never are. Sometimes we break briefly into each other's lives, when we get up to stretch, offering fragments of talk to fill the emptiness. But in the end each of us is alone, withdrawn into our newspapers and our crossword puzzles and our sacred urban privacy.

³The room intimidates us. It is a dreary place, done in thirties Bureaucratic, too dull to sustain more than a few minutes of mental effort. On the subconscious level, however, it exerts a strong and uncanny hold. It is the universal waiting room. It is the induction center and the clinic; it is the assembly hall and the office where forms are filled out. Thoughts come unbidden there, sneaking back from all the other moments—in the army, at camp, on the first day of school—when we were part of a crowd and therefore lonely.

⁴The mere taking of roll call by a jury clerk will summon back the countless times when we have waited for our name to be yelled out—loud and just a little wrong. Like every person whose job is to read names aloud, the jury clerk can't read names aloud. Their shapes mystify him. They are odd and implausible names, as diverse as the countries that they came from, but surely the clerk has met them all before. *Hasn't* he? Isn't that what democracy—and the jury system—is all about? Evidently not.

⁵We are shy enough, as we wait for our name, without the extra burden of wondering what form it will take. By now we know most of the variants that have been imposed on it by other clerks in other rooms like this, and we are ready to answer to any of them, or to some still different version. Actually we don't want to hear our name called at all in this vast public chamber. It is so private, so vulnerable. And yet we don't want to *not* hear it, for only then are we reassured of our identity, really certain that we are known,

wanted, and in the right place. Dawn over Camp Upton, 1943: Weinberg, Wyzanski, Yanopoulos, Zapata, Zeccola, Zinsser . . .

[6]I don't begin my jury day in such a retrospective state. I start with high purpose and only gradually slide into mental disarray. I am punctual, even early, and so is everybody else. We are a conscientious lot—partly because we are so surrounded by the trappings of justice, but mainly because that is what we are there to be. I've never seen such conscientious-looking people. Observing them, I'm glad that American law rests on being judged by our peers. In fact, I'd almost rather be judged by my peers than judged by a judge.

[7]Most of us start the day by reading. Jury duty is America's gift to her citizens of a chance to catch up on "good" books, and I always bring *War and Peace*. I remember to bring it every morning and I keep it handy on my lap. The only thing I don't do is read it. There's something about the room . . . the air is heavy with imminent roll calls, too heavy for tackling a novel that will require strict attention. Besides, it's important to read the newspaper first: sharpen up the old noggin on issues of the day. I'm just settling into my paper when the clerk comes in, around ten-twenty-five, and calls the roll ("Zissner?" "Here!"). Suddenly it is 1944 and I am at an army base near Algiers, hammering tin to make a hot shower for Colonel McCloskey. That sort of thing can shoot the whole morning.

[8]If it doesn't, the newspaper will. Only a waiting juror knows how infinite the crannies of journalism can be. I read "Arrival of Buyers," though I don't know what they want to buy and have nothing to sell. I read "Soybean Futures," though I wouldn't know a soybean even in the present. I read classified ads for jobs that I didn't know were jobs, like "keypunch operators." What keys do they punch? I mentally buy 4bdrm 1½bth splt lvl homes w/fpl overlooking Long Island Sound and dream of taking ½bath there. I read dog news and horoscopes ("bucking others could prove dangerous today") and medical columns on diseases I've never heard of, but whose symptoms I instantly feel.

[9]It's an exhausting trip, and I emerge with eyes blurry and mind blank. I look around at my fellow jurors. Some of them are trying to work—to keep pace, pitifully, with the jobs that they left in order to come here and do nothing. They spread queer documents on their knees, full of graphs and figures, and they scribble on yellow pads. But the papers don't seem quite real to them, or quite right, removed from the tidy world of filing cabinets and secretaries, and after a while the workers put the work away again.

[10]Around twelve-forty-five the clerk comes in to make an announcement. We stir to attention: we are needed! "Go to lunch," he says. "Be back at two." We straggle out. By now the faces of all my fellow jurors are familiar (we've been here eight days), and I keep seeing them as we poke around the narrow streets of Chinatown looking for a restaurant that isn't the one where we ate yesterday. I smile tentatively, as New Yorkers do, and they smile tentatively back, and we go our separate ways. By one-fifty-five we are seated in the jurors' room again, drowsy with Chinese food and American boredom—too drowsy, certainly, to start *War and Peace*. Luckily, we all bought the afternoon paper while we were out. Talk about remote crannies of journalism!

[11]Perhaps we are too hesitant to talk to each other, to invite ourselves into lives that would refresh us by being different from our own. We are scrupulous about privacy—it is one of the better gifts that the city can bestow, and we don't want to spoil it for somebody else. Yet within almost every New Yorker who thinks he wants to be left alone is a person desperate for human contact. Thus we may be as guilty as the jury system of not putting our time to good use.

[12]What we want to do most, of course, is serve on a jury. We believe in the system. Besides, was there ever so outstanding a group of jurors as we, so intelligent and fairminded? The clerks have told us all the reasons why jurors are called in such wasteful numbers: court schedules are unpredictable; trials end unexpectedly; cases are settled at the very moment when a jury is called; prisoners plead guilty to a lesser charge rather than wait years for a trial that might prove them innocent. All this we know, and in theory it makes sense.

[13]In practice, however, somebody's arithmetic is wrong, and one of America's richest assets is being dribbled away. There must be a better way to get through the long and tragic list of cases awaiting a solution—and, incidentally, to get through *War and Peace*.

COMMENT

Zinsser uses jury duty to comment on traits of American life. He explores the experience fully to reveal these various traits, and also uses the experience to show what New Yorkers and, most important, people in general feel as they sit in "a little island of apartness." The strength of his comments on American life, New Yorkers, and individuals lies in the details of the experience. Zinsser does not merely recall the roll call at the Army base in 1943: he gives the names. He names the book he has brought to read, and tells us what he read in the newspaper to show "how infinite the crannies of journalism can be." And he is specific about each moment of the long wait. Through these details he has made an idea and a feeling concrete.

QUESTIONS FOR STUDY AND DISCUSSION

1. How does Zinsser establish a point of view? Why is a specific point of view important to the concreteness of the essay?

2. What details would have meaning for the New Yorker only? What does Zinsser assume about the age and experience of his readers?

3. Why would Zinsser "almost rather be judged by my peers than judged by a judge"?

4. Is Zinsser describing an experience, or arguing a thesis, or possibly doing both?

5. What creates tone in the essay? Do you find shifts in tone?

6. What does the essay reveal about Zinsser as a person? How important to the essay is your discovery of him as a person?

VOCABULARY STUDY

Write a sentence using each of the following pairs of words, and explain the difference between them:

a. *fragments, parts*
b. *intimidates, threatens*
c. *bureaucratic, governmental*
d. *uncanny, strange*
e. *implausible, unconvincing*
f. *vulnerable, weak*
g. *crannies, holes*
h. *scrupulous, careful*
i. *bestow, give*

SUGGESTIONS FOR WRITING

1. Describe a waiting room and your feelings in it. Make your details as concrete as possible. Use your description to make a comment about the place itself and your general situation.

2. Compare Zinsser's use of concrete details and the feelings he reveals with those of Dorothy Rodgers. In particular show how the details in each essay contribute to our understanding of their feelings.

figurative language

Much of our language is *figurative*—that is, not literal but metaphorical—sometimes without our realizing it is. Certain figures of speech may once have called a picture to mind but have become stale. Here are a few examples:

blaze of glory   *hard as nails*   *drunk with power*

The first of these is a *metaphor*—a figure of speech in which one thing is talked about as if it were something else. The metaphor does not tell us that glory is like a fire: it speaks of glory as if it actually were a fire. "Hard as nails" makes the comparison directly through the word *as,* and we therefore call it a *simile.* Another important figure of speech is *personification,* which gives animate or human qualities to something inanimate or nonhuman:

The tree *cowered* in the storm.

Figurative language is one way of making feelings specific, particularly when there is no physical experience to represent an idea or feeling. The experience of love is different from one person to another; persons writing about love may express their special feelings through familiar objects that connote feelings instead of naming them. The poetess Emily Brontë, in the following lines, explores contrasting feelings through contrasting objects and states what each object connotes to her:

> Love is like the wild rose-briar;
> Friendship like the holly-tree.
> The holly is dark when the rose-briar blooms,
> But which will bloom most constantly?

LIVING ON VANCOUVER ISLAND

Lisa Hobbs

Lisa Hobbs was born in Australia in 1930. She was on the staff of the *San Francisco Examiner* for ten years, then joined the foreign staff of the *San Francisco Chronicle*. She studied Asian affairs at Stanford University on a fellowship. In 1969 she traveled in Vietnam, Laos and Cambodia. She now lives with her family on Vancouver Island, and is a feature writer for the *Vancouver Sun*. Her book, *Running Towards Life* (1972), tells of her experiences on Vancouver Island, off the southwest coast of British Columbia, in Canada, after living in California.

[1] The days melted one into the other. There were no great highs and lows as we had known them in the city. There were no battles of personalities at teachers' meetings, no jockeying for top position in newspaper articles, or television interviews. No interior victories or defeats; no agonizing post-mortems as to what we might have done, said or thought; no meeting our neighbors or fellow men as rivals, competitors with a knife at our throats; no meeting with friends and acquaintances imprisoned in mutual masks of distrust and loneliness. No outside authority dominating the hours of our day, telling us to do this or that and make sure it's ready on time.

[2] All we did was *experience*. We experienced silence, a silence that only the forces of nature could break—the wind brushing against the trees, or the shrieks of the sea gulls over the water, or the thunder of the creek against the rocks as the stream burgeoned with the increasing rains. We experienced darkness, a velvety primordial darkness; one looked to the moon or the stars for light. When we shut off our hydro-power, we stumbled body against body within our cottage like the blind. We experienced elemental cold when we arose and shared with cavemen the lust for heat. We huddled over our stove, rubbing our hands and turning our bodies, sighing with pleasure, and then went out into the cold.

[3] We wore clothes that protected our bodies from cold and injury. To outsiders we would have looked grotesquely amusing; we

neither noticed nor cared. Occasionally, we would come unexpectedly one on the other, or be hauling a piece of lumber together and, seeing each other with fresh eyes, would start to laugh and end up collapsed sitting in the mud or on a carpet of cedar needles, laughing not in derision but in joy. We were very aware of what we had almost missed.

[4]I did what I could but I can't pretend to have done much of the building. Despite our move, I had a series of writing commitments that had to be fulfilled, and we were delighted to have them, for our expenses were heavy and our capital diminishing. Yet, forced absences, at first back to San Francisco and later Vancouver, did nothing to decrease our mutual sense of being in command of our bodies and our lives. Each time I returned it was with a growing sense that I was coming home, home where I was finding, and would find ever increasingly, the deepest of satisfactions and creative fulfillment.

[5]Once home I threw myself into the pursuit of helping Jack. He had built a cable line from the middle of the jetty up over the stream and up the side of the hill to the pad. On the pad he had constructed a wooden winch. He would load the lengths of lumber onto the cable line and I would start the muscle-wracking process of hauling it up. Standing there in the wind and the rain, soaked to the skin, our hands blistered and our shoulders aching, we learned more than we could have by reading fifty books dealing with the realities of pioneer life. How false is the image projected by most history books and entertainment, particularly television. Nobody in his right mind would willingly return to that period: Getting up in a cold house, lighting a fire and waiting for its heat to cook some breakfast, dressing for the day's work in the cold and then leaving a warm house that will be like an icebox upon returning—soaked and shivering—five or six hours later, cutting wood, washing from a bucket of warm water heated on the stove, cooking the dinner meat in the fireplace because the wood consumption was too high to keep both the fireplace and the kitchen stove burning, washing dishes in the tin bucket, later using the same tin bucket for the laundry.

[6]We decidedly did not want to be pioneers or go back to those times. And yet it was through experiencing many of the elements of those times that we found ourselves. There were some mornings when we gave up; hearing the wind or looking at the rain we said to heck with it, stoked the fire and stayed indoors. But we found to our

surprise that our bodies had begun to assert themselves. At first it was as if they knew our wills were weak and would readily respond if a protest against the cold or wet was sent up. Yet with time, it was as if the body gained a deep contentment from a task performed and could accept with full pleasure the rest, warmth and sustenance it received only after that task was satisfactorily fulfilled. The body seemed to become subservient, but harmoniously so, to the beauty of the environment, to our quiet contemplation of the meaning of life.

[7]We were constantly learning new things. For instance, one of our endless needs was for firewood. Scores of logs, looking as if they would supply sufficient firewood for a year, float past our jetty every month. It took more trial, error and effort than we would care to recall before we knew what we were doing in the firewood department. We found out that most of the logs that float by are cedar, hemlock, balsam and, from time to time, spruce, but that fir is the best. No Presto logs ever flowed by! Cedar burns like paper and continually pops and cracks while giving off little heat. Hemlock will not burn unless its combustion is supported by other wood and unless where it has had a chance to dry out, seemingly from the beginning of time. We also burned a lot of spruce at the beginning. It isn't too bad for firewood, but now that we can tell it from other logs we no longer use it. Burning balsam is like trying to burn a wet rag.

[8]Today, when a fir log floats by, Jack or one of the boys hurries out in the boat and tows it in. At high tide we float it in as close to the house as possible, cut it into "biscuits" about sixteen inches long, and then later split them for firewood. Jack says after four years he can now smell a fir log when it burns and is no longer surprised by a fire that neither sounds nor burns like a breakfast cereal.

[9]This constant learning of new things was a major part of our expanding in consciousness; it was combined with many changes. There was the alteration in time that I mentioned earlier. Our outside activities were dominated by the availability of light, by the rising and setting of the sun. If a log had to be brought in off the inlet at high tide, and high tide was at 2 A.M., then it was the tides and the moon that set our sleeping and awakening. In allowing natural forces to determine our concept of time, we found a new lightness, an easy capacity to sleep and awake. We no longer needed eight and nine hours sleep at a stretch, although that is how much sleep we normally had. But if we had to break this pattern, the break was in harmony with the pattern of our lives.

[10]All this—the experience of living in harmony with nature, the shedding of false imagery through our clothes and possessions, the meeting of neighbors and fellow men as friends not competitors, the daily physical acts of hauling lumber, scrambling up the mountainside, splitting wood—thrust us into a new consciousness of wholeness. It was not so much that we stood still and sloughed off our old lives, old attitudes and old ingrained habits of thought and action; it was more as if we had sped forward or stepped up into a different world in which our old life did not really matter, for it was as if it had never existed.

COMMENT

The language of the essay is moderately figurative. Some of the metaphors are so common that we probably do not visualize them, nor is it necessary that we do to understand the passage:

> The days *melted* one into the other. There were no great *highs and lows* as we had known them in the city. There were no *battles* of personalities at teachers' meetings, no *jockeying* for top position in newspaper articles, or television interviews.

Figurative language is a means to concise expression; it would take many words to state the idea that the metaphor expresses in so few. Certain metaphors in the essay are, of course, meant to be visualized. The following sentence contains metaphorical language that must be imagined to be understood. We have italicized the most vivid of these words:

> We experienced silence, a silence that only the forces of nature could break—the wind *brushing* against the trees, or the *shrieks* of the sea gulls over the water, or the *thunder* of the creek against the rocks as the stream burgeoned with the increasing rains.

QUESTIONS FOR STUDY AND DISCUSSION

1. What words and phrases in paragraphs 3–10 are figurative and must be imagined for the sentences to be understood?

2. How much does the author depend on figurative language to describe physical processes? What details of her experience make her feelings concrete to the reader?

3. What experiences have led you to give up "false images" of yourself? Do you believe a change in environment is necessary to lose these?

4. What parts of your life would you willingly give up, and why?

VOCABULARY STUDY

Examine the dictionary definition of the following words. For each, seek an *antonym* (a word that expresses an opposite or nearly opposite meaning). Use these antonyms in sentences of your own: *burgeoned, derision, diminishing, assert, subservient, sufficient, ingrained.*

SUGGESTIONS FOR WRITING

1. Describe an experience that changed your sense of time or forced you to shed "false images" of yourself. You might choose an experience that taught you to see the city in a new way or that changed your thinking about city or rural life.

2. The author says about pioneer life: "How false is the image projected by most history books and entertainment, particularly television." Describe a television show or a movie that presents a false image of an institution like the family or a group of people—high school students, teachers, policemen, for example. Contrast the false image with the reality as you have experienced it.

UNTYING THE KNOT

Annie Dillard

Annie Dillard was born in 1945 and grew up in Pittsburgh, Pennsylvania. She attended Hollins College. She has written poetry and is a contributing editor to *Harper's Magazine;* she is also a columnist for The Wilderness Society. Since 1965 she has lived in the Roanoke Valley of Virginia.

[1] Yesterday I set out to catch the new season, and instead I found an old snakeskin. I was in the sunny February woods by the quarry; the snakeskin was lying in a heap of leaves right next to an aquarium someone had thrown away. I don't know why that someone hauled the aquarium deep into the woods to get rid of it; it had only one broken glass side. The snake found it handy, I imagine; snakes like to rub against something rigid to help them out of their skins, and the broken aquarium looked like the nearest likely object. Together the snakeskin and the aquarium made an interesting scene on the forest floor. It looked like an exhibit at a trial—circumstantial evidence—of a wild scene, as though a snake had burst through the broken side of the aquarium, burst through his ugly old skin, and disappeared, perhaps straight up in the air, in a rush of freedom and beauty.

[2] The snakeskin had unkeeled scales, so it belonged to a nonpoisonous snake. It was roughly five feet long by the yardstick, but I'm not sure because it was very wrinkled and dry, and every time I tried to stretch it flat it broke. I ended up with seven or eight pieces of it all over the kitchen table in a fine film of forest dust.

[3] The point I want to make about the snakeskin is that, when I found it, it was whole and tied in a knot. Now there have been stories told, even by reputable scientists, of snakes that have deliberately tied themselves in a knot to prevent larger snakes from trying to swallow them—but I couldn't imagine any way that throwing itself into a half hitch would help a snake trying to escape its skin. Still, ever cautious, I figured that one of the neighborhood boys could possibly have tied it in a knot in the fall, for some whimsical boyish reason, and left it there, where it dried and gathered dust. So I carried the skin along thoughtlessly as I walked, snagging it sure enough on a low branch and ripping it in two for the first of many times. I saw that thick ice still lay on the quarry pond and that the skunk cabbage was already out in the clearings, and then I came home and looked at the skin and its knot.

[4] The knot had no beginning. Idly I turned it around in my hand, searching for a place to untie; I came to with a start when I realized I must have turned the thing around fully ten times. Intently, then, I traced the knot's lump around with a finger: it was

continuous. I couldn't untie it any more than I could untie a dough-nut; it was a loop without beginning or end. These snakes *are* magic, I thought for a second, and then of course I reasoned what must have happened. The skin had been pulled inside-out like a peeled sock for several inches; then an inch or so of the inside-out part—a piece whose length was coincidentally equal to the diameter of the skin—had somehow been turned right-side out again, making a thick lump whose edges were lost in wrinkles, looking exactly like a knot.

[5] So. I have been thinking about the change of seasons. I don't want to miss spring this year. I want to distinguish the last winter frost from the out-of-season one, the frost of spring. I want to be there on the spot the moment the grass turns green. I always miss this radical revolution; I see it the next day from a window, the yard so suddenly green and lush I could envy Nebuchadnezzar down on all fours eating grass. This year I want to stick a net into time and say "now," as men plant flags on the ice and snow and say, "here." But it occurred to me that I could no more catch spring by the tip of the tail than I could untie the apparent knot in the snakeskin; there are no edges to grasp. Both are continuous loops.

[6] I wonder how long it would take you to notice the regular recurrence of the seasons if you were the first man on earth. What would it be like to live in open-ended time broken only by days and nights? You could say, "it's cold again; it was cold before," but you couldn't make the key connection and say, "it was cold this time last year," because the notion of "year" is precisely the one you lack. Assuming that you hadn't yet noticed any orderly progression of heavenly bodies, how long would you have to live on earth before you could feel with any assurance that any one particular long period of cold would, in fact, end? "While the earth remaineth, seedtime and harvest, and cold and heat, and summer and winter, and day and night shall not cease": God makes this guarantee very early in Genesis to a people whose fears on this point had perhaps not been completely allayed.

[7] It must have been fantastically important, at the real begin-nings of human culture, to conserve and relay this vital seasonal information, so that the people could anticipate dry or cold seasons, and not huddle on some November rock hoping pathetically that spring was just around the corner. We still very much stress the simple fact of four seasons to schoolchildren; even the most modern

of modern new teachers, who don't seem to care if their charges can read or write or name two products of Peru, will still muster some seasonal chitchat and set the kids to making paper pumpkins, or tulips, for the walls. "The people," wrote Van Gogh in a letter, "are very sensitive to the changing seasons." That we are "very sensitive to the changing seasons" is, incidentally, one of the few good reasons to shun travel. If I stay at home I preserve the illusion that what is happening on Tinker Creek is the very newest thing, that I'm at the very vanguard and cutting edge of each new season. I don't want the same season twice in a row; I don't want to know I'm getting last week's weather, used weather, weather broadcast up and down the coast, old-hat weather.

[8] But there's always unseasonable weather. What we think of the weather and behavior of life on the planet at any given season is really all a matter of statistical probabilities; at any given point, anything might happen. There is a bit of every season in each season. Green plants—deciduous green leaves—grow everywhere, all winter long, and small shoots come up pale and new in every season. Leaves die on the tree in May, turn brown, and fall into the creek. The calendar, the weather, and the behavior of wild creatures have the slimmest of connections. Everything overlaps smoothly for only a few weeks each season, and then it all tangles up again. The temperature, of course, lags far behind the calendar seasons, since the earth absorbs and releases heat slowly, like a leviathan breathing. Migrating birds head south in what appears to be dire panic, leaving mild weather and fields full of insects and seeds; they reappear as if in all eagerness in January, and poke about morosely in the snow. Several years ago our October woods would have made a dismal colored photograph for a sadist's calendar: a killing frost came before the leaves had even begun to brown; they drooped from every tree like crepe, blackened and limp. It's all a chancy, jumbled affair at best, as things seem to be below the stars.

[9] Time is the continuous loop, the snakeskin with scales endlessly overlapping without beginning or end, or time is an ascending spiral if you will, like a child's toy Slinky. Of course we have no idea which arc on the loop is our time, let alone where the loop itself is, so to speak, or down whose lofty flight of stairs the Slinky so uncannily walks.

[10] The power we seek, too, seems to be a continuous loop. I have always been sympathetic with the early notion of a divine power

that exists in a particular place, or that travels about over the face of the earth as a man might wander—and when he is "there" he is surely not here. You can shake the hand of a man you meet in the woods; but the spirit seems to roll along like the mythical hoop snake with its tail in its mouth. There are no hands to shake or edges to untie. It rolls along the mountain ridges like a fireball, shooting off a spray of sparks at random, and will not be trapped, slowed, grasped, fetched, peeled, or aimed. "As for the wheels, it was cried unto them in my hearing, O wheel." This is the hoop of flame that shoots the rapids in the creek or spins across the dizzy meadows; this is the arsonist of the sunny woods: catch it if you can.

COMMENT

Dillard uses the knotted snakeskin as a metaphor for existence. She makes her point directly: she can no more "catch spring by the tip of the tail" than she can untie the knot—"there are no edges to grasp. Both are continuous loops." She builds carefully to this statement, the full meaning emerging in the details of her account. The open feeling of spring stands for a larger experience: the sense of "open-ended time." Like Lisa Hobbs who sees herself and the world as if for the first time, Dillard wants to see the world anew at each moment, though she knows that experiences repeat themselves. That is why she does not want to "catch spring by the tip of the tail." It would fix the experience instead of keeping it open. Having explored these ideas, she can finish her analogy—"Time is the continuous loop"—and she thinks also of a divine power that is everywhere always. It is the oneness and at the same time the variousness of nature that she seeks to express through figurative language.

QUESTIONS FOR STUDY AND DISCUSSION

1. The power of nature, and its openness, are symbolized in many ways in the essay. How is it symbolized at the end?

2. The author moves from ordinary experience to the extraordinary. What words and phrases suggest the extraordinary and mysterious qualities of life as the essay proceeds?

3. What use has the author made of the Bible (Daniel 4:25) in paragraph 5?

4. In how many ways is the knotted snakeskin used in the essay? That is, how many references do you find to entanglement and overlapping?

5. How does the author characterize herself through her response to the snakeskin and the world of Tinker Creek?

6. What use does the author make of personification?

VOCABULARY STUDY

Write a paraphrase of the final paragraph, translating similes, metaphors, and other figures of speech into literal language.

SUGGESTIONS FOR WRITING

1. Write about your feelings and thoughts concerning a season of the year. Focus your discussion on an object you associate with this season. You may want to explore the various qualities of the object and what these tell you about the season.

2. Develop one of the ideas of the essay from your point of view and personal experience.

usage

We earlier mentioned the formal and informal uses of English.
Each of us has a formal and informal language, each suited to
specific occasions. At such formal occasions as weddings, funerals,
and interviews with deans and employers, we speak a language
different from our language at home or with our friends. Though the
standards of formal and informal language are sometimes different
from one group of people and one part of the country to another,
there is agreement on extreme differences—for example, that the
language of insurance policies is formal, and that the language of
television comedy is informal. One important measure of the
difference is sentence structure. Formal sentences are often
complex, sometimes with considerable subordination, as in this
sentence:

> Having glanced at the major trauma of the telegraph on conscious
> life, noting that it ushers in the Age of Anxiety and of Pervasive
> Dread, we can turn to some specific instances of this uneasiness
> and growing jitters.—Marshall McLuhan, *Understanding Media*

In McLuhan's sentence a series of modifiers builds to the core
sentence. An informal sentence, by contrast, is usually looser,
perhaps starting with the core sentence and ending with the
modifying phrases, as in this sentence you are reading. Or it may
coordinate the three main ideas instead of subordinating:

> *We have glanced* at the major trauma of the telegraph on conscious life, *and noted* that it ushers in the Age of Anxiety and of Pervasive Dread, *and we can turn* to some specific instances of this uneasiness and growing jitters.

A sentence whose core idea comes at the end is sometimes called *periodic.* By contrast, a *loose* sentence begins with the core idea and finishes with modifying phrases:

> We can turn to some specific instances of this uneasiness and growing jitters, *having glanced* at the major trauma of the telegraph on conscious life, and *noting that* it ushers in the Age of Anxiety and of Pervasive Dread.

This sentence is still rather formal, owing to the abstractness of the vocabulary. Formal English sometimes deals with specific concrete ideas and experiences, and uses a simple vocabulary; informal English usually does.

Slang and jargon associated with special trades or sports are usually found in informal discussions. People who work on assembly lines or repair telephone equipment or automobiles share a special language—in particular, special terms and expressions. So do teenagers, jazz musicians, college professors, and baseball fans. This language is uncommon in formal writing, mainly because the audience for that writing is usually a very general one. It is important for writers to keep in mind what terms or expressions their audience knows. Expressions associated with rock music will be understood by an audience limited to rock fans; however, a general audience will need these terms explained. The failure to keep one's audience in mind probably accounts for mixed usage, which confuses one segment of the audience and then another. Much writing does effectively combine formal sentences with an informal vocabulary; the effectiveness of the writing depends on the ability of the audience to understand both. Unless we know that our audience will be a special one, it is a good idea to think of it as general— drawing on many kinds of backgrounds and interests. This advice bears most on diction, for it is vocabulary that gives readers the most trouble—especially inexact and overblown words and expressions that conceal, rather than clarify, our thoughts.

JOB HUNTING

Art Buchwald

Art Buchwald was born in Mount Vernon, New York, in 1925, and was educated at the University of Southern California. During the Second World War he served in the Marine Corps. He has written for many newspapers; his satirical columns have been collected into many books. His chief target has been the Washington scene but he has also written about contemporary social problems.

Vice President of Development
Glucksville Dynamics
Glucksville, California

DEAR SIR,

I am writing in regard to employment with your firm. I have a BS from USC and PhD in physics from the California Institute of Technology.

In my previous position I was in charge of research and development for the Harrington Chemical Company. We did work in thermonuclear energy, laser beam refraction, hydrogen molecule development, and heavy-water computer data.

Several of our research discoveries have been adapted for commercial use, and one particular breakthrough in linear hydraulics is now being used by every oil company in the country.

Because of a cutback in defense orders, the Harrington Company decided to shut down its research and development department. It is for this reason I am available for immediate employment.

Hoping to hear from you in the near future, I remain

Sincerely yours,

EDWARD KASE

DEAR MR. KASE,

We regret to inform you that we have no positions available for someone of your excellent qualifications. The truth of the matter is that we find you are "overqualified" for any position we might offer you in our organization. Thank you for thinking of us, and if anything comes up in the future, we will be getting in touch with you.

Yours truly,
MERRIMAN HASELBALD
Administrative Vice-President

Personnel Director
Jessel International Systems
Crewcut, Mich.

DEAR SIR,

I am applying for a position with your company in any responsible capacity. I have had a college education and have fiddled around in research and development. Occasionally we have come up with some moneymaking ideas. I would be willing to start off at a minimal salary to prove my value to your firm.

Sincerely yours,
EDWARD KASE

DEAR MR. KASE,

Thank you for your letter of the 15th. Unfortunately we have no positions at the moment for someone with a college education. Frankly it is the feeling of everyone here that you are "overqualified," and your experience indicates you would be much happier with a company that could make full use of your talents.

It was kind of you to think of us.

HARDY LANDSDOWNE
Personnel Dept.

To Whom It May Concern
Geis & Waterman Inc.
Ziegfried, Ill.

DERE SER,

I'd like a job with your outfit. I can do anything you want me to. You name it Kase will do it. I ain't got no education and no experience, but I'm strong and I got moxy an I get along great with peeple. I'm ready to start any time because I need the bread. Let me know when you want me.

Cheers
EDWARD KASE

DEAR MR. KASE,

You are just the person we have been looking for. We need a truck driver, and your qualifications are perfect for us. You can begin working in our Westminister plant on Monday. Welcome aboard.

CARSON PETERS
Personnel

COMMENT

Buchwald writes in a clearly satirical voice when he writes in his own person. He is not writing in his own person in these letters, but we do hear him indirectly—in the language he has given the correspondents. Buchwald's humor arises in the changes we see in Kase's letters and in the situation itself. Humor must develop out of real problems in the world we know: we will not find humor long in invented qualities and situations. Those problems may be serious—the problem Buchwald deals with is a serious one today. We can laugh with Buchwald because we are laughing not at Kase but at ourselves and at the dilemma of our world.

QUESTIONS FOR STUDY AND DISCUSSION

1. How do Kase's letters change in language? What are the most important changes? What changes do you notice in sentence structure?

2. What situation is the source of Buchwald's humor? What exactly is he satirizing?

3. What do Kase and his correspondents reveal about themselves in the impressions they give of themselves?

VOCABULARY STUDY

Find substitutes for the formal diction in the letters to Kase. Discuss how their substitution would change the humor or point of the letters.

SUGGESTIONS FOR WRITING

1. Write three letters of application for the same job. Change your language to give a different impression of yourself. Use these letters to make a satirical point, as Buchwald does.

2. Write an exchange of letters like Buchwald's, satirizing a current social problem through them. Fit the language of each letter to the character and attitude of the writer.

THE GENERATION AS MODEL YEAR

Truman E. Moore

Truman E. Moore was born in 1935 and grew up in Myrtle Beach, South Carolina. He is a free-lance writer and photographer and the author of several books—*The Slaves We Rent* (1965), *The Traveling Man* (1972), and *Nouveaumania* (1975), in which the essay included here appears. He studied journalism at the University of North Carolina and has attended New York University Graduate School.

[1] American nouveaumania, with its insatiable appetite for change and novelty, has in the last fifty years increasingly demanded that human beings, like manufactured goods, have model years. This urge has been largely satisfied by the excessive labeling of generations.

From *Nouveaumania: The American Passion for Novelty and How It Led Us Astray* by Truman E. Moore. Copyright © 1975 by Truman E. Moore. Reprinted by permission of Random House, Inc.

[2] The *American College Dictionary* calls a generation a "whole body of individuals born at the same time," a definition that left journalists and social scientists at liberty to discover a new wave of Americans as often as they pleased. Sociologists agree, however, that the duration of a generation is about thirty years, or the time it takes for the father to be replaced by the son. The generation has been classically considered to be the embodiment of the spirit of the times or the age. This means that there should be about three "ages" in a century.

[3] But in the first sixty years of this century, the United States has, with characteristic excess, experienced four "ages": the age of the moguls and tycoons that preceded World War I, the Roaring Twenties, the proletarian thirties, and following the transition of World War II, the age of suburbia and the organization man. In 1960, sociologist Bennett Berger, counting the beat generation and sensing the imminent birth of yet another generation, remarked that the United States seemed to have an age and a generation about every ten years, a rate which has since increased.[1]

[4] David Riesman put the blame for the tendency to define generations on the mass media. The labeling of generations, he said, had been "speeded up in recent years by the enormous industry of the mass media which must constantly find new ideas to purvey, and which have short-circuited the traditional filtering down of ideas from academic and intellectual centers. We can now follow an interpretation of the suburbs from an article in the *American Journal of Sociology* to an article in *Harper's* to a best selling book to an article in *Life* or a TV drama—all in the matter of a couple of years—much in the way in which . . . a 'beat generation' [is] imitated almost before [it] exists."[2]

[5] The attempt to name the generation and characterize the "age" became both a media and an intellectual pastime. Nor were young people entirely passive in the process. They rapidly acquired the notion that they ought to be completely different from the "older" generation, and willingly cooperated in the game of presenting a steady succession of new models for the satisfaction of their own egos and the entertainment of their elders.

[6] In 1946 the youth of the day were called the New Lost Genera-

[1] Bennett Berger, "How Long Is a Generation?," *British Journal of Sociology* (March 1960).
[2] David Riesman cited, *ibid.*

tion. Five years later they were called a generation of aesthetes. Also in 1951, a Texas college professor said they were without responses, and the term "silent generation" became widely used. The beat generation entered the national consciousness in 1952, and in 1953 William Styron, after rejecting "scared," called American youth a "waiting generation." A year later *Life* magazine said they were the luckiest generation. The 1961 generation was called both explosive and cool. In 1962 *Life* invented a generation out of young people who had already achieved unusual success in their fields. The "takeover generation," as they were called, consisted of only a hundred people, mostly white males. A swarm of photographers—I among them—was dispatched across the country to photograph this powerful mini-generation. They appeared in a foldout spread, each person about twice the size of a commemorative postage stamp.

[7] The students and young people of the sixties really needed no such contrivance. They could boast of a record-breaking production of new generations (or life styles, as they were more popularly known), to fire the journalistic imagination. Reporters flocked to the campuses and discovered a new generation every year or two. Civil rights workers, hippies, yippies, show-biz radicals, revolutionaries, and various religious converts appeared and disappeared in rapid succession. The media called the 1963 generation tense, and in 1964 it was New Lost again. In 1965 it was the generation under the gun, and the youth of 1966 were open, restless, and rebellious. In 1969, they were called cheated and unsilent. In 1970 they were without fathers, and in 1971, romantic. For adults, the sixties were swinging.

[8] In 1972, one young man told a newspaper reporter that he had been "into drugs," then had joined a commune, and ate only organic food. Now he was "into Zen" after going from other involvements ranging from stealing to loving Jesus. At nineteen he was, like many of his fellow students, a generation freak dabbling in life styles.

[9] As the seventies wore on, the production of generations slowed down. The media grew impatient and one had the feeling that if the next generation did not appear, it would have to be invented. The press and television began to speak of the young with thinly veiled displeasure. The campuses were quiet, they reported. Apathy had returned. The September issue of *Esquire,* usually devoted to the college scene, was given to other material in 1973.

The editors felt that the kids weren't doing anything and put them on notice that they were expected to "go bite a dog or something."

[10]James S. Kunen, author of *The Strawberry Statement,* disparaged the inactivity of the students of 1973 and even declared that his own class of '70 was copping out, not a new generation after all.[3] A college freshman—class of '78—acutely aware that his class was not leading a wave of changes, reflected that "It was a little disheartening to find yourself drinking your parents' liquor and listening to their old records."[4] Most students manage to see their own activities as a progression. A New York University student told a reporter, "More people have turned to drinking because they have already experienced drugs and are ready to move on to another level."[5] Presumably a higher one.

[11]Many of the "old ways" are returning to campus. The prom, dropped in many colleges in the late sixties because it was old-fashioned, came back in 1974, complete with waltzes and fox trots. Students also returned to the library and grades were again important, giving a *New York Times* reporter first sight of what may be called the new generation. He found that students were filled with such anxiety over grades that they developed a neurosis and a tendency not only to cheat but to sabotage the work of other students seen as competition. There were no comparative figures to substantiate the existence of a cheating or a grade-grind generation, but it was interesting that the reporter found a new trend in an age-old college problem.[6]

[12]While labels are only broad generalizations and are often put forth frivolously, the label that sticks to a generation is important to those to whom it applies, for, as Berger noted, the successful designation determines who is behind the times, who is "with it," and who is ahead of the times. One's sense of esteem may be damaged by a derogatory designation. The youth of the fifties, for example, were hurt by the silent-generation label so firmly applied to them, and they displayed a vague sense of apology and guilt.

[13]When I was a freshman in 1953, a worldly senior told me of the glorious days in the late forties when the veterans had been on

[3]James S. Kunen, "The Rebels of '70," *New York Times Magazine* (October 28, 1973).
[4]Steven Gordon Crist, undated article in airlines magazine (ca. 1973).
[5]*Villager* (September 27, 1973).
[6]Iver Peterson, "Race for Grades Revives Among College Students," *New York Times* (November 21, 1974).

campus, of how great it was then, and how dead it was now. Veterans were supposed to have been a terrifically energetic generation of students, hellbent on success, a phenomenon attributed to the maturing effects of their wartime experiences. The football team even had a winning season. "There's no school spirit now," he said, "not like there used to be."

[14] I recall quite vividly a political-science class in which the professor, with a trace of disdain, explained to us that in other countries, particularly in Latin America, students played an active role in influencing their governments, sometimes by setting things on fire and overturning cars. We're guilty, I thought, of not committing unlawful acts! I tried in vain to imagine the students I knew rioting in the streets, fitting us into grainy newsreels in my mind.

[15] The only things the students of the Silent Generation burned were prep rally bonfires. And once a year fraternity pledges, bloated with beer and Dad's money, chopped a perfectly good piano to pieces and burned it in the middle of their lawn. It was in antics like this, along with snowball fights with the campus police, and panty raids in the spring, that the students of the fifties made their noise. We were trapped between the glory of the past and the hazy but persistent demands of the present, facing an unpalatable future outlined by William Whyte in *The Organization Man,* published the year before I graduated. We were expected to furnish the nation with a new generation more wonderful than the previous one—new and better, as it were. *Send me men to match my cars and appliances.*

[16] Richard Lingeman, writing about his memories and experiences in the fifties, put his finger on the source of much of the prevalent guilt and regret. "We had," he observed, "no new life style to purvey . . ."[7]

[17] The invention of new generations hardly contributes to the individual's sense of value. Berger pointed out that "a firm identity seems to manifest itself as pigheadedness and a stable one as stubbon rigidity."[8] Thus the American, already undermined by swiftly changing versions of humanity, is criticized if he possesses the qualities he needs most. To be excluded from the current age is to be obsolete, no matter how "into it" or "with it" an individual

[7] Richard Lingeman, "There Was Another Fifties," *New York Times Magazine* (June 17, 1973).
[8] Bennett Berger, "Teen-Agers Are An American Invention," *New York Times Magazine* (June 13, 1965).

might feel. If he insists on trying to stay in style, he will look like that over-fifty executive in the *New Yorker* cartoon introducing himself to a young lady at a party as "part of an exciting new breed of old men."

[18] Our emphasis on generations implies obsolescence of the older Models. Unfortunately, Americans lack a sure sense of self-identity with which to counter the depreciating effects of this kind of rapid devaluation.

[19] Our uncertainty is the creator of the stereotype of the American abroad, bellowing and ranting in hotels and restaurants over the illogic of the currency, the inadequacy of the bathrooms, the absence of fluent speakers of English. It is the picture of a man in utter confusion whose violent reactions arise from his having no sure sense of himself. He hides his internal incongruity in his blustering.

[20] Humorists have always enjoyed the meeting of rustic Americans with the careful traditions of England and the Continent. The threat that the American feels among the people of older civilizations comes from the feeling of inauthenticity he experiences when confronted with a present linked coherently with the past. Henry James said that American society was "thinly composed," a condition he contrasted with the "thick, indubitable *thereness*" of English society.

[21] The American lacks the sure grip that is the property of the past-connected man. Stephen Spender wrote that "Americans fear the European past" and added with equal insight that "Europeans fear the American future." History, even our own, is treated here as a pile of wornout events. (I encountered a Kansas couple in a French department store. They had just finished an extensive tour and I asked them how they had liked it. "Well," said he, "they just showed us a lot of history.")

[22] Our separation from the past adds an American flavor to modern man's sense of alienation. We celebrate our freedom from the restraints of the Old World without connecting it with our malaise in the New World.

[23] During the expatriot era of the twenties, when the rootlessness of our national life became unbearable to many, they sought to withdraw from their own society, back to Europe, seeking their culture's lost childhood. Though many artists and writers felt cut off, they remained abroad, seeking some living tissue to replace a

vital part of their heritage misplaced in the transfer of European civilization to America.

[24]Today we still feel the impulse to go look at Europe, to go "home" to places where we have never been, looking at familiar sights we have never seen. Our minds are filled with incomplete images of things past, half-formed visions we strain to see, hoping to find guidance in what we brusquely dismiss as "just a lot of history."

[25]Our shaky identity structure is exploited by advertisers through the use of testimonials in which some well-known figure endorses a product or service, such as Joe DiMaggio's promotion of a savings bank, and the packaging of Mark Spitz. The association of a product with a clearly defined public image can have meaning only when our private image of ourselves is hazy.

[26]In the absence of fully developed models of behavior or style, Americans are easily manipulated by those who claim to know the rules and can definitely state what is correct. The English are frequently held up as models, or as experts on taste. Americans are not quite sure of what "English" style really is, yet many carry the image of themselves as distantly associated with England and subject to that influence. There is, for example, an after-shave lotion called British John Bull, bottled by a New York firm. There is no relation between this product and any quality or suggestion of character remotely British, nor is there any way for such a relationship to exist. The lotion was assigned a nationality with the safe assurance that few would question its citizenship. To what people is such a product directed? Does John Bull need to be identified as British? And what exactly, in the manufacturer's opinion, does a Briton smell like?

[27]The English obsession with what is "proper" is not easy for Americans to understand. When an Englishman says "That is a proper hat," he means that is exactly what a hat should be and no other will serve. Americans can't really think this way because we carry too many images of what a hat might be without being sure of which one, if any, is correct.

[28]It is our confusion over identity, the absence of reliable models, that has given American character its malleability so plainly displayed in our readiness to be persuaded and manipulated by people who are only famous, to be overly respectful or hostile to other cultures that are only older, or to be repeatedly and variously marked by labels which are only rough generalizations.

COMMENT

Truman Moore's discussion of the American habit of labeling generations tells us something important about the impact of names and slogans on our thinking about ourselves. We know how people can take on the qualities attributed to them in words of hate and contempt; women recently have protested the widespread use of "girls" to describe grown people, as blacks have protested the word "Negro" because of the connotations the word carries from the past. Awareness of connotations is basic to full awareness of "usage." The words and labels Moore discusses influence the behavior of the people they describe: that is one of his points, but it is not the main one. He is mainly concerned with the causes of this influence in American life, and he builds the discussion to a statement of these causes, reserving the final paragraph for a statement of the main cause. The strength of his analysis depends on the strength of his examples and the use he makes of secondary evidence—the testimony of other analysts like Bennett Berger (paragraph 3). But it is Moore's primary evidence that is central to the essay—his own experiences and observations of his fellow students and later ones, and his observations of advertising techniques like the testimonials of famous athletes.

QUESTIONS FOR STUDY AND DISCUSSION

1. What use does Moore make of the contrasting ideas and definitions of the word *generation*? What causes of the change in idea or definition does he discuss in the opening paragraphs?

2. Is Moore in agreement with Riesman and other sociologists whom he quotes? How does he indicate his agreement with or attitude toward them?

3. What explanation does Bennett Berger give for the influence of labels on people? How does Moore support Berger's analysis of this influence? Do you agree with this analysis?

4. Is Moore in agreement with Richard Lingeman's observation, "We had no new life style to purvey," referring to the fifties?

5. What use does Moore make of the "American abroad" in the concluding paragraphs? What does the contrast between America and Europe show about American culture or attitudes in this century?

6. What does Moore mean by "identity," and what in the concluding paragraphs helps to explain the word?

7. What is the main cause of the influence labels have on the self-images of Americans?

VOCABULARY STUDY

1. *Nouveau* is the French word for *new*. Write a paragraph explaining how Moore defines the phrase *nouveaumania* in the whole essay.

2. Write a sentence for each of the following pairs of words, singling out the most important difference in meaning:
   a. *moguls, tycoons*
   b. *contrivance, gimmick*
   c. *neurosis, obsession*
   d. *unpalatable, tasteless*
   e. *depreciating, declining*
   f. *incongruity, ambiguity*
   g. *blustering, threatening*
   h. *manipulated, used*
   i. *malleable, flexible*

SUGGESTIONS FOR WRITING

1. Discuss the impact of names and labels on your image of yourself and your behavior. Use this discussion to evaluate Moore's conclusion about "identity" in America.

2. Discuss the extent to which you and your fellow students share qualities and attitudes that may be said to characterize a "generation." Use this discussion to support or criticize Moore's statements about the labeling of generations.

3. Discuss the extent to which paragraph 11 describes your high school or college friends and yourself. Use this discussion to develop a thesis of your own.

THE FINE ART
OF PUTTING THINGS OFF

Michael Demarest

Michael Demarest was born in Long Island, New York, in 1924, and was educated in England at Rugby and Oxford. Since World War II, when he served in the U.S. Merchant Marine, he has written for newpapers and magazines. In nearly twenty years at *Time,* he has been a foreign correspondent, editor, and senior writer. He won the John Hancock Award in 1973 for financial and business reporting, and the J. C. Penney–University of Missouri Award for his 1974 *Time* cover story on American pets. Demarest is a member in good standing of the Procrastinators' Club of America, Inc.

[1] "Never put off till tomorrow," exhorted Lord Chesterfield in 1749, "what you can do today." That the elegant earl never got around to marrying his son's mother and had a bad habit of keeping worthies like Dr. Johnson cooling their heels for hours in an anteroom attests to the fact that even the most well-intentioned men have been postponers ever. Quintus Fabius Maximus, one of the great Roman generals, was dubbed *"Cunctator"* (Delayer) for putting off battle until the last possible *vinum* break. Moses pleaded a speech defect to rationalize his reluctance to deliver Jehovah's edict to Pharaoh. Hamlet, of course, raised procrastination to an art form.

[2] The world is probably about evenly divided between delayers and do-it-nowers. There are those who prepare their income taxes in February, prepay mortgages and serve precisely planned dinners at an ungodly 6:30 p.m. The other half dine happily on leftovers at 9 or 10, misplace bills and file for an extension of the income tax deadline. They seldom pay credit-card bills until the apocalyptic voice of Diners threatens doom from Denver. They postpone, as Faustian encounters, visits to barbershop, dentist or doctor.

[3] Yet for all the trouble procrastination may incur, delay can often inspire and revive a creative soul. Jean Kerr, author of many successful novels and plays, says that she reads every soup-can and jam-jar label in her kitchen before settling down to her typewriter. Many a writer focuses on almost anything but his task—for example, on the Coast and Geodetic Survey of Maine's Frenchman Bay and Bar Harbor, stimulating his imagination with names like Googins Ledge, Blunts Pond, Hio Hill and Burnt Porcupine, Long Porcupine, Sheep Porcupine and Bald Porcupine islands.

[4] From *Cunctator's* day until this century, the art of postponement had been virtually a monopoly of the military ("Hurry up and wait"), diplomacy and the law. In former times, a British proconsul faced with a native uprising could comfortably ruminate about the situation with Singapore Sling in hand. Blessedly, he had no natter-

ing Telex to order in machine guns and fresh troops. A U.S. general as late as World War II could agree with his enemy counterpart to take a sporting day off, loot the villagers' chickens and wine and go back to battle a day later. Lawyers are among the world's most addicted postponers. According to Frank Nathan, a nonpostponing Beverly Hills insurance salesman, "The number of attorneys who die without a will is amazing."

[5]Even where there is no will, there is a way. There is a difference, of course, between chronic procrastination and purposeful postponement, particularly in the higher echelons of business. Corporate dynamics encourage the caution that breeds delay, says Richard Manderbach, Bank of America group vice president. He notes that speedy action can be embarrassing or extremely costly. The data explosion fortifies those seeking excuses for inaction—another report to be read, another authority to be consulted. "There is always," says Manderbach, "a delicate edge between having enough information and too much."

[6]His point is well taken. Bureaucratization, which flourished amid the growing burdens of government and the greater complexity of society, was designed to smother policymakers in blankets of legalism, compromise and reappraisal—and thereby prevent hasty decisions from being made. The centralization of government that led to Watergate has spread to economic institutions and beyond, making procrastination a worldwide way of life. Many languages are studded with phrases that refer to putting things off—from the Spanish *mañana* to the Arabic *bukra fil mishmish* (literally "tomorrow in apricots," more loosely "leave it for the soft spring weather when the apricots are blooming").

[7]Academe also takes high honors in procrastination. Bernard Sklar, a University of Southern California sociologist who churns out three to five pages of writing a day, admits that "many of my friends go through agonies when they face a blank page. There are all sorts of rationalizations: the pressure of teaching, responsibilities at home, checking out the latest book, looking up another footnote."

[8]Psychologists maintain that the most assiduous procrastinators are women, though many psychologists are (at $50-plus an hour) pretty good delayers themselves. Dr. Ralph Greenson, a U.C.L.A. professor of clinical psychiatry (and Marilyn Monroe's one-time shrink), takes a fairly gentle view of procrastination. "To many

people," he says, "doing something, confronting, is the moment of truth. All frightened people will then avoid the moment of truth entirely, or evade or postpone it until the last possible moment." To Georgia State Psychologist Joen Fagan, however, procrastination may be a kind of subliminal way of sorting the important from the trivial. "When I drag my feet, there's usually some reason," says Fagan. "I feel it, but I don't yet know the real reason."

⁹ In fact, there is a long and honorable history of procrastination to suggest that many ideas and decisions may well improve if postponed. It is something of a truism that to put off making a decision is itself a decision. The parliamentary process is essentially a system of delay and deliberation. So, for that matter, is the creation of a great painting, or an entrée, or a book, or a building like Blenheim Palace, which took the Duke of Marlborough's architects and laborers 15 years to construct. In the process, the design can mellow and marinate. Indeed, hurry can be the assassin of elegance. As T. H. White, author of *Sword in the Stone,* once wrote, time "is not meant to be devoured in an hour or a day, but to be consumed delicately and gradually and without haste." In other words, *pace* Lord Chesterfield, what you don't necessarily have to do today, by all means put off until tomorrow.

COMMENT

Demarest's sentences and diction are formal, although his essay deals with everyday experiences. He does not chat with us about the art of putting things off: he prefers to deal with the subject seriously. But the serious point he has to make about procrastination does not prevent him from being humorous, as his frequent play on words shows: "Even where there is no will, there is a way." Thus the formality of the language invites us to consider Demarest's ideas seriously, but he manages to avoid a sober attitude toward the subject, toward his reader, and toward himself.

QUESTIONS FOR STUDY AND DISCUSSION

1. Demarest mixes abstract with concrete words, often for humorous effect. What examples of this mixed diction can you cite?

2. Why does Demarest refer to visits to the barber, the dentist, and the doctor as "Faustian encounters"?

3. What point is he making about bureaucratization? Is he making this point seriously?

4. What points is he making about putting things off?

5. What shifts in tone do you notice, and how are they managed?

VOCABULARY STUDY

1. Identify words that you would expect to find in formal speech and writing. State what words might be used in their place in informal speech and writing.

2. Use your dictionary to find out whether the following pairs of words are different in meaning or in level of usage or possibly both:
   a. *ruminate, ponder*
   b. *echelons, ranks*
   c. *reappraisal, revalue*
   d. *rationalizations, excuses*
   e. *assiduous, hard-working*
   f. *truism, platitude*

SUGGESTIONS FOR WRITING

1. Demarest distinguishes two classes of people in his second paragraph. Describe your attitude toward putting things off and state the class you belong to and why you do.

2. Organize an essay for a specific audience on one of the following statements. Use your experience and observations to qualify it or to support it fully:
   a. "The best liar is he who makes the smallest amount of lying go the longest way—who husbands it too carefully to waste it where it can be dispensed with."—Samuel Butler
   b. "One of the most striking differences between a cat and a lie is that a cat has only nine lives."—Mark Twain
   c. "One can never pay in gratitude; one can only pay 'in kind' somewhere else in life."—Anne Morrow Lindbergh
   d. "You might as well fall flat on your face as lean over too far backward."—James Thurber

INDEX OF AUTHORS AND TOPICS

Where there are several page numbers for a topic, italics indicate the main discussion.